AF538910

Eyewitness Kashmir

Teetering on Nuclear War

ARUN JOSHI

India Research Press

India Research Press
Flat No.6, Khan Market, New Delhi - 110 003
Ph.: 24694610; Fax : 24618637
e-mail : contact@indiaresearchpress.com ; bahrisons@vsnl.com
www.indiaresearchpress.com

2007

ISBN : 10 digit 81-8386-004-4
ISBN : 13 digit 978--81-8386-004-8

Cataloguing Publication Data
Eyewitness Kashmir : Teetering on Nuclear War
by Arun Joshi

Includes references and index.
1. Security - India / South Asia 2. Military - India / South Asia
3. Kashmir. 4. Threat / Accession. 5. Kashmiri People. 6. Threat
7. Turmoil 8. Liberation
i. Title ii. Author

Printed in India at Focus Impressions, New Delhi-110 003.

Dedicated
to
Mrs. Shobhana Bhartia
(Vice Chairperson and Editorial Director,
Hindustan Times)
whose leadership has given new and
dynamic dimensions to journalism

Contents

Acknowledgements

Writing this book was as good a challenge for me as it is for the best brains in the world to resolve the Kashmir crisis. There were alternatively periods of prolonged inertia and heightened enthusiasm to write on Kashmir, but the wish to record the moments I had seen in Kashmir were persistent. This exercise started when the typewriter was the reporter's best friend, and now that it has been completed, computer technology is already evolving by the minute.

Friends in Kashmir urged me to write and relatives offered help. My thanks to Aarti Tikoo—a colleague, a friend, a soul mate—whose daily pestering and encouragement made this work possible.

I also owe a lot to my friend, Yusuf Jameel, who gave me all the help I requested for.

I am grateful to Marshall Cavendish Academic for making this book the first in their Asian Commentary Series. My special thanks go to Mr. Anthony Thomas, Mr. Roy See, and the copy editor Ms. Lily Loy, who spent much time refining the manuscript and making it what it is.

But the biggest credit goes to the people of Kashmir, who showered help upon me, their adopted child. In return, I am grateful to be able to tell their story.

Preface

Kashmir is unique, unexplored and mysterious. It alternates between throbbing life and unexpected lapses into the abyss of passivity, darkness and death. That is the contradiction of Kashmir: it both embraces and repels one. Kashmir is difficult to understand because it defies established logic, acknowledged perceptions and common sense. Such is the potent impact of this land blessed with unmatched natural beauty for which its sons and daughters can find no words to describe.

For outsiders, the enigma is even greater. There is, however, no disputing the fact that it mesmerizes one and all. And as if that were not enough to bemuse the world, the secessionist war that Kashmir has been witnessing since the late 1980s, has added to the conundrum. It has become a challenge for politicians and diplomats and engages the finest minds, across the globe, bent on seeking understanding of the issues in which it is enmeshed. Statesmen and analysts find themselves lost in the craggy terrain of the Himalayas. Their propositions, so clear and lucid on paper, fail to stand up to the realities on the ground.

Kashmir now has the dubious distinction of being a nuclear flashpoint. The two competing nations, India and Pakistan, are nuclear powers. Both have territorial, strategic, political and emotional stakes in Kashmir. If Pakistan feels incomplete without Kashmir, India is equally persuaded of its legal claim to this territory. *Jis Kashmir ko khoon se seencha, woh Kashmir hamara hai* (The land which was watered by blood of our soldiers belongs to us Indians). These rallying battle cries of 1947–1948 when Indian troops pushed back the tribal raiders of Pakistan—now find an echo in every household in India. The

15-year-old secessionist war simmers on, with body bags of soldiers delivered to their homes in all parts of India.

Perceptions have changed. From being a paradise, Kashmir has become, sometimes, a death-trap for the unsuspecting tourist. The Valley is now a source of terror and violence. The violent rape of this land has spawned graves across the entire extent of its territory. Foreigners have made their appearance on its stage: militants from Pakistan, Afghanistan and even Sudan have fought against Indian security forces. None of these are Kashmiris. Yet they have fought over Kashmir and Kashmiris have become and still are victims of the crossfire. There have been occasional attempts to rescue Kashmir from the mess in which it finds itself today but the future is murky.

During my stay in Kashmir as a child and then as a reporter, I have witnessed the changes. The land has been used by one and all for furthering vested interests. The common man is sensible and sensitive. He loves his land and his family and he yearns for a measure of economic and political stability to live out his life in dignity. He watches with envy the solutions hammered out at the White House or Camp David for the Israel-Palestine conflict and the world burning midnight oil on the Iraq crisis. He agonizes over the way Kashmir smoulders and the failure of his leaders to draw useful lessons from the Good Friday agreement of Ireland. Instead, he is confounded by the maelstrom of Indian and Pakistani rhetoric and the shrill voices of his own, Kashmiri, leadership. He is confounded by the way truth is twisted and turned to exploit emotions.

I have seen all this happening over and over again. The moment the table for the talks are set up and solutions are laid and hope appears to glimmer on the horizon, someone, from somewhere, the visible and not so visible hands, reach out to cause devastation and everything caves in. More often than not this tragedy is unleashed by the inflexibility of all the parties concerned and their obdurate prejudices. All are guilty.

This book has attempted to tease out the strands of deceit which the players have woven to dupe the masses and gather profits and glory for themselves. It is the failure of the Kashmiri leadership that allows India and Pakistan to use their leverage. Kashmiris ask for their say in the matters concerning them—their future, the future of their posterity and the very existence of Kashmir as a unit—but then so many extraneous issues are thrown in that the real issue gets buried.

Kashmir is embroiled in the debate: should peace be established before a lasting solution can be found or should a solution be found before peace can be established. Where do we go from here? The question has yet to be answered.

List of Abbreviations

9/11	September 11, 2001 when planes crashed into the World Trade Centre in New York and the Pentagon in the worst terrorist attack on American soil.
AAC	Awami Action Committee
ACS	Additional Chief Secretary
Advani	L. K. Advani
AFP	Agence France Press
AIIMS	All India Institute of Medical Sciences
ANI	Asian News International
APHC	All Parties Hurriyat Conference
BBC	British Broadcasting Corporation
BJP	Bhartiya Janta Party
Blair	British Prime Minister, Tony Blair
Brig.	Brigadier
BSF	Border Security Force
Bush	US President George W. Bush
CBI	Central Bureau of Investigation
CIA	Central Intelligence Agency (of America)
CID	Criminal Investigation Department
CPI-M	Communist Party of India (Marxist)
CRPF	Central Reserve Police Force
CS	Chief Secretary
CSD	Canteen Stores Department
DFP	Democratic Freedom Party
DGP	Director General of Police

DIG	Deputy Inspector General
Farooq	Farooq Abdullah
Garry	Girish Chandra Saxena
Geelani	Syed Ali Shah Geelani
Gen	General
Harkat	Harkat-ul-Ansar
Hizb	Hizb-ul-Mujahideen
HM	Hizb-ul-Mujahadeen
HMT	Hindustan Machine Tools
HT	*Hindustan Times*
HUA	Harkat-ul-Ansar
Hurriyat	All Parties Hurriyat Conference
IAF	Indian Air Force
IAS	Indian Administrative Service
IB	Intelligence Bureau
ID	Identity Card
IG	Inspector General
Indira	Indira Gandhi
IPS	Indian Police Service
ISI	Inter Services Intelligence (of Pakistan)
ISL	Islamic Students' League
Jaish	Jaish-e-Mohammad
JEM	Jaish-e-Mohammad
JKAP	Jammu Kashmir Armed Police
JKNLF	Jammu Kashmir National Liberation Front
JKNPP	Jammu Kashmir National Panthers Party
KAS	Kashmir Administrative Service
KPs	Kashmiri Pandits

KT	*Kashmir Times*
Lashkar	Lashkar-e-Toiba
LeT	Lashkar-e-Toiba
LoC	Line of Control
Lone	Abdul Ghani Lone
Lt. Gen	Lieutenant General
Maj. Gen	Major General
MAT	Muslim Aquaf Trust
MC	Muslim Conference
Mehbooba	Mehbooba Mufti
MLA	Member Legislative Assembly
MUF	Muslim United Front
Mufti	Mufti Mohammad Sayeed
MP	Member of Parliament
NATO	North Atlantic Treaty Organization
NC	National Conference
NDA	National Democratic Alliance
NDTV	New Delhi Television
NSG	National Security Guards
Omar	Omar Abdullah
Pak	Pakistan
PCC	Pradesh Congress Committee
PCR	Police Control Room
PDF	People's Democratic Forum
POTA	Prevention of Terrorism Act
PDP	People's Democratic Party
PoK	Pakistan Occupied Kashmir
PRO	Public Relations Officer

PSC	Public Services Commission
PTI	Press Trust of India
PUCL	People's Union of Civil Liberties
Qazi	Qazi Nissar
Rajiv	Rajiv Gandhi
RAW	Research and Intelligence Wing (India's Foreign Intelligence Agency)
RPC	Ranbir Penal Code
RSS	Rashtriya Swaym Sewak Sangh
SAARC	South Asian Association of Regional Cooperation
Sheikh	Sheikh Mohammad Abdullah
SOG	Special Operation Group
SHO	Station House Officer
SSP	Senior Superintendent of Police
STF	Special Task Force
TDP	Telugu Desam Party
TRC	Tourist Reception Centre
UK	United Kingdom
UN	United Nations
UNI	United News of India
UP	Uttar Pradesh
US	United States
Vajpayee	Former Indian Prime Minister Atal Bihari Vajpayee
VOA	Voice of America
WMDs	Weapons of Mass Destruction
WTC	World Trade Centre

Timeline

Jan 1931	Kashmiri Muslims launch a struggle against Dogra rule in Kashmir Valley. Sheikh Mohammad Abdullah founds Muslim Conference.
Feb 1938	Muslim Conference converted into National Conference; Hindus and Sikhs included to give a secular façade to the movement against Dogra rule in Jammu Kashmir.
1946	National Conference launches 'Quit Kashmir' movement. Sheikh Abdullah arrested.
1947	Tribal invasion of Kashmir. Dogra King Maharaja Hari Singh accedes to India. An emergency government formed with Sheikh Abdullah as Prime Minister.
1948	India refers tribal invasion of Kashmir to the UN.
1949	India and Pakistan cease-fire on Kashmir.
1951	An interim constitution adopted for Jammu and Kashmir.
Aug 9, 1953	Sheikh Abdullah dismissed as Prime Minister and arrested. His Deputy, Bakshi Ghulam Mohammad succeeds him as Prime Minister.
1956	The Constituent Assembly adopts the constitution and declares itself an integral part of India.
Dec 1963	The Holy Relic of Prophet Mohammad is stolen from the highly revered Muslim shrine Hazratbal in Srinagar and demonstrators thronged the streets seeking restoration of the holy relic to the shrine.

1964	Recovery of the holy relic. Sheikh Abdullah is released and asked by Indian Prime Minister Jawaharlal Nehru to visit Pakistan and meet Pakistan's dictator Field Marshall Ayub Khan. The mission is not fulfilled because of Nehru's death on May 27.
Aug 1965	First Indo-Pak War on Kashmir. Cease-fire in September.
1965	Jammu Kashmir National Liberation Front formed.
Dec 1971	Indo-Pak War, liberation of Bangladesh.
Jul 1972	Indian Prime Minister Mrs. Indira Gandhi and her Pakistan counterpart Zulfikar Ali Bhutto sign Simla Agreement in which it is agreed that the two countries resolve the Kashmir issue bilaterally.
Jan 1975	Kashmir Accord signed between Mirza Mohammad Afzal Beg and G. Parthasarthy which enables Sheikh to return to power.
Feb 1975	Sheikh Abdullah becomes Chief Minister of Jammu and Kashmir.
Mar 1977	Congress withdraws support from Sheikh Mohammad Abdullah and Sheikh resigns.
Jul 1977	Assembly Elections, the National Conference wins a clear majority and Sheikh Abdullah is back as Chief Minister.
Sep 8, 1982	Sheikh Abdullah dies. His son Farooq Abdullah takes over as Chief Minister.
1983	Assembly Elections held. National Conference wins and Farooq retains Chief Ministership.

Jul 2, 1984 Farooq Abdullah's government is dismissed as 12 NC MLAs defect and help Congress in installing Farooq's brother-in-law Ghulam Mohammad Shah as Chief Minister.

Mar 1986 Congress withdraws support from the G. M. Shah Government. Governor's rule imposed on Jammu and Kashmir. Muslim United Front formed.

Nov 1986 Congress and Farooq Abdullah's National Conference become allies and form coalition government.

Mar 1987 Assembly Elections. The NC-Congress combine win a two-third majority and MUF loses. Large-scale rigging is alleged. Youth get frustrated and start insurgency.

Jul 1988 First bombs explode in Srinagar, marking the beginning of the militancy.

Dec 1989 Rubiya Sayeed, youngest daughter of then Indian Home Minister Mufti Mohammad Sayeed is kidnapped by JKLF. She is released five days later in exchange for five hard-core activists of the JKLF. This is the first victory of the militancy.

Jan 1990 Farooq Abdullah resigns. Governor's rule imposed. Jagmohan takes over as Governor. The Assembly is suspended.

Feb 1990 Assembly dissolved.

May 21 1990 Jagmohan removed as Governor, former RAW chief Girish Chandra Saxena takes over as new Governor.

Oct 15, 1993	Hazratbal shrine occupied by militants. Army lays siege. People protest the siege. BSF opens fire at protestors in Bijbehra-37 killed, 72 wounded.
1994	Farooq Abdullah seeks restoration of greater autonomy for the State.
1995	Charar-e-Sharief shrine burnt.
1996	Omar Abdullah contests for the first time in Parliamentary Elections and wins from Srinagar.
1999	Pakistani forces intrude into the Indian territory in Kargil in the north of Kashmir. War follows that lasts for 50 days and Pakistan withdraws troops to its side after US intervention. Omar Abdullah is re-elected in the Parliamentary Elections and becomes a minister in the Government of India.
Dec 1999	Maulana Masood Azhar, who later formed Jaish-e-Mohammad, and Mushtaq Zargar, top militant of Al-Umar Mujahadeen, are released from jails in Jammu and Kashmir in exchange for the passengers of the hijacked IC 814. The plane was hijacked from Kathmandu, Nepal and taken to Kandahar in Afghanistan.
2000	Hizb-ul-Mujahadeen announces unilateral cease-fire and holds first round of talks with the Government of India in Srinagar. The cease-fire is withdrawn by Pakistan-based HM leader Syed Salahauddin as the Government of India refuses to involve Pakistan in talks. Prime Minister Atal Bihari Vajpayee announces unilateral cease-fire in November.

May 2001	The November 2000 cease-fire is withdrawn.
Dec 13, 2001	Terrorists attack Indian Parliament in Delhi. India mobilizes troops to border.
2002	Assembly Elections. National Conference loses and a multi-party government headed by Mufti Mohammad Sayeed is set up.
Apr 2003	Prime Minister Atal Bihari Vajpayee extends hand of friendship to Pakistan from a rally in Srinagar.

Principal Players

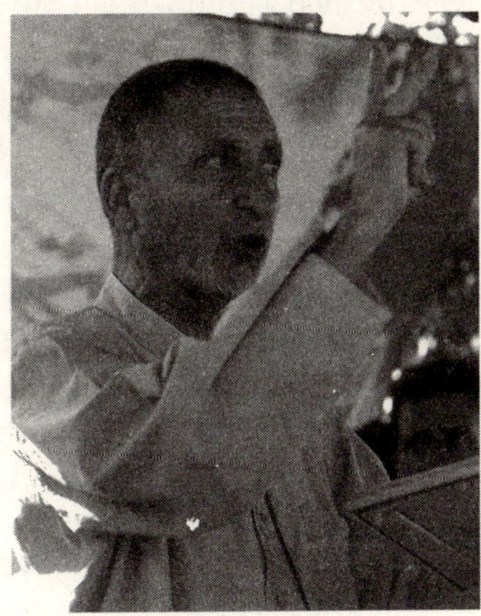

Abdul Gani Bhat

Abdul Gani Bhat

Abdul Gani Bhat, the former Chairman of All Parties Hurriyat Conference, was born in 1933 in Botingu village, outside the apple-rich town of Sopore in Kashmir. He received his elementary education in Sopore itself. Bhat holds an MA in Law and Persian. He practised as a lawyer between the years 1962 and 1963, before joining the Education Department as lecturer in 1963 itself.

During his stint at the Education Department, he was also active in separatist politics. In 1986, he was dismissed by the then Chief Minister, Ghulam Mohammad Shah, now in opposition, on the charge of practising secession. At the time of his dismissal he was serving as Head of the Department of Persian in Baramulla College.

When his services were terminated, Bhat and other dismissed employees formed a union called Muslim Employees Front, which later merged with the Muslim United Front. He was jailed in 1987 for agitating against the rigging of polls by the ruling National Conference and its ally Congress Party. He is vehemently opposed to the NC even now.

Bhat revived the Muslim Conference in the year 1989 after the outbreak of armed militancy in Kashmir. Prior to this, together with a number of other leaders of the Hurriyat Conference faction led by Moulvi Abbas Ansari he initiated talks with Deputy Prime Minister L. K. Advani. Bhat would demand resolution of the Kashmir issue under the relevant resolutions of UN Security Council or by consensus through tri-partite talks, involving India, Pakistan and the representatives of the people of Jammu and Kashmir. The move, though opposed by the rival faction of the Hurriyat, and other hardline separatist groups will have far-reaching implications on Kashmir politics and Bhat's role in the 'ice breaking' has been dominant.

He has been arrested several times since 1985. In 1990, he was arrested and lodged in jail for three years. Bhat has been a driving force behind the APHC since its formation in 1993. He has been very widely covered by local, national and international media for his excellent oratory.

Syed Ali Shah Geelani

Syed Ali Shah Geelani, the firebrand Jamait-i-Islami leader has represented the rightwing organization in the All Parties Hurriyat Conference (APHC) since its inception in the year 1993 but a year ago he fell out with some of the other leaders over the question of holding a bilateral dialogue with the Centre. Geelani questioned his comrades' wisdom and insisted that the Indian government was not sincere and that unless Pakistan was involved in the talks no tangible results could be expected from the process. Soon, with other disgruntled activists and second-rung leaders of the Hurriyat he organized the breakaway faction of the amalgamation.

Geelani was born in Zoori Munz village, in tehsil (an administrative unit) Bandipora, in the northern Baramulla District on September 27, 1929. He has spent more than ten years in different prisons within and outside the state for espousing the cause of Kashmir's accession to or merger with Pakistan.

Geelani joined Jamait-i-Islami in 1950, and his first arrest came in August 28, 1962. He was imprisoned for 13 months and during the same period his father, Syed Peer Shah Geelani,

Syed Ali Shad Geelani

died. He was not allowed to attend the funeral of his father; he would never forget or forgive those who prevented him from having a last glimpse of his beloved father.

On the charges of having 'secret contacts' with Pakistan, Geelani was jailed for 22 months in the year 1965.

Geelani, however, contested in the state legislative assembly thrice from his home constituency—in the years 1972, 1977 and 1987—and won each time, the first two times on the Jamait ticket and the last one as a candidate of the Muslim United Front (MUF). With the onset of militancy in Kashmir, he resigned from the State Assembly in 1989. So did two other MUF members.

Since 1989, he has been the active leader of pro-Pakistan thought, which wants the Kashmir issue to be resolved through the implementation of the UN Security Council resolutions. He has been incarcerated several times since 1989, and has spent two complete years behind bars from 1990 to 1992.

Geelani is viewed as a hard-liner within Kashmir's separatist echelons. His precondition for any dialogue with New Delhi is that Pakistan be involved in the tripartite dialogue on Kashmir.

Mohammad Yasin Malik

Mohammad Yasin Malik hails from Srinagar's congested Maisuma locality, the hotbed of separatist campaigning. Born on April 3, 1966, Malik was interested in modelling when the elections of 1987 changed the course of his life. Malik remained associated with the Islamic Students' League from 1985 to 1987. He was one of the polling agents of Mohammad Yusuf Shah alias Syed Salahauddin, the supreme commander of Hizb-ul-Mujahideen. Salahauddin unsuccessfully contested in the assembly polls from the Amira Kadal constituency in Srinagar. Yusuf had contested polls on the ticket of the Muslim United Front. Owing to mass rigging, Salahauddin lost, and his polling agents, including Yasin Malik were made to suffer in various prisons by the ruling National Conference Party at that time.

Malik along with Mushtaq Zargar, Ashfaq Majid, Javed Mir and Sheikh Hamid crossed over to Pakistan-administered-Kashmir where they met key figures in the JKLF and others outside it. They were given training in the use of small arms. The five, before returning home, joined Amanullah Khan's Jammu Kashmir Liberation Front and once in Srinagar launched a full-fledged armed struggle in Kashmir. Malik and the others soon became household names in the Valley.

Upon Ashfaq Majeed's death in a grenade explosion, Malik became the chief commander of JKLF. He dodged police and security forces several times, but finally was arrested along with some of his commanders from the Barzulla locality of Srinagar on August 6, 1990. He was released in 1994, primarily on medical grounds, and immediately after his release, he called for a unilateral cease-fire by his group. The cease-fire is still in force.

In 1995, Malik broke away from Amanullah Khan and became the Chairman of the faction he was heading. He nominated his close lieutenant, Javed Mir, as his Deputy. Since his release, Malik has been very vocal against New Delhi. He initially resisted being part of the APHC, but finally joined the bandwagon during one of the Friday congregations at the revered Hazratbal shrine. Recently, he bade adieu to the Hurriyat Conference after remaining silent over the bickering within the amalgamation. He is one of the few surviving pioneers of the armed secessionist movement launched in the Kashmir valley in 1988. But Islamic fighters, known to India as foreign mercenaries, and pro-Pakistan outfits now form the background of today's militant struggle; they dominate his JKLF faction. Within the APHC, the JKLF, considerably weakened since its glorious days, is the only outfit which still stands for its avowed goal of independence of Kashmir, unlike most other outfits which advocate Kashmir's accession to or merger with Pakistan. But Malik himself has assumed significance since his joining the Itehadi Force which is instrumental in the formation of a new alliance of the separatist groups outside the APHC. While in the APHC, he was always in the forefront whenever important decisions were to be taken by the amalgamation's executive council, of which he was a member.

Sheikh Abdul Aziz

Sheikh Abdul Aziz was the executive member of APHC, representing the People's League in the separatist conglomerate, before its split. He is now actively involved in the new alliance of the separatist groups and parties called the Itehadi Force. Aziz was born in 1951 in the saffron-growing Pampore area on the outskirts of Srinagar and right from his childhood he had a separatist bent of mind. Aziz has spent more than 16 years in different jails in Jammu and Kashmir, and outside.

Sheikh Aziz is a science graduate and the present chairman of People's League (Aziz group). Known for its pro-Pakistan stand, the PL wants Kashmir's merger with Pakistan. Aziz says he wants implementation of the UN resolutions on Kashmir for resolution of the issue.

At the age of 17 he joined the Young Men's League. He joined the People's League in 1974 as its District President. When the Kashmiri separatist campaign turned violent in 1989–90, Sheikh Aziz threw in his lot with them. He took up arms and became the Chief Commander of Al-Jihad militant group. He was the second 'most wanted' militant commander in Kashmir, after Syed Salahauddin of Hizb-ul-Mujahideen.

Sheikh Aziz was arrested in a surprise raid by the Indian army at Neloora village in Pulwama in 1993 and detained for seven years. Two years ago on being released at the persistent demand of the APHC, Aziz was asked by the People's League to represent the party in the APHC's executive council. As he was vehemently opposed to cease-fire politics, he was rearrested. After remaining in prison for several months, he was set free in 2004.

Moulvi Omar Farooq

Moulvi Omar Farooq

Moulvi Omar Farooq was only 17 when unidentified gunmen assassinated his father Moulvi Muhammad Farooq at his lakeside residence in Nageen, on the outskirts of Srinagar. Only days after his father's death on May 21, 1990, Omar was made the head priest of Kashmir, a job which he performs to the satisfaction of his supporters and admirers by giving Friday sermons at Srinagar's main mosque, Jamia Masjid.

At the tender age of 17, he had to bear the weight of his father's political party, Awami (People's) Action Committee on his shoulders. Omar is the Chairman of AAC, and he attends to party affairs almost daily. He has already carved a niche for himself in Kashmir, in particular, in downtown Srinagar.

Omar has the distinction of being the first Chairman of All Parties Hurriyat Conference (APHC). He was unanimously urged to continue for another term, before Syed Ali Geelani took over the reigns from him. Omar has represented APHC in many world forums like the Organization of Islamic Conference-OIC. Omar's is a secular outlook, a driving force for many outside the Kashmiri separatist politics. Omar represents the young and moderate face of the Hurriyat. He has held two rounds of talks with Mr. Advani and says that Pakistan, if necessary, could be involved in the dialogue process at a later stage. He is still pursuing higher studies in Islamic sharia and has undertaken several tours for completing his research work in Iran and the Central Asian Republic. He is very well-versed with e-mail and Internet and has made several friends on the net. Whenever he finds himself free he surfs the net in search of the latest information on varied subjects ranging from Islam to politics.

Moulvi Abbas Ansari

Moulvi Abbas Ansari

The Shiite cleric-turned-politician is considered another moderate face of the Hurriyat Conference who took cudgels with Syed Geelani and other hardliners within the amalgamation by taking the lead in holding talks with the Centre. Not long ago he would insist that without involving all the three parties to the dispute no lasting solution could be arrived at on the issue of Kashmir. He says that the changing political scenario in South Asia and beyond and the ground situation prevailing in Jammu and Kashmir itself forced him to opt for friendship with Delhi but his critics accuse him of betrayal.

Before he landed himself in this situation, the 70-year-old leader had been popular among sections of Kashmiri Sunni and Shiite population alike for his steadiness in local politics. He is admired for the consistent stand which he takes in politics, unlike his contemporaries who are subject to political vagaries.

He became active in politics in Kashmir on his return from Najaf (Iraq) where he reportedly studied Islamic law at premier Shiite institutions for eight years beginning in 1963. Incidentally, in December that year the holy relic of Prophet Muhammad was stolen from Srinagar's Hazratbal mosque. The incident sparked off widespread protests across Kashmir and Moulvi Abbas was among the religious-political leaders who created the stir. Presently, he heads the Anjuman-e-Itehadul Muslimeen, a religio-political group dominated by Shiite Muslims of the Valley, and a constituent of the Hurriyat Conference.

Abdul Gani Lone

The moderate face of the Hurriyat Conference was silenced on May 21 , 2002 when Abdul Gani Lone fell to assassins' bullets at Srinagar's Idgah.

Born in Lona Haray village in northwestern Kupwara district close to the Line of Actual Control, Lone had joined Kashmir politics as a student leader. He later became a legislator and then a minister in the Congress Party government at Srinagar. He exerted influence in pockets along the Kupwara-Handwara belt, which he nursed almost throughout his political career. A veteran legislator and chief ideologue of the Hurriyat Conference, he was the key man in the Indian Government's efforts to start a dialogue with the amalgamation. Lone had reportedly been contacted through Syed Mir Qasim, a veteran Kashmiri mainstream politician and former State Chief Minister in whose regime Lone was a minister. Lone favoured dialogue but insisted on the UN resolutions on Kashmir. Soon he found himself at the centre of controversy following his criticism of the role of foreign militants in Kashmir in whose presence he thought the initiative of seeking a peaceful solution to the issue might not see the light of day. Soon he paid with his life.

Until his assassination, Lone served as Chairman of the People's Conference, which he launched, in the late 1970s of the twentieth century primarily to demand greater autonomy for the State. From the time when he joined Kashmir politics as a Congress leader, Lone had often changed his stand on the issue facing the Himalayan State.

Mohammad Yusuf Tarigami

The man who floated the idea of a unilateral cease-fire in October 2000 before it actually came from Prime Minister, Atal Behari Vajpayee, CPI (M)'s State Secretary was returned from his home constituency Kulgam as member of the State Assembly in the September-October 2002 elections contested in the recent Lok Sabha elections from Anantnag and lost. Tarigami is a young and well-meaning Kashmiri politician. A staunch votary of greater autonomy, Tarigami has been an ardent critic of the Farooq Abdullah government. One of the few political figures in Kashmir who draws crowds because of his image as a fighter for the people's cause. But that is the story of yesteryear. His critics say that he was a creation of the political vacuum that has prevailed in the Valley, as a result of the militancy. What, however, cannot be denied is that Tarigami has played a key role in Kashmir's modern politics.

Shabir Ahmad Shah

Outside the Hurriyat Conference, he is the only credible separatist leader. Shabir Shah is known as Kashmir's Nelson Mandela because of the long detention he, as the leader of the People's League, underwent for his unwavering stance on the right to self-determination. The 49-year-old leader was expelled from the Hurriyat Conference when, in violation of a collective decision taken by the amalgamation executive, he met the then visiting US ambassador to India, Frank Wisner, and later on former Indian Prime Minister, V.P. Singh to discuss the issue of Kashmir. Subsequently, he launched the People's Democratic Freedom Party, which believes in seeking a peaceful resolution to the Kashmir problem. He too has been instrumental in launching the Itehadi Force.

Farooq Abdullah

Sheikh Abdullah's eldest son who took over as Chief Minister in 1982, in typical dynastic succession style, upon the death of his father, could not measure up to the personality and political vision of his father. He displayed no signs of being a serious politician or a man who could launch or lead struggles. He is a comfort-loving, globe-trotting man who loves the company of beautiful women.

Farooq Abdullah

Farooq is a doctor by profession. But he was not successful either as a doctor or as a politician. He was dragged into politics by his father who first got him elected to the Indian Parliament in 1980 and later appointed him as President of the National Conference. Before his death, Sheikh Abdullah, had prepared the ground for Farooq to take over as Chief Minister.

For a while Farooq made a mark in politics because of his father's goodwill. He won the 1983 elections and after his government was dismissed in July 1984, he was perceived as a victim of the conspiracies of Delhi. People were with him. But he squandered away a lot of that goodwill and popularity when he aligned himself with the Congress in 1986 to regain power. It is said about him that he is a fish without water when out of power. He had to pay a heavy price for his lust for power. The elections in 1987 were rigged; militancy erupted in the State.

He failed because he displayed no signs of a good politician, kept himself busy with anything but politics and administration. The party under him crumbled and despite his being Sheikh Abdullah's son and the cadre strength of the National Conference, he could not gather the courage to stand up in Kashmir when the Valley was in turmoil. He spent most of his time with his family in London. He is married to a British woman, Molly. The party became disillusioned and the cadres began to lose faith in themselves. But the common people in Kashmir gave the NC yet another chance in 1996 and Farooq Abdullah was elected Chief Minister. His party obtained a two-third majority in the Assembly elections in 1996. But this time too Farooq could not cash in on the goodwill. He became more suspect in the eyes of the Kashmiris when he aligned himself with the Hindu fundamentalist party, the BJP and made his son Omar Abdullah a minister. He could not control the security forces. Militancy and counter-insurgency operations made life hell for the people. Except for a few and occasional voices of protest, he could not do anything for the people and in 2002, on the eve of the elections, he made Omar president of the NC. But they had their differences. As a result, the National Conference suffered a crushing defeat in the elections. It has lost power and now sits in the opposition. Yet, in spite of it all, Farooq Abdullah has retained his charisma. He is still the biggest crowd puller for his party over which he presides.

Omar Abdullah

Omar Abdullah wanted to become a pilot, but could not. He landed himself in hotel management and was dragged into politics by his father who made him contest from the Srinagar parliamentary constituency in 1998. He won. In mid-term elections in 1999, Omar was again elected and this time became minister in the BJP-led NDA government.

Omar was brought up in England and has found himself in difficulty when speaking Kashmiri; he became unpopular

Omar Abdullah

with the senior leaders of the party, especially when he became President of the National Conference. He crashed in the Assembly elections. He lost his own seat in Ganderbal, that is part of the Srinagar parliamentary constituency, from where he had been elected twice, before that. His defeat was demoralizing for the party and his style of working alienated loyal workers. But in Kashmiri politics, he is seen as a man of promise, a clear thinker with the capability to deliver because of his stint as Minister in the Indian Government. He is a straight talking person and that is his asset. He was elected to the Lok Sabha for a third time in the April-May 2004 elections.

Sheikh Mohammad Abdullah

Born to a poor family in Kashmir in 1905, Sheikh rose to become the most eminent ever leader of the Kashmiris. He did his postgraduate studies in mathematics from Aligarh Muslim University and joined as a teacher under Mahraja Hari Singh's rule. Protesting against his transfer to Muzzaffarabad from Srinagar, Sheikh quit the government job and joined politics. He organised a group of like-minded youth and launched the Muslim Conference in 1931. The basic fight of the Muslim Conference was against the Hindu king and monarchy. However, under the influence of Congress leadership, he converted the Muslim Conference into the National Conference to give it a secular character. He was greatly influenced by Congress leaders Mahatma Gandhi and Jawaharlal Nehru.

When tribes invaded Kashmir in 1947, power was handed over to Sheikh Abdullah. He was made Prime Minister of the emergency Government. But in 1953, he was deposed on suspicion of working with Pakistan. The conspiracy trial lasted for several years during which his National Conference was disbanded and renamed the Plebiscite Front which sought the right of self-determination for the people of Jammu and Kashmir.

In 1975, he was lured back to the Indian mainstream after then Indian Prime Minister Indira Gandhi decided to hand power over to him. Congress which was then ruling the State quit power and backed Sheikh Abdullah's appointment as Chief Minister. Immediately, thereafter, the National Conference was revived.

Sheikh Abdullah led the rebellion against the monarchy in Jammu and Kashmir and became the icon of the aspirations of the people of Kashmir. It was thanks to his mesmerizing influence on the masses that Kashmiris agreed to the accession of the Muslim majority state to India.

But he proved to be rather unpredictable in politics and landed himself in a series of controversies that resulted in his fall from favour with Delhi. He was in the political wilderness for 22 years from 1953 to 1975 before he was resurrected by Indira Gandhi into Indian mainstream politics. But those 22 years of his political wilderness and the plebiscite movement were to sow the seeds of secession in Kashmir. His slogan for secession of Kashmir from India was imprinted on the minds of generations of Kashmiris and, when in 1975 he rejoined national mainstream politics, he lost a great deal of his support. But his towering personality and his contribution of land to the tiller during his first spell of rule in 1947 to 1953, kept his critics under check. But with his death on September 8, 1982, the critics have gained a new lease on life and the new generation is characterizing him as a traitor.

Mehbooba Mufti (left) and Mufti Mohammad Sayeed (right)

Mehbooba Mufti

Daughter of Mufti Mohammad Sayeed, Mehbooba Mufti is the real architect of the victory of the People's Democratic

Party founded by her father in July 1999 in the 2002 Assembly elections. Her relentless campaign against the National Conference, her visits to places where militants have lost their lives, her preoccupation with issues of unemployment and poverty have endeared her to the people. She established herself in politics by scoring a victory in the 1996 Assembly elections. She won on a Congress ticket and quit the party and the MLAship in July 1999 to help her father form the PDP. She was elected from Pahalgam Assembly constituency in 2002 where her mother Gulshan had lost in 1996. In the 2004 parliamentary elections, she contested from Anantnag constituency and won.

She is seen as a rising star in Kashmir politics. Within her party, she is both envied and admired.

Mufti Mohammad Sayeed

A law graduate from Aligarh Muslim University, Mufti Mohammad began his political career with Congress in the 1960s. He carved a niche for himself as a rebel against the might of the National Conference and the family of Sheikh Abdullah whom he has relentlessly pursued with a deep-seated hatred. For all his machinations, he did not immediately succeed as Chief Minister. In 1999, he parted company with the Congress and formed his own party, the People's Democratic Party and intensified his campaign against the National Conference.

The hate campaign against the National Conference succeeded and his party unexpectedly won 16 seats in the Valley; it then aligned with Congress and some small parties to form the Government. He soon proceeded to do what he had accused the National Conference of doing—he rigged the polls in the 2004 parliamentary elections to help his daughter Mehbooba Mufti win from the Anantnag parliamentary constituency.

Having realized his lifetime dream of becoming Chief Minister, he is proceeding to build a base for his daughter, in the same way that Farooq Abdullah had done for his son, Omar Abdullah. His role in Kashmiri politics has primarily been that of a persistent challenger of the National Conference. He is now bent on suppressing and shattering the NC, and thereby break the main political party of the Kashmir Valley.

Part I

1

The Global Perspective

On the geopolitical world map, Kashmir is circled in red as the most dangerous place in the world. It is called a nuclear flashpoint and triggers panic in the hearts of world leaders whenever Indian and Pakistan armies clash on borders. In the year 2002, US and UK leaders[1] landed almost every month in Delhi and Islamabad to ensure that the two contestants for the Himalayan territory did not go to war.

The nuclear tests undertaken in turn by India and Pakistan in the summer of 1998, in a typical game of tit for tat which the two countries have perfected in political, diplomatic and military one-upmanship have tagged them as irresponsible nations. While the masses of their populations struggle to eke out a living, their respective governments have poured hundreds and thousands of billions of dollars into their nuclear programmes. The proliferation of nuclear weapons in the region has exacerbated the task of seeking solutions. This build-up of atomic weapons has given Pakistan the means to blackmail the world on the issue.[2] Islamabad has drawn close attention to the 'Kashmir dispute' and seeks international intervention: a posturing that pleases the United States of America. Pakistan wants to embark on this path with the twin objectives of keeping Washington happy and averting US pressure on its own terrorist network, which it finds difficult to dismantle, because of the rising power of the Muslim fundamentalist groups.[3] India, for her part, attributes the whole problem to the export of terrorism from Pakistan. The world has to some extent come to believe India especially as September 11 has brought increased focus on Pakistan's deep involvement with terrorist networks. Its role in raising the Taliban and supporting Al-Qaeda networks has unravelled, much to the embarrassment of the people and rulers of the country that came into being with the division of India in 1947 on religious lines. It is now a known fact that many of Al-Qaeda's top leaders were operating from Pakistan. Pakistan herself, too, has seen the pitfalls in promoting terrorism, Pakistan's military ruler President Pervez Musharraf, who once hailed the terrorists in Kashmir as 'freedom fighters'[4] and wanted the world to draw a distinction between the two classes, has himself voiced concerns over the world punishing Pakistan.[5]

At the height of tensions on the global scene, when the US was preparing for an all out war against Iraq to oust Saddam Hussein amidst world criticism, barring the United Kingdom and a few other countries in Europe, Kashmir appeared to have been sidelined. In reality this was not the case. Even as America and its allies were expending their energy and vocal power in diplomacy at the Security Council and NATO, Kashmir was being connected to the overall security situation in the world.[6]

The American allies of the past, France and Germany found themselves cast alongside Russia and China in opposing the war–as a means of punishing Iraq–without substantial evidence against the country which President George W. Bush in his State of the Union speech in 2002 had listed along with Iran and North Korea as the 'axis of evil.'

As the diplomatic skirmishes deteriorated into a futile name calling exercise between the European leaders especially when Germany and France provided their own formula for disarming Saddam Hussein by strengthening the human and technical capacities of the UN mandated inspectors to look for nuclear as well as Weapons of Mass Destruction (WMDs), the Muslim world was petrified by the rigidity of the US over the issue. Washington had made it clear that it would not wait for a second UN resolution nor allow the split in NATO to stand in the way of unleashing war against Iraq. It was also endorsed by the British Prime Minister Tony Blair. He had built a moral case against Iraq making it clear that the US and UK were not merely interested in the disarmament of Iraq but also in effecting a regime change. Millions of protesters world-wide interpreted the war as a game writ in blood for oil by the US and its closest ally the UK.

The US was convinced that war was the only option of punishing Saddam Hussein whose links with Al-Qaeda were being cited as the reason for the punishment that it was proposing. US Secretary of State Colin Powell who had put his prestige behind this assertion at the UN Security Council on February 14, 2003, saw any delay in action against Saddam as consolidating the terrorist network that could pose a serious threat to world peace and stability. Al-Qaeda was the punishing link. Pakistan saw it coming to her as well. And this conviction was strengthened with the American ousting of Saddam in the second Iraq War that began on March 20, 2003, and lasted for 50 days. After all, Pakistan had been the greatest supporter of this terrorist network and its sleeping cells across the globe had been capable of razing the WTC in New York and bombing night clubs in Bali and hotels in the Indonesian capital Jakarta and provoke terror attack alerts at Heathrow airport and the White House. The US had already started warning Pakistan after a series of attacks on foreigners in naval bases, churches and hotels. The US suddenly found new evidence of Pakistan's raising the level of infiltration into the Indian part of Jammu and Kashmir while having maintained for long that Pakistan was doing enough to keep in check the terrorists from infiltrating into the Indian side. The writing on the wall was apparent to all. Pakistan was not so blind as to ignore the warning signals emanating from Washington the world capital, which once it had decided on a course of action never sought justification for doing what it did. Afghanistan and Iraq are living examples.

This was despite the fact that Pakistan had served as an outpost for America for its war against terrorism after 9/11. Pakistan had opted for that role out of obligation. It knew what the US could do and how refusal to cooperate with an angry superpower in the unilateral world could spell doom for the cash-strapped nation facing a threat from its eastern neighbour. Islamabad understood the tough line which President George W. Bush was taking on terrorism. He had warned those nations who did not side with Washington in the war against terrorism that they would be viewed as being on the side of terrorists.

Pakistan sought the path of prudence in siding with the US war. It was its aim to gain legitimacy in American eyes and obtain thereby the lifting of economic and military sanctions. (These had been imposed after May 1998 for the nuclear blasts). That was how Pervez Musharraf had sought for survival for himself and the nation of which he had become the self-appointed President in July 2001, ironically days before he arrived in India for what is now known as the failed Agra summit. The Indian Prime Minister Atal Bihari Vajpayee regretted that even the backdrop of the monument of love—Taj Mahal—the white marbled marvel built by Mughal emperor Shahjahan for his beloved wife Mumtaz in Agra—had not been able to melt the ice. Musharraf remained frigid and rigid.

President Musharraf who had changed sides after the 9/11 attack on the World Trade Centre and the Pentagon in which Muslims who were devoted to the holy cause had destroyed the symbols of the economic and military power of the US by smashing aircrafts into the buildings and thereby awakened the world to new horrors, was indeed a worried man. He told a gathering of industrialists and businessmen in Lahore on January 19, 2003 that, after Iraq, it could well be Pakistan's turn. Pakistan could have saved itself from the impending predicament had it not been bent on the path of self-destruction in Kashmir.

Musharraf told the leaders of business and industry: 'We will have to work on our own to stave off the impending danger. Nobody will come to our rescue, not even the Islamic world. We will have to depend on our own muscle.' This was a clear admission that things were wrong for Pakistan which had come under unwanted spotlight as a nation with a huge number of terrorists and terrorist organizations operating from its soil. President Musharraf could predict that even the Muslim world would not come to the rescue of Pakistan for he had seen how Iraq had been isolated and the rest of the Islamic world was watching the US aggression against Iraq, even though the streets in some of the Islamic countries had been filled with anti-American protesters. In the end, everyone had fallen in line. A new empire was born. The US was not plundering the wealth of Iraq nor did it have any intention of sending colonialists there, after the pattern of empires of the 19th and 20th centuries. But it was trying to subjugate a nation whose ruler had defied Washington. The US was also sending a message to other nations that it would brook no defiance. These signals were being beamed to Iran. Pakistan too did not miss the point.

This shift in global politics and especially in the US was a worrying scenario for Pakistan. It was caught in a bind. It could not abandon the path it had chosen for Kashmir-sponsoring men and material for jihad in Kashmir nor could it continue with the same impunity what it called diplomatic, political and moral support for the 'freedom fighters' in Kashmir because the world had come to openly condemn the role Pakistan was playing in destabilizing India through terror. Even the erstwhile supporters of Pakistan within Kashmir had predicted that Pakistan would meet the same fate as Afghanistan at the hands of the US. These were cold realities, which had come to bite at Islamabad, though rather belatedly.

All this was of meagre comfort to India as it is seen as the weaker party when the focus shifts to the internal problem in Kashmir. It accepts that mistakes have been made in the past vis-a-vis Delhi and Srinagar. It refuses to concede any role to Pakistan in addressing the tensions arising from within. While confronting global opinion it maintains that there is no problem and the whole trouble is inspired by Pakistan. But India knows, in historical terms, that errors had been committed. For example, the leadership of the 1980s and 1990s had blamed Congress and Jawaharlal Nehru for taking Kashmir to the United Nation Security Council and halting the military operations against tribal invaders in 1947-48. The charge is that Nehru had internationalized an issue that was primarily an internal problem. This problem developed into a crisis because of the promise that Nehru had made to the people to settle the issue of the choice of the country they wanted to live in through self, determination. That has given reason to the separatists who, by quoting Nehru on the issue, have sown the seeds of secession and reminded Kashmiris and the rest of the world of India's sincerity.

Endnotes

1 US Secretary of State, Colin Powell, Deputy Secretary of State, Richard Armitage; UK Foreign Secretary Jack Straw.

2 In 2002, when Indian and Pakistani troops were standing eyeball to eyeball, after the assault on the Indian Parliament on December 13, 2001, Pakistan President Pervez Musharraf, who is also the army chief of his country, had declared that, if need be, Pakistan would not hesitate to go for nuclear weapons. This was perceived by the international community as a ploy by Pakistan to put international pressure on India to withdraw its troops from the border. This threat was held out in May 2002 when it appeared imminent that India might resort to nuclear power. Gen. S. Padmanabhan, Chief of Staff of the Indian Army had acknowledged on his retirement at the

beginning of 2003 that India could have gone to war with Pakistan in May 2002. Pakistan had held out the threat because India had established supremacy in conventional war, as adequately demonstrated in the 1965 and 1971 wars.

3. President Musharraf has clearly stated on several occasions that he is the ally of the US in the war against terrorism and at the same time he has been pitching for a solution for Kashmir. In his speech on PTV September 19, 2001 immediately after September 11, he stated that Pakistan was going to side with the US. He made it clear that one of the reasons for doing so was "our Kashmir cause."

4. During the Agra Summit at his breakfast meeting with editors of leading newspapers of India in July 2001, President Musharraf had said that there is a clear distinction between terrorists and freedom fighters. "In Kashmir it is a freedom struggle and not terrorism and those fighting there are freedom fighters." He has repeated this on many occasions.

5. Speech given by President Musharraf to industrialists in Lahore on January 19, 2003.

6. It was the observation of Pakistan and that of the leaders of the separatists groups in Kashmir that, with India and Pakistan going nuclear, the threat of atomic war had increased. Kashmir was referred to as a nuclear flash-point. British Prime Minister Tony Blair in several of his speeches on Iraq and terrorism has always spoken of Kashmir and categorized it with Palestine and other conflict zones across the globe.

2

The Historical Perspective

Paradoxically, the year 1947 does not mark the real date of secession which dates back to March 16, 1846—the day of the signing of the Amritsar Treaty which Kashmiri Muslims have come to see as the beginning of their slavery. There is an argument that Kashmiris had perpetually been under foreign rule. So Dogra rule had not been their first experience of alien rule. But the marked difference is that Dogra rule had been the result of a sale deed and no community likes to see itself as a purchasable commodity. Defeat in battle, on the other hand, was something totally different. From day one, Kashmiris had chafed under Dogra rule. The terms of the treaty were rubbing salt into the wounds of the people. By a purchase deed, Gulab Singh had become owner of the minds and bodies of the people and even of their very sweat and blood. Intense hatred characterized the entire period of the Dogra rule for the Dogra kings hailing from Jammu were alien to the basic principles of government and further incensed the Kashmiris with their deliberate acts of injustice. Concessions were made by the Dogra rulers solely at the behest of the British who had their own ends to achieve as subsequent history has demonstrated beyond doubt. The British role is one of the major contributory factors to the turmoil that the Himalayan State is experiencing today.

The fermenting resentment found an outlet with the arrival of Sheikh Abdullah on the scene in the 1930s. Sheikh Abdullah was a young postgraduate who could find no better job than that of a school teacher. He had been drawn to politics by his refusal to accept transfer orders from Srinagar to Muzzaffarabad. He found common cause with Mohammad Yusuf Shah and Muslim leaders of Jammu: Ghulam Abbas Choudhary and

Zafarullah in raising the banner of revolt against the Dogra king. They were essentially asking for better treatment of Muslims in education, government services and living conditions. Their primary aim was not to overthrow the monarchy but, as the pace of events in Kashmir was influenced by contemporary developments in British India, where the voices raised against British rule were getting louder, that unspoken aspiration also became their objective. The weakening of the empire and the dallyings of the leaders of the Indian revolution of both the Congress and the Muslim League were making their impact on the minds of the leaders in Kashmir.

Complacency is the sin that rulers commit inadvertently. This lesson from history has been read by all the rulers, only to be forgotten by them at the critical moment. The Dogra kings were no exception. The Maharaja Hari Singh was as much a victim of his make-believe world as any other ruler of the past. The convulsions of revolution in India, might have appeared to him, as events confined to a distant land and the high walls of the Himalayas prevent the winds of change from blowing onto the plains. But these whirlwinds were to produce avalanches which threatened to dwarf even the Himalayas. That is precisely what happened when the 'Quit India' movement found a loud echo in 'Quit Kashmir.' Events might have taken their natural course with the king being overthrown and the rebels succeeding him as the new ruler. This was not destined to be the case for Jammu and Kashmir. The revolution ended in the division of the continent for different objectives, into India and Pakistan, with the British looking out for their strategic interests, keeping watch on Central Asia to check the influence of the Russian empire under the Czars. There was also a clash in the personalities and ambitions of the two men which could have shaped the state's future. The Maharaja wanted to stay independent, as was also the ambition of Sheikh Abdullah. The

Muslim League Leader Mohammad Ali Jinnah wanted Kashmir to be a part of Pakistan. Jinnah's foot soldiers in the peripheries of Poonch and Mirpur were up in arms. This tribal invasion was preceded by the blockade of essential commodities from the Rawalpindi-Baramullah road even though Pakistan had signed the stand-still agreement with the Maharaja while India was adamant that it would not help the king who was rapidly losing both ground to tribal invaders and the loyalty of his subjects in Kashmir, unless he signed the accession. There are many doubts surrounding the veracity of the instrument of accession. Those doubts have persisted and the instrument of accession and its finality are questionable in the eyes of the world because Kashmir is far from being an integral part of India, Delhi's repeated assertions notwithstanding. The major part of the fault lies with the Maharaja himself. He got control of all the portfolios for the state except defence, foreign affairs and communications. This has irked some because it stood in the way of full merger of the state with the Indian union. For separatists, it was an endorsement of Delhi's insincerity.

From Delhi's viewpoint the matter was absolutely settled and it remained only to address the forcible occupation of the territory under the thumb of Pakistan which for some reason was called *Azad Kashmir* (Independent Kashmir), though people there were no better than hostages to the wishes and dictates of Pakistan. The Jammu Kashmir Liberation Front (JKLF) which stands for the independence of Kashmir was barred from contesting polls at the Assembly in *Azad Kashmir*. Every aspirant had to pledge loyalty to Pakistan and accept its sovereignty to qualify to become a contestant in the polls in November 2000. Pakistan and democracy are two hostile terms.

Kashmiri separatists like Syed Ali Shah Geelani, blinded by their love for Pakistan, have the liberty to run down India day in and out, preaching open revolt against India and still get away with it. Had Geelani attempted anything similar even once against Pakistan upon Pakistani soil, he would not have lived to see another day. Perhaps, all of them know this in their hearts but their fanaticism and inexplicable love for Pakistan, prevents them from speaking the truth and acknowledging the virtues of Indian democracy however flawed it might be. Though much is left to be desired in Jammu and Kashmir conditions are better and brighter there, compared with the political system in Pakistan and Pakistan occupied Kashmir (PoK).

It is the fanatics on both sides who have kept relations between the two nations sour and often this animosity has deteriorated into wars over Kashmir.

3

The Ethnic-Religious Divide

Jammu and Kashmir is beset by profound divisions. Apart from PoK and the territory that Pakistan has handed over to China as a gift for the Karakaram pass road, the majority of the population in the Jammu and Ladakh regions are deeply opposed to the secessionist movement in the Valley, the backbone of which is made up of by the Muslims there. Since Jammu and Kashmir is the only Muslim majority state in India, attention is riveted on them and their cause, while Jammu and Ladakh escape the attention of the world. Even Delhi ignores these two regions.

This convulsive development is involving other dimensions as well. With Osama bin Laden's call for Jihad and the suicide bombers having made their explosive presence in the state, the Kashmir issue is also seen as part of the global phenomenon of war between believers and infidels. There is hardly any other region in the world which has so many in-built complexities—where the people are divided along religious, regional and ethnic lines and where wars have been fought and more are in preparation.

It is a big challenge for cartographers to map Jammu and Kashmir. The Valley is populated purely by Muslims, more so after the exodus of Kashmiri Hindus, better known as Kashmiri Pandits in the early 1990s followed by the Sikhs at the beginning of this century when select members of their community became targets of the militancy. Bill Clinton probably would remember his visit to India in March 2000 more for the nightmare massacre of 35 Sikhs in Chittisinghpora, a sleepy village in South Kashmir about 70 kms south of Srinagar, than anything else. Sikhs were gunned down on the night of Clinton's arrival in India and to date no one knows who had perpetuated the deed. Like everything else in Kashmir, there are conflicting reports of the massacres, one official and the other from the separatists.

But even within the exclusively Muslim Valley, there are divisions in culture. First, among Sunni Muslims who form about 95 per cent of a five million population, many of whom would not qualify to be Muslims in the strictest sense of the definition prescribed by Islam for its followers elsewhere. They visit shrines and worship relics, something which is considered un-Islamic in the Islamic world and condemned by others within the Muslim community. Such practices have their roots in Sufi culture at the core of which is the principle of the mutual brotherhood between religions.

Despite 14 years of militancy, there has, however, been little change in their attitudes and styles of worship. Then there are the Ahmediyas, who are often disparagingly referred to as 'non-Muslims' which is, for them, a term of abuse. The Shias who are historically different from the Sunnis are also present in the Valley. Cultural differences and differences in the way they worship are, however, not the only dividing lines. Within the Valley, there are also the Gujjars and Bakerwals whom Muslims consider backward and view with extreme suspicion as being more inclined towards India. They are seen as aliens to the secessionist movement and rarely trusted. It is for this reason that they are often chosen as targets by the militants. The Gujjars have spread over to other regions. Further to the north, they are hated by both the Shias as well as the Buddhists, in Ladakh, for economic reasons and are prohibited from pasturing their herds in the trans-Himalayan grasslands in Kargil which adjoin the Doda district of the Jammu region. The Buddhists in Zanskar in Kargil and Leh deeply resent the Shias whom they consider as members of the Kashmiri Muslim community who are ever ready to prey on their land and economic avenues. All these differences, notwithstanding, the Muslims are becoming more fundamentalists and being drawn to *jihad*.

By virtue of their religion, Kashmiri Muslims are part of the wider Muslim *ummah* or Muslim nation. They share in the pain of the atrocities wreaked upon Muslims in Kosovo, Palestine, Chechenya, Iraq and Afghanistan. In return, they receive petrodollars for insurgency activities. Kashmiri Muslims are not immune to the *jihad* movement or holy war until victory or martyrdom, which is gaining ground. Their political aspirations are being submerged in the call of Islam; they admire Hamas and its volunteer force of suicide bombers and satellite channels have raised their motivation to higher levels. Born amidst the rattle of bullets and explosions, and fed upon TV images of suicide bombers tearing apart their perceived oppressors, those who belong to this generation are more beguiled by *jihad* and martyrdom than the pleasures of a prolonged, youthful life, preferring to exchange earthly existence for immediate entry into paradise.

In the Jammu region, the majority Hindu community which has always resented the Kashmiri Muslims for having dethroned the Hindu Dogra king, is now confronted by a Muslim population which has turned its back on its regional Dogra identity in favour of being identified as part of the Muslim Ummah, sharing the secessionist dreams of their co-religionists of the Valley. For its part, Jammu is affronted by its diminishing role in state politics. Although their region forms the backbone of the economy of the State, Jammu Hindus feel that second class treatment is being meted out to them by their Kashmiri rulers. There are voices, among them, calling for a separate state for Jammu demarcated by the geographical boundaries of the region. But the Muslims are opposed to this. Hence the demand for a separate state has complicated matters and deepened the religious and regional fissures.

The Buddhists in the cold desert region of Ladakh see their future in separation from rest of the state, particularly the Valley. They want their identity to be preserved under the direct rule of Delhi. This brings them in confrontation with the Valley Muslims whose case on the international forum is thereby weakened as such a position only lends further weight to Delhi's argument that the problem is restricted to Muslims and confined solely within the Valley.

Had the matter been settled through the plebiscite which the Government of India should have held under the UN resolution of January 5, 1948, much of the uncertainty would have disappeared and at least, territorially, there would have been no dispute. The will of both India and Pakistan is suspect in the matter. India was as much uncertain of the outcome as Pakistan. India never announced the plebiscite, Pakistan never withdrew its troops from the parts under its occupation, as envisaged under the terms of the United Nations resolution for both the countries claiming Kashmir to be their own, prior to the holding of the plebiscite. That legacy has periodically helped pro-Pakistan forces to exploit the situation. As it happened, Sheikh Abdullah, Nehru's best bet in Kashmir turned the tables once he was deposed on suspicion of hobnobbing with foreign powers to wrest Kashmir from Indian sovereignty. His arrest and the concomitant rise to power of Bakshi Ghulam Mohammad won peace for the state, and helped pacify the bickering within the National Conference. But what he failed to do was to stem the separatist sentiment despite his legendary generous handing-out of doles and job orders on cigarette wrappers. When he was removed under the Kamraj Plan, India discovered to its great dismay that life in Kashmir would be permeated with undying separatist sentiments.

Sheikh Abdullah was continually in and out of jail. His appeal might ebb and flow but he remained a force to be reckoned with; he was a nightmare for his successor Ghulam Mohammad Sadiq. What Sadiq could never do was to prevent the pro-secessionist constituency from growing. Proof of this, if needed, could be found in the rallying cries of 'We want Pakistan, our leader Ayub Khan' raised daily by hundreds of demonstrators thronging the streets of Kashmir. And this was happening even though India was pouring in billions into Kashmir to buy loyalties. For a nation that had been sold for Rs 75 lakhs in 1846, loyalty was not to be traded, however astronomical the sum. India was far from retaining it and Pakistan far from getting it.

There could never be an easy solution to a crisis of such magnitude. It is imperative that a solution be found if the world is not to be thrown into a quagmire of war and bloodshed or the new world order ruined without any guarantee of a secure future for the new generations whom we want to settle in outer space where the risks of Columbia and Challenger-style crashes are fewer than those on earth. Kashmir is a tiny dot on this planet but it has the potential to explode and consume at least half of the world.

Kashmir, in its present shape is the direct outcome of the personality clashes and failures of leaders of the past. Jawaharlal Nehru and Mohammad Ali Jinnah could not reconcile their ambitions. This led to the emergence of Pakistan, at the cost of millions dead, looted, and raped. This dark chapter is still casting its long dark shadow and it is now the third generation which has inherited their legacy of mutual hatred and distrust. Where one's own victories in cricket matches taste sweet, the defeat of the neighbour is yet sweeter. This poisoning of the social fabric has given birth to religious riots, in which humans are reduced to the levels of beasts. Religious zealotry has spawned the entire spectrum of terrorism which plagues both India and Pakistan. The tests of military might which have resulted in the dismemberment of Pakistan have not brought about repentance. Remorse, if any, has been ephemeral. And so the cycle of revenge continues.

Neither India nor Pakistan would face each other across the table. Domestic politics dictate that they each hold tenaciously to their position, baulking at the very prospect of seeking a solution. Kashmiris have allowed themselves to become a pawn even though they are living in the world's most dangerous spot on earth, one which—and they know it better than any others—was a haven of peace not long ago.

Nehru-Jinnah chose the confrontational track that was matched in the ego clashes between the Maharaja Hari Singh and Sheikh Mohammad Abdullah- one a monarch and the other a rebel. Both wanted a free and safe state and both had dreams for its progress and prosperity. In the final analysis their roles contributed to the selfdestruction of the Himalayan state.

Dogra rule was introduced with the signing of the Treaty of Amritsar on March 16, 1846 between Gulab Singh and British. The British who had acquired Kashmir Valley by dismembering the Sikh rule in Kashmir handed over the territory to Dogra king for Rs. 75 lakhs. The Treaty gave the king full rights over the land and the people of the state. The Kashmiris deeply resented this but were helpless against Dogra might which had the blessings and full backing of the British in India. Kashmiri poet Iqbal summed up the plight of Kashmiris in his beautiful poetic version:

> 'Oh breeze if you pass by Geneva,
> Deliver this message of ours to the League of Nations
> They sold peasants, crops, rivers and gardens;
> In short, sold a whole nation and so cheap at that.'

Dogra rulers could not endear themselves to Kashmiris at anytime throughout their century-long rule. Ruthless and overbearing they were good warriors but not good rulers, capable of action only when under pressure. The Maharaja declared himself the sole owner of all lands, forests and mountains. He did not concede any property rights to any of his subjects. He ensured stability through repression and was the unchallenged authority. But down the line, that did not remain the case. The atrocities which the Dogra rulers inflicted on Kashmiris stirred deep liberal and nationalistic sentiments. The Dogra King's efforts to control the Kashmiri nation in his interest proved disastrous.[1]

The Maharaja Hari Singh who became king in 1929 had no time for the niceties of governance preoccupied as he was with his pleasure, hunting and ambitions. He had been adept at the art of ruthlessness. However, he could not grasp that the birth of the nationalist movement in Kashmir was the direct outcome of his oppressive rule. Times had changed and so had attitudes. This was not a mere change of dates on the calendar; spirits were changing and people were beginning to believe that rights existed for them. The under-currents of the political movement sweeping through in India where British rulers were facing tough times were felt in the Valley. The Maharaja tried to assuage the feelings but in the process created more problems than he actually solved.

He had not anticipated that the rise of Sheikh Mohammad Abdullah on the political scene of Kashmir would spell his undoing. It was not the Sheikh but the ideology and principles which he represented that had taken control of the Maharaja's people and for whom the Sheikh had become a hero.

The Sheikh was a challenge to the king on the very streets of the Valley. He had struck a chord in the hearts of the masses.

His speeches had a messianic appeal and a body of folk-lore and ballads had even sprung up around the Sheikh as he moved in and out of prisons for defying the rule of the Dogras.

Both the Maharaja and Sheikh Abdullah were rulers of their respective kingdoms. Hari Singh ruled the physical territory, while Sheikh Abdullah reigned in the hearts of the people. Therein lay the confrontational path on which both of them were hurled from opposite directions until they collided and caused the disintegration of the state. However much they might have wished otherwise, their confrontational course was to cause irreparable damage.

This clash of personalities did not allow them to look beyond their immediate interests. This myopic vision of the two spelt doom for Jammu and Kashmir. The Maharaja could not bear hearing of Sheikh Abdullah for the latter was the source of disaffection among his loyal subjects. The Maharaja did not want to acknowledge that it was he and his ruthless rule that had brought success and glory to Sheikh Abdullah and his tribe of challengers. There was none to tell him the truth. Surrounded by flattering courtiers intent on keeping him happy in the belief that all was well and that the Sheikh and his band were elements that could be lightly dismissed. He woke up to the truth only when things had already taken a downward turn for the end of his rule.

The Maharaja was consumed by his hatred for the Sheikh and his patron Jawaharlal Nehru. He could not admit that his subjects had come to challenge his rule and were actually dictating their own terms.

He thought that he had been fair to them, giving them far more leverage than any subject might expect from a ruler. He had constituted the Assembly and given the people a say in decision making. But if they still protested then he knew no other remedy but to resort to what he knew best: oppression.

What troubled the King even more was that at the time of the partition of India, the Sheikh had squashed his dream of becoming the ruler of independent Jammu and Kashmir undisturbed by Pakistan and India. His ambitions and dreams were stoked by his courtiers and soothsayers. The King fell into their trap, forgetting that if soothsayers alone held the key to the truth then kingdoms would never have crumbled or kings dethroned.

It was a combination of ambition and fear that characterized the Maharaja's desire to keep the state independent. He never sought to conceal the fact that he had no liking for India or the Congress leadership and Nehru in particular. His ambitions were stoked by the silence of Mohammad Ali Jinnah, the protagonist of Pakistan over the issue of Jammu and Kashmir remaining independent. His courtiers and especially Prime Minister R. C. Kak had advised him that this was the best option. A Maharaja who was not in touch with his subjects could not grasp the seriousness of the situation. He was a Hindu, whereas the majority of his subjects were Muslim. He vacillated on every occasion finding it difficult to make a choice until one was thrust upon him by events. He had signed the accession with India only after the tribal invasion. It was Pakistan which had forced his hand.

> 'I was present when the accession was signed. It was the same accession that other kings had signed. So there is no dispute over the contents of the instrument of accession,' Karan Singh, the only son of Hari Singh, had commented in 1993 when American diplomat Rabin Raphael had made a statement that the 'accession was not final.'

Who could be more authoritative on the subject than Karan Singh, who had witnessed the momentous events in the state's history?[2]

Had the Maharaja worked in tandem with Sheikh Abdullah who represented the aspirations of the people of the Valley and had they thrashed out together a democratic arrangement for the sovereignty of the state without allowing their personalities to come in the way of mutual understanding and had they both tamed their ambitions and accepted the ground realities—Jammu and Kashmir today would appear very differently on the global map—both geographically and politically. The course of South Asian history would have been very different. That was not to be. Rather, Kashmir is a source of potential turmoil to the rest of the world.

Endnotes

1. Kashmiri Muslims were discriminated against in government services. They were also treated as second class citizens who were made to toil on the land of big landlords (mostly Hindus) and in compensation would get virtually nothing. Any voice of dissent was ruthlessly curbed. The July 1931 protest against the Maharaja's rule was resisted by firing in which 30 Kashmiris were killed. That laid the foundation for the struggle against Maharaja's rule.

2. Karan Singh, son of Hari Singh made the following comment at a press conference when he visited Srinagar in the middle of the Hazratbal crisis in November 1993. The author was present at the conference. Karan Singh: 'I was sitting by the side of my father when the accession papers were signed and these were no different from the accession signed by other states.'

Part II

4

The Day I Became a Muslim

There is no image of Pakistan or Kashmir in my mind prior to my father's transfer and posting as professor to Government Degree College, Anantnag, a town in south Kashmir famous for defining critical moments in Kashmir's history thanks to Mirza Afzal Beg[1] and Shabir Shah.[2]

This town, located to the south of Srinagar, is now encountering many problems because of its parallel identities. The people there call it Anantnag, a name derived from Sanskrit meaning "The Land of Countless Springs". Muslims name it Islamabad and some newspapers in Kashmir even use Islamabad in the dateline while Pakistan TV satisfies both by whimsically combining the two Anantnag-Islamabad.

It was October 1964 and I had no clear idea as to what Kashmir looked like. The only thing my mother told me was that we were going to a place where there was a majority of Muslims. She had very bitter memories of the community. My mother came from what is now Pakistan, and had lost a brother soon after the partition of India. She was a victim of partition—a word which evoked grim, blood-soaked memories of Hindus butchered at the hands of fanatic Muslims in Pakistan and of the tortuous journey she had to undertake with her family from Pakistan to Amritsar.

It was sobering to think of going to the land of Muslims. My youngest sister was to be born two months later and at almost the same time my mother lost her father. This confirmed her conviction that the land of the Muslims was inauspicious for her. But I realized that her impression about the Muslims and Kashmir were to be greatly transformed in those two months.

Anantnag was bitterly cold and chilly; we had never before experienced a winter of such intensity. I was then in the second standard. It was my responsibility, as the only boy at home, to interact with the outside world and part of it was to fetch vegetables and other necessities for the family.

The surroundings leading to our rented accommodation, in a bylane close to Reshi Bazar in Anantnag were squalid and the narrow lane was always dirty. Yusuf,the youngest son of my landlord accompanied me to Lal Chowk (Anantnag, like Srinagar, also has a square by this name) and I remember that he took me to a shop where I made the first ever purchase of my life: two kilogrammes of potatoes and a packet of salt. Munir[3] became my best friend at the 'Happy Home' school run by Lakshmanjoo Raina, a retired teacher. There was nothing extraordinary about the school. It looked more like a shop where we used to sit on mats on the floor. Still, it was considered the best school in town because it was run by a Kashmiri Pandit, a community well-known for its impeccable standards in learning and teaching. There used to be morning assembly, but what struck me, then, even as a child was that the Indian national anthem was not sung at the school. It was run by a Hindu and most of the children there were Hindus, the community that takes patriotic pride in being true Indians.

The absence of the national anthem left me with a strange sense of disquiet. Why could we not sing it? It was the first thing we did daily in my school in Jammu, why not in Kashmir?

There was a palpable fear in the minds of the people in Kashmir about this. In the coming years as I attempted to improve my understanding of Kashmir and its people, I was to learn that they did not want to identify themselves with India. The Muslims labelled the Kashmiri Pandits *Daali batta*, mocking their diet of *dal* (pulses) which was for them a symbol of weakness. Vegetarians are perceived to be a weaker race than mutton eaters, though I personally rarely found any difference between the diet of the Muslims and the Hindus. Both communities were fond of eating mutton and that too in excess and *halal* only.

Munir became my friend because most of the other Kashmiri children were unable to understand my language, and would make fun of me. Even the students of Punjabi descent would join them. It was the robust Munir who would come to my rescue. He first taught me how to throw snowballs, upon my first snowfall and so shook off my fear of snow.

It was in my struggle to cope with life in an alien environment that I discovered how compassionate the Muslims in the Valley were. Rather they still are. My mother was bed-ridden and she was being taken care of by our landlady and her daughter. I could not understand Kashmiri but their actions said it all. My mother was moved by their deeds of kindness. They would fetch water and also serve me and my two sisters breakfast. When the news of my maternal grandfather's death was broken to mother, the ladies came to comfort her as she wept and wailed inconsolably.

But the severity of the winter made me sick of the place. I vowed that, given a chance, I would never come back to this place which the people hailed as paradise on earth. To me it seemed nothing short of hell on the planet. Finally the school was closed for the winter vacation.

When the Jammu-Srinagar national highway was cleared of snow, we left Anantnag for Jammu. The highway very often gets closed by heavy snowfall during winters. At Jammu, I prayed day and night that my father would be posted back to Jammu. But that did not happen. We returned to Kashmir at the end of winter. I remember crying throughout our bus journey from Jammu to Anantnag. My mother could guess that something was wrong. In the meantime, my father had moved to another house. We now lived in the main Rishi Bazar, blessed with somewhat better surroundings.

Yusuf enters my memories at this point. In school, however, I found myself in the arms of Munir who was only too happy to see me back.

'It is good that you have come back, there will be lots of fun now,' he said in halting Urdu. He was right. Summer in Kashmir was different. The weather was pleasant and my visits to Nagbal—a cluster of springs, became frequent. Munir would go to adjoining Sher Bagh—also a cluster of springs, the waters of which flowed out of Nagbal. I felt bad that the people in Sher Bagh—Muslims—should bathe in the waters already used by Hindus. That was what Kashmiriyat was or it may have been the outcome of the Dogra rule: Kashmiri Pandits were placed high on pedestals from which they looked down in condescension upon Muslims as inferior beings. Anyway those were times of great fun. I had picked up Kashmiri. That pleased Munir above everything else. One day he recited *Kalma* to me and asked me to repeat it. In all innocence, I obliged my friend: *'La he Illa Illala, Mohammadun Rasoolala'* (There is no God but Allah and Muhammad is His Apostle). He hugged me tightly and kissed me. I was stunned by his reaction. 'What is it?' I queried, he replied again in all innocence: 'Now, you have become a Muslim.' I thought of protesting. Then suddenly his father appeared on the scene. Munir proudly narrated to his father Ghulam Rasool how he had 'converted' me. His father, I remember slapped him hard, and told him, 'You study in a school where you read Hindi, do you become Hindu then? Everyone loves his religion. No one becomes a Muslim simply by reciting *Kalma*. Don't play this trick again,' Munir was warned. He apologized profusely. His remorse was visible. He felt so bad that he could not meet my eyes for the next few days. 'I shouldn't have done that,' he apologized. His feelings were sincere and nothing pleases anyone more than the respect shown towards one's faith. I was pleased.

Munir's apology and the severe scolding that he got from his father were an intimation of Kashmiri Muslim values: their concern not to hurt the religious feelings of others. More than that, it was a demonstration of the principles which informed their relations with others. It was embedded in the way they inculcate their children, from earliest childhood, in the teachings at schools and the reprimands of the kind administered by Munir's father all of which imbue their lives with these outstanding values.

There were many more such experiences which I was to encounter in the Valley in the coming years and that were to confirm my faith in the goodness of the Kashmiri Muslims. It was something that could not have left anyone untouched. I was no exception. That, did not mean that there was absolute calm in the Valley and that secessionist feelings were non-existent, at that point in time. They were there. But they were not violent. The Muslims were secular in their attitude and extraordinarily tolerant towards the Hindus, but when it came to India; they had their qualms, rather strong ones at that. During the 1965 Indo-Pak war, the people in Rishi Mohalla where we used to live would not listen to All India Radio or Radio Kashmir Srinagar. I can still fluently mimic the opening sentence of the news reader: *Yeh Radio Kashmir Srinagar hai, aab aap Moti Lal Khazanchi se Khaberein Suniye* (This is Radio Kashmir Srinagar, now you can hear the news from Moti Lal Khazanchi).[4] In the streets, I would very often overhear contemptuous words about All India Radio. *'Yaih dale batt radio kaya vani, tala boz Pakistan kaya chhoo vanan?'* (What will this radio of Kashmiri Pandits say? Let's hear what Pakistan radio has to say).

The conduct of Kashmiri Muslims and their attachment towards Pakistan often baffled me. The very neighbours who preferred listening to Radio Pakistan and believed everything transmitted from it, were the ones who would visit us and ask if my family needed anything. 'Don't worry, we are here' were the reassuring words that bolstered the confidence of our family.

It was to be an ongoing paradox to which I could never get the right kind of answers. And so it goes on.

Islamia Schools and the Jamait-i-Islami

Islamia schools run by Jamait-i-Islami which prepared recruits for spreading fundamentalism and militancy were growing in the Valley. Some pupils were attracted to these schools because of the dedication and commitment of their teachers to the cause of the Islamization of the Valley. No inducement was great enough to deflect them from their chosen course.

That was reflected in their teachings and therein lay the strength of these institutions. Islamic education was a binding factor. Islam is the most superior religion was the fundamental message. Their teachers had ample evidence to substantiate their point of view. They would mock at the strict religious purification rituals undertaken by the Hindus contrasting them to the simplicity fostered by Islam. The vices of Hinduism were detailed. The caste and the pariah system in Hinduism were depicted as signs of the terminal decay of this religion contrasted to the discipline and brotherhood of Islam.

Muslims in Kashmir are a well-knit society where a landlord and the labourer who worked his land would share the same hookah, taking turns to puff from it. The cups of tea were shared and the concept of four eating from the same '*trami*' (an outsized plate) at weddings and other functions reinforced their faith in the equality that their religion offered.

The divide in Hindu society was exaggerated to tighten the grip of the fundamentalism on the minds of the pupils. At the same time, pupils were taught that a theocratic state like Pakistan was better than one ruled by Hindus like India. The role of Hindu fundamentalist organizations like the Jan Sangh was exaggerated to amplify its horrors. Echoes of this discourse reverberate in speeches of separatist leaders. Today, Syed Ali Shah Geelani[5] makes it a point, in his speeches, to draw attention to the way Muslims in Jammu were massacred in 1947. The Gujarat riots of 2002[6] are the latest in the series quoted[7] to pour scorn on 'Hindu-India', and the brutality of the Indian face finds its stereotype in the 'brutal' soldiers of the Indian Army which has prevented Kashmir from becoming part of Pakistan in 1947. There is no lack of arguments. Jammu and Kashmir had a majority of Muslims and in accordance with the two-nation theory the state should have become a part of Pakistan. The accession signed by Maharaja Hari Singh[8] was called devious. Moreover, the state was more akin to Pakistan in terms of geography. 'Our roads and boundaries are more with Pakistan than India and all our rivers flow into Pakistan,' was the fundamentalist argument. The students were learning this rapidly and common sense told them to believe their teachers.

The Punjab Traders: Newcomers to the Valley

The people of the Valley had minimal exposure to the world outside. Visiting tourists from various parts of India or foreign countries were the only interaction the Valley had with the outside world. But these were mainly links of a more or less commercial nature.

Very few people could afford air travel. The only road link between Jammu the winter capital and Srinagar, the summer capital was the National Highway which was prone to closures during periods of rain; in the winter season landslides often occurred at Nashari, Sher Bibi and Khooni nullah while windstorms were frequent at Shaitan nullah, throwing buses off the road into deep gorges killing and wounding people. The journey was a dreadful one. Sometimes the highway would remain closed for days altogether. Even in the finest of seasons, the journey by road would take not less than 12 hours from Jammu to Srinagar, a distance of 294 kms.

The people of the Valley knew nothing of the Indian perspective. The Indian democracy was a sham for the people as they had never tasted of its fruits. For them India was an oppressor whether it was Jawaharlal Nehru, Lal Bahadur Shastri or Indira Gandhi ruling from Delhi. The only people who sang the praises of India were those who had been installed as rulers of Jammu and Kashmir by New Delhi. Yet, it was almost a tradition among the rulers, be it Sheikh Abdullah, and later his son Farooq Abdullah or Ghulam Mohammad Bakshi to praise Delhi when in power and curse it once they were out of it. But they were so discredited that they never commanded any real respect from the people.

Another factor that was turning the tide against India, at that time, rather quietly as compared to the violent times in which we now live, was the presence of traders from Punjab who had settled in the Valley. They had somehow managed to set up their businesses and even obtained state subject status by securing permanent resident certificates by bribing the officials. Jammu & Kashmir State Subject Law 1925 explicitly prohibits outsiders from obtaining ownership of land or property. The inhabitants of the Valley resented the rise of these traders up the social and economic ladder. They had come as what locals would contemptuously call *sade cheh aana* (six and a half annas worth 40 paisa). They came as pavement hawkers selling their wares at the uniform price tag of *sade cheh aana*. They attracted customers because their goods were sold at cheap rates. They, however, made profits and rose economically. Soon, from pavements they moved to self-owned shops. These shops expanded into shopping complexes and as their businesses grew, they further diversified from one field to another. They were tightening their grip on the economy of the Valley and this was being watched with great resentment by the locals who, somehow, envied the rise but never thought of learning the enterprise that could have propelled them to greater financial and social heights.

Kashmiri Isolation

The sense of distrust was becoming pervasive. It was a crisis which kept deepening. Kashmiri Muslims, as I understood, are disinclined both by training and upbringing to seek out life beyond the Valley. They have deep-seated reservations and apprehensions which keep them within the confines of the Valley. That is the misfortune that they have brought upon themselves. Partly, it was aggravated by the snide remarks that they have heard and of being called '*Aya Haato*', a disrespectful form of addressing someone, in Kashmiri in the plains of Punjab. That has made them detest the Indians. This is reflected in their conversations where they would invariably refer to the maltreatment of Delhi not only towards themselves, as Kashmiris, but their leaders as well.

Sheikh Mohammad Abdullah: The Plebiscite Front

Even though he was not the ruler, Sheikh Mohammad Abdullah was the hero of the masses. They called him *Sher-e-Kashmir* (Lion of Kashmir) and see in him the embodiment of their resistance to the rule of Delhi in Kashmir. Jamait-i-Islami and its *madaris*, however, always painted Sheikh Abdullah as a Kashmiri leader who had betrayed his people at a crucial point in time when he made the choice, in 1947, of accepting Indian suzerainty over Kashmir rather than choosing the natural country: Pakistan. Nowadays he is more ilified than ever before.

Despite this vilification campaign against Sheikh Abdullah, the leader has enjoyed a tremendous following among the people. His words were mesmerizing and the Plebiscite Front which was formed after his arrest revived the demand for the settlement of Kashmir issue according to the United Nations resolutions. It received massive support.

The Plebiscite Front was run by the Sheikh's crony, Mirza Afzal Beg, a diminutive figure as compared to tall Sheikh Abdullah, but a master of wit and an old hand in devising political strategies for his close friend and leader. The two however, were bitter enemies in the end. Mirza Afzal Beg and the Sheikh parted ways in 1978. They were never to be friends again.

One of the rare glimpses of Mirza Afzal Beg's wit is often cited by his supporters.[9]

Many in Kashmir believe that the Plebiscite Front was the main factor responsible for creating the distance between Delhi and Srinagar. It drove the wedge between Kashmir and India. The Plebiscite Front was the organization with which the Kashmiris identified themselves just as they were later to do with the sentiments represented by the All Parties Hurriyat

Conference (APHC).[10] They had become disillusioned with the Indian ways of working in Kashmir: pumping money to buy loyalties. The gaps between India and Kashmir were widening on the political plane and the recurring communal clashes in other states were doing no service to India in the Valley. Almost every month there were Hindu-Muslim clashes in the streets of Moradabad and Maharashtra and Gujarat.

Whatever might have been the Sheikh's predilections with the changing times, the man who stood almost six feet tall, had the interest of the people of the Valley at his heart. He had no secular pretensions when it came to helping his people. He was also a master strategist. Sheikh Abdullah had converted his Muslim Conference into the National Conference when he saw Nehru and Gandhi's Congress holding sway over the people of India. He felt that he was being submerged among the leaders of the Muslim League of Mohammad Ali Jinnah as within his own community he was only one among many. On the other hand, vis-à-vis Congress and the National Conference, he would be the only Muslim leader and from Kashmir, at that. So converting the MC into the NC was his master-stroke. The way he abolished the landlord system that had been a burden for the Hindus, and gave preference to Kashmiri bureaucracy in all matters and the way he promoted even the incompetent to top posts reflected his inner desire to lift Kashmiri Muslims. He created the super-time scale for Kashmir Administrative Service (KAS). It is the equivalent of the Indian services of the Indian Administrative Service (IAS) to help Kashmiri Muslim officers. These policies were later blindly followed by all Kashmiri Muslim leaders with the result that Jammu Hindus ended by finding themselves off the civil secretariat. Their share in the decision-making was gradually reduced and continues to be diminished. Life-sized portraits of Sheikh Abdullah adorned the walls of people who made it a point to identify themselves with him, his philosophy and political thought. But in most of such houses, the Sheikh's portrait was hung side by side with that of Pakistani dictator Ayub Khan.[11]

Hum Kya Chahte, Pakistan, Hamara leader Ayub Khan (We want Pakistan and our leader is Ayub Khan and later it was Yahya Khan). These slogans were often heard by the people in the streets of Anantnag in the 1960s.

Why was the Sheikh so important to Kashmir and why he remains so important even today for the people of the Valley, sharply divided between those who still remember him as a messiah for the Kashmiris and who was elevated to the status of '*Hazrat*' and those who condemn him as traitor? But no one disagrees that the Sheikh was the most eminent leader Kashmir ever produced. Even the Jamait-i-Islami ideologue Syed Ali Shah Geelani has conceded this.

Islamabad has not forgotten or forgiven Sheikh Abdullah's rebuff and refusal to join Pakistan in 1947. One of the reasons for Pakistan's continuing support of the insurgency in Kashmir in one form or the other is to wreak its revenge.

To others among his own people, he was a big let down. The circumstances in which he was deposed remains a mystery. It is a story of betrayal on both sides. There is a speech at Ranbir Singhpora, a town close to the Pakistan border in Jammu, where he declared that options were open for Jammu and Kashmir and that India did not have complete suzerainty over the State. He disputed the accession that he had endorsed. His deposition on August 9, 1953 was a switch button case. It was not the culmination of a process. It was reported that he had just gone to a retreat in Gulmarg where his meeting with a United States envoy had complicated matters for him. Suspicion about him had increased and he was removed from the Kashmir political scene and imprisoned. During the years of incarceration, his image was tarnished and the people switched their allegiance to Bakshi Ghulam Mohammad whom some consider the most pragmatic and secular leader of the times. The Sheikh's people had given him all their love and affection but in 1975, he fell for power. He forgot all his promises and pledges and was bedazzled by the lure of power.

I was present at a rally which Sheikh Mohammad Abdullah held in Kathua.[12] He made his entrance like a roaring lion and there was a splendid welcome for him. I had seen him before. I was impelled by curiosity, wondering what he looked like and how he might alter the course of things within the State. His speech was focused largely on 'accountability.' There was high sounding talk of punishing the corrupt and bringing relief to the people. But although the people of Kashmir, who had worshipped Sheikh Abdullah, did fall in line, they did not forgive him in their inner hearts for his betrayal. They had seen him as the symbol of Kashmiri resistance, self-respect and aspirations and he had just taken the power and done nothing. That political betrayal they could not swallow for the rest of life. Still they came forward by the thousands, to mark their respect for the man when he died. How could they not show their gratitude to the man who had, overnight, made tens of thousands of them owners of the land which they had tilled and toiled for generations? It was Sheikh Abdullah who had shown them the path of self-respect before he himself showed his vulnerability to the trappings of power. Kashmiris often trace the roots of the current violence in the State, to the 1975 betrayal by Sheikh Abdullah. It was this which had made them hostile to the National Conference and the Sheikh dynasty as one may call it. Their reasoning is simple. The Sheikh had compromised freedom for the sake of power and the desire to further the personal fortunes of his family.

Endnotes

1. Mirza Afzal Beg was a close confidant of Sheikh Mohammad Abdullah, who led the Plebiscite Front when the Sheikh was jailed after his government was dismissed in 1953. Beg, regarded as the real brain in the National Conference, had also signed the Kashmir Accord with Parthasarthy, envoy of Indira Gandhi in 1974. This Accord paved the way for the Congress handing over power in Jammu and Kashmir to Sheikh Abdullah in February 1975.

2. Shabir Shah was also born in Anantnag. He is a born separatist who spent more than 20 years in jail. He is currently head of the Jammu and Kashmir Democratic Freedom Party and believes that dialogue between India, Pakistan and the representatives of Kashmir should be held to resolve the Kashmir issue.

3. Munir Qayoom Geelani was my first Muslim friend at Happy Home School. He now runs a shop in Anantnag.

4. Moti Lal Khazanchi was a famous news reader on Radio Kashmir, Srinagar. He was a household name in Kashmir Valley before the TV news replaced the popularity of the radio news.

5. Syed Ali Shah Geelani is a prominent pro-Pakistan voice in Kashmir. Born in Sopore and an unrelenting anti-India and pro-Pakistan campaigner in Kashmir.

6. During the Gujarat riots more than 2000 Muslims were brutally massacred, and their women raped in the western Indian state of Gujarat in March 2003 after more than 40 Hindu pilgrims returning from Ayodhya were set afire and burnt alive in train at Godhra, a small town in Gujarat. This is considered a blot on Indian secularism because in these riots the BJP Government in the state led by a Hindu fundamentalist Narendra Modi had sided with the rioters.

7. Geelani reminded the Kashmiris about the Gujarat riots in his speech in Baramullah, a north Kashmir town in September 2003. Arun Joshi, 'Geelani urged to be rival; Hurriyat Conference chief '(*Hindustan Times*, September 13, 2003).

8. Maharaja Hari Singh was the last Dogra king of the state, who signed the Instrument of Accession in October 1947 to seek the Indian help in pushing back the tribal invaders from Pakistan.

9. Sheikh Abdullah visited the ailing Mirza Afzal Beg. It was time for the Beg to take his medicine which the servant had just brought in. Sheikh, wishing to demonstrate his affection for his dying friend, offered to give the medicine himself to Beg. 'Where is the spoon?', he is reported to have asked and Beg could not hide his smile and chimed in, 'Sheikh Sahib there are so many "chamchas" (sycophants) around you, why do you require one more chamcha?' The Sheikh blushed.

10. All Parties Hurriyat Conference is a secessionist conglomerate of more than 23 groups, was set up in 1993 to give a political colour to the secessionist movemment in Kashmir.

11. Mohammad Ayub Khan was Field Marshal Administrator of Pakistan who ruled Pakistan from October 1958 to March 25, 1969. He signed the Tashkent agreement with Indian Prime Minister Lal Bahadur Shastri in Tashkent in January 1966. India and Pakistan fought the first war in 1965 when Ayub Khan was the ruler of Pakistan.

12. Bakshi Ghulam Mohammad was one of the closest confidants of Sheikh Mohammad Abdullah. Bakshi became Prime Minister of Jammu and Kashmir after the Sheikh was deposed in August 1953 and he ruled the state until 1964.

5

The Abdullah Dynasty

The Lion Ceases to Roar

It was Sunday afternoon—September 5, 1982. Ordinarily, there were no newspaper deliveries in Jammu, on Sundays. So it was a holiday at the *Kashmir Times*[1] office, housed in a dingy, decrepit building in the Shahidi Chowk area of Jammu. It was a newspaper that didn't have anything to boast of except for a letter press and a half-broken typewriter, the proud possession of Ved Bhasin.[2]

I was moonlighting for the United News of India (UNI)[3] and the *Indian Express* apart from working with Bhasin's newspaper, or rather I was the reporter-cum-sub-editor-cum-proof-reader.

Subash, who was working with the UNI, rushed in, almost shouting, 'Sheikh Abdullah has had a massive heart attack.' He had seen it on the teleprinter. The story had been sent by J. N. Raina, the UNI correspondent of Kashmir, a thorough journalist, who had sources in every nook and corner. At that point, the phone began to ring and he called out, 'There's a call for you from Vedji.' I woke up with a start; I was at the UNI office having a nap, after lunch.

The voice at the other end was crisp. 'Come, we are bringing out an edition today. Sheikh is seriously ill.' Within ten minutes I was at the *Kashmir Times* office, where I saw Vedji trying to organize things for the next edition. Tara Chand, who was a sort of Man Friday to Ved Bhasin and regarded as one of the architects of the newspaper's management, was pacing restlessly up and down. 'Tara Chand, you go and get Deep.'

Deep was Ved Pal Deep, a great Dogri[4] poet and a genius.

Ved Bhasin was trying to contact his journalist friends Mohammad Sayeed Malik[5] and Zafar Meraj.[6] The word was that Sheikh might die at any moment. There were many things that had to be attended to. One was the obituary. Sheikh Abdullah, the man who had challenged the might of Dogra rule, was dying. The man who had led the Kashmiris and made them aware of their rights, was dying. Doctors attending on him, the name of one of whom I still remember Dr. J. S. Bajaj were at his bedside along with Begum Akbar Jehan, Sheikh's wife.

Sheikh had fallen ill after a district development board meeting in Doda, a mountainous district in the north-east of the Jammu region and south of the Kashmir Valley in July that year. He had never recovered from it. What would happen now? That was the question uppermost in our minds. It was in the autumn of his life that he had appointed his son Farooq Abdullah as Health Minister. There was a common belief that Farooq would succeed *Sher-e-Kashmir* or the Lion of Kashmir. That was considered something natural. Sheikh's intention had been patent when he made Farooq President of the National Conference. This remarkable event has been recorded by one of Kashmir's most noteworthy journalists, Yusuf Jameel has described the event which is summarized here.

It was no different from the crowning of a king, a real coronation. Farooq Abdullah walked up to the well-decorated dais at Iqbal Park.The multitudes who had filled the spacious grassland in uptown Srinagar stood up in veneration.

Cries of 'Long live Abdullah' and '*Qaid-e-Sani*' (Leader of the times) Zindabad filled the air in honour of Sheikh Mohammad Abdullah who was stepping down to make way for his son and at the same time accept the successor with equal reverence. The National Conference's red flag with the white plough fluttered above the dais as if it were a witness of the historic occasion.

That was in August 1981. There was a smile on Farooq's face but soon he was overwhelmed with emotion. As the announcement of his takeover as the new President of National Conference was made, he waved to the audience and then moved up to his legendary father Sheikh Mohammad Abdullah.

Sheikh rose and gave his son a passionate hug. The Lion of Kashmir too broke down, perhaps for the first time in public. Farooq's mother Begum Akbar Jehan and almost every other person sitting on the dais was in tears—tears of joy. Begum known as Mader-e-meharban (kind mother's) dream was coming true at last.

Then followed the national anthem of *Kashmir Lehra aey Kashmir ke Jhande* penned by Maulana Mohammad Sayeed Masoodi, one of the founders of the National Conference. This song had boosted the morale of the people of Kashmir when the Valley was subjected to unspeakable terror and torture by Pakistani raiders.

When Farooq had taken the oath of loyalty to the party and to the principles of democracy, socialism and Hindu-Muslim Sikh unity which it preached, the supporters and admirers surrounded him jostling to garland him and others just to touch him. The galaxy of political stalwarts from within and outside the state, journalists and friends looked on.

Farooq badshah banega (Farooq will become king one day), was the cryptic remark of veteran journalist Kuldip Nayar who stood among the spectators at that time.

But there were strong signals that the road would not be smooth for his son after his death. Sheikh's son-in-law Ghulam Mohammad Shah, and Transport Minister who thought that he was the real successor to his father-in-law, was waiting along the sidelines for an opportune moment to strike back.

Ved had charged me to keep track of things to find out exactly when Sheikh died. I knew nothing about Sheikh except for those glimpses I had caught of him in the streets of Anantnag, when he was still championing the cause of the Plebiscite Front or the occasion when he visited my college in Kathua, a small town in southern Jammu and Kashmir or the times when I had seen him at public functions. I had shared the admiration of the people for this legendary personality who had had the courage to face up to every situation. I had also shared the hate that the Jammuites had felt for him for being *'anti-Jammu.'* There were many stories circulating about him in the streets of Jammu: that he was biased and nurtured anti-Hindu feelings. This man was dying. Sheikh did not die that day but three days later and Deep's labour was rewarded with the publication of that remarkable front-page editorial, sans his name.

The death of Sheikh was a national tragedy. Despite his penchant for setting up dynastic rule within the state, Sheikh Abdullah was by far the most eminent leader that Kashmir has ever produced. He could lead his people, and command their respect and loyalty. It was he who had delivered them from autocratic rule, restored their self-respect and helped them gain a confidence they had lost through the habit of living in servitude.

He helped to rid them of this curse. With the signature of the 1975 accord he had completely aligned himself with India and alienated himself forever from Pakistan. There was no doubt about it. Sheikh had been reduced to the level of a traitor in the eyes of Pakistan which had earlier epitomized him as leader of the Kashmiri resistance against India. Pakistan had done so in the name of the plebiscite, hoping that the Muslims in the Valley would vote Pakistan, given a choice. Sheikh Abdullah was bringing international pressure to bear on India with his high-profile attempts to settle the Kashmir issue. And most of the world was on Pakistan's side. The compulsive need of a Kashmiri to side with the victor had forced him to sign the 1975 Accord and give up his demand for the plebiscite, particularly in the face of the Indian victory in the 1971 Indo-Pak conflict and the subsequent division of Pakistan and the creation of Bangladesh.

He knew that there would be turmoil after his death. In a speech delivered at the inauguration of a bridge across river Tawi in Jammu in August 1980, he had predicted, 'Kashmir would be a war zone and big powers would make it a battle-field.' He had the foresight of a natural leader and a keen observer of both national and international events.

Indira Gandhi[7] knew that though she appeared to have tamed the lion for India, this was a lion who had the capacity to keep in check the forces of antagonism and contention, whether they were ideologically aligned with Pakistan or otherwise. As long as Sheikh held sway over the masses, these recalcitrant forces would not raise their heads. During his first stint as Prime Minister in the 1950s, he did not hesitate to throw anyone sporting green headgear into jail. Green was the symbol of Pakistan. No other leader in Kashmir had been capable of such forceful action and that is why the death of Sheikh Abdullah was such a loss for the whole of the Indian nation. Events after his death have proven that.

Kashmir had lost its most popular leader and thousands turned up at his funeral. President Giani Zail Singh[8] and Prime

Minister Indira Gandhi were there to offer their condolences. Her real purpose however was to ensure the smooth transition of power. She knew that Farooq was no match for his father, a fact of which Farooq himself was fully congnizant. But he was the best choice for her for now. Farooq's inexperience had become, for the moment, his chief asset. Indira Gandhi wanted to capitalize on that. It was a decision which she was to regret later, one for which she had been personally responsible. The shrewdest of us may make mistakes. This was to be Indira's.

At 8.00 p.m. on September 8, Farooq Abdullah himself appeared on Radio Kashmir to announce his father's death cautioning that the 'people should control their sentiments and in this moment of crisis not do anything that would hurt Sheikh Sahib.'

Mrs. Gandhi was pondering over her future moves on the *shikara* (luxury boat) that took her to Hazratbal,[9] even as the funeral procession of tens of thousands of people was making its way there by road. It was from there that Sheikh had launched himself into politics and it was there that he had harangued the Kashmiris. Hazratbal had been the scene of his political triumphs and it was there that he wished to be buried.

Sheikh Abdullah was gone. Farooq would be made Chief Minister on September 8, 1982. But Sheikh had left his legacy to a son who lacked his father's political acumen, foresight, dedication and tenacity to grapple with the complexity of politics in Kashmir at a time when it was to come into international focus.

He tried often to project the image of a strong person who was not to be lightly dismissed but his political career was marked by uncertainty from the outset. Often, he demonstrated a lack of political judgement. Soon after he became President of the National Conference, he brought up the theme of the opening of the Rawalpindi road. This is an emotional issue for many Kashmiris. Kashmiri politicians have laid claim to the road linking the Kashmir Valley to Rawalpindi now in Pakistan. It was an issue which they often raised whenever they were in a tight spot. But Farooq was an elected MP in the Lok Sabha and knew that whatever promises he had made in 1980 could not be fulfilled. Mrs. Gandhi could never be expected to agree to such a proposition.

Nonetheless, Farooq asserted this demand in the streets of Jammu even though there were no takers for it. Farooq was subject to rapid swings in whims. When he was elected unopposed to the Lok Sabha from Srinagar in 1980, he travelled to Jammu and was seen together with Congress leaders at the rallies of Indira Gandhi. 'She is the only leader who can lead this nation. We must help her. It is the duty of youth to back her,' he told me on the eve of the Congress rally at Parade Ground Jammu where Mrs. Gandhi had come to campaign for his party candidate Girdhari Lal Dogra,[10] in the 1980 Lok Sabha polls.

The Dogra was shrewd and recruited all those who had completed the tenth grade as clerks or primary school teachers during his term as finance minister of the state in the 1960s and 70s. He did this in order to prevent them from obtaining higher education and pre-empt them from becoming, eventually, his political opponents. Farooq had forgotten the bitterness of the past when Congress had withdrawn support from his father in 1977. He knew that Congress was all set to rout the Janta Party[11] which had been fragmented into so many parties but was emerging once again with Jan Sangh under the name of the Bhartiya Janta Party or BJP.

Farooq was ineffectual as an MP. He did not take up any issues that could have turned the tide against the Centre or take up the causes of the people. His acquaintance with Delhi life at 90, Shahjahan Road was somewhat a replica of his life in London. He soon gave up these quarters to Devi Dass Thakur, who later turned against him. Both of them had become good friends during the 1977 campaign and had jointly campaigned for the National Conference in Jammu region where the party was at its weakest as compared to the Kashmir Valley where it successfully halted the surge of the Janta Party led in Kashmir by Mirwaiz Moulvi Farooq, the chief priest of Kashmir and Chairman of the Awami Action Committee. The party did its utmost but managed to obtain only one seat. Abdul Rashid Kabuli[12] was the only one who could win it from Kashmir. He later joined the National Conference and finally deserted that party too to become a functionary in the Bhartiya Janta Party, which he also left, eventually.

For a while then, Farooq had made a mark thanks to the goodwill built up by his father. He won the 1983 elections and when his government was dismissed in July 1984, he was seen as the victim of conspiracies of Delhi. People were with him. But he lost a lot of goodwill and popularity when he aligned himself with Congress in 1986 to regain power.

Throughout his tenure in the Lok Sabha, from March 1980 to August 1982, Farooq had his eyes on the chair of Chief Minister. He knew that sooner or later it was going to come to him and when he was made National Conference President, he knew that his ambitions were about to be realized. It was a momentous moment for Farooq Abdullah when his father made him the President of National Conference.

Resettlement Bill No. 9

Indira Gandhi resumed her political manoeuvring the moment she left Kashmir. She was looking for some means of keeping a hold on Farooq Abdullah. The Prime Minister had learnt from her father Jawaharlal Nehru, a Kashmiri himself, who had studied in London and settled in Allahabad in Uttar Pradesh, never to allow the regional party leaders to gain ground or influence. Farooq was committing the unpardonable sin of standing up to Indira as a leader of Kashmiris. He refused to oblige her. It was in April 1982 that the Jammu and Kashmir Legislative Assembly had passed what is called the Resettlement Bill which envisaged that the people who had fled the state during the bloody days of partition in 1947 to Pakistan and Pakistan occupied Kashmir could come back and resettle within the state. Even their descendants could claim the privileges which were available to the natives of Jammu and Kashmir. They were entitled to preferential treatment, within this state, as the Indians and they could buy immovable property, compete for government jobs and also contest and vote at all elections.

The bill was moved by a private member Abdul Rahim Rather, who later rose to become a minister in the Farooq Abdullah government and is currently leader of the National Conference. Rather told me that he was guided by the humanitarian considerations rather than anything else. He was moved by the plight of an elderly person in his constituency in Charar-e-Sharief[13] in the central Kashmir district of Budgam who had come from Pakistan to see his friends and relatives. When his visa expired, he did not wish to return to Pakistan. He wanted to die in the land where he had been born. But there were legal barriers involving the Line of Control (LoC) that divided his state between two hostile neighbours, India and Pakistan. He would have to go back.

'I approached the passport office and got him some relief of stay for a few more days. But that did not end his misery,' Rather recalled to me. 'There were many such cases, so I decided to move a bill in the Assembly.' Rather moved the bill in 1982. But, as might be anticipated, the bill raised controversy and uproar in the House. Cutting across the party lines, Congress and BJP said that the bill would open the floodgates for Pakistanis. The Hindu leadership of Jammu sensed something suspicious about the bill. It was referred to a select committee for deliberation on the legal and constitutional aspects and to determine whether it was in violation of any Indian law. The bill was listed as number 9, so it came to be known as Bill No. 9. Rather was determined to get it passed and for that he had to face many risks. 'There were threats that I would be murdered and my family wiped out,' he narrated to me. 'I withstood all these threats and finally when it was put to the vote it was passed.'

The National Conference viewed it as a victory. Critics said that the National Conference had brought this bill to consolidate its Muslim constituency throughout the state as Sheikh Abdullah's Government had no bright spot to focus on. The Sheikh Government was rated as immeasurably corrupt. Some of its ministers were said to have amassed huge assets in their own name and in the names of their family members.

When the bill had received clearance from the state legislature, it was sent to Governor B. K. Nehru, uncle of Indira Gandhi. He had known the storm that the bill had raised in the Assembly. He sat over the bill. The Governor's consent is needed for any bill before it becomes a law on the statute book. Indira was aware of the bill pending with the Governor. She urged her uncle to send the bill back to the legislature. The aim was to find out Farooq's response. If he insisted on passing the bill, that meant he would be pursuing the policies of Sheikh Abdullah and if he did not, then the possibility of an alliance with him might be explored for the 1983 Assembly elections. The previous Assembly had been elected in 1977 when Sheikh was bedridden and Farooq had campaigned for his party. The party had won a massive victory and all the challengers including the Congress

Party which had withdrawn support for Sheikh Abdullah after its debacle in the general elections in the country in March 1977, had withered. The National Conference had bounced back with a vengeance. Indira did not want that to happen again. She had become wary of the NC and its motives. She had decided to woo Sheikh Abdullah to the mainstream of national politics and hand over power to him and offer the full support for his party even though the NC did not have even a single MLA in the House, in the hope, though it may sound very crude, that Sheikh would not live long. Sheikh, once back in power, had shown a resilience that probably derives from power itself. He survived long enough to become a source of misgiving for Indira Gandhi.

Since Sheikh's son was young and had long innings to play, she wanted to work out an arrangement of a permanent coalition with him before the polls and for doing so the irritant of the Resettlement Bill had to be removed. It had to be shown to be irrelevant. B. K. Nehru, a cousin of Jawaharlal Nehru who was Governor of Jammu and Kashmir from 1979–84, sent the bill back to the State Legislature for 'reconsideration' and at the same time on September 30 referred it to the Attorney General for Presidential reference. The bill was then sent to the constitutional bench of the Supreme Court of India, whose jurisdiction to the state and legal affairs of the state had been extended in the post-1953 era.

The bill was passed for a second time in the state legislature on October 4, 1982. The Legislature passed it in Srinagar and Jammu observed a complete bandh, the kind of which I have not seen for ages in the city and its surroundings. There were both political and human angles to the opposition to the Resettlement Act in Jammu. Sheikh Abdullah had not allowed the waves of refugees coming from Muzaffarabad and other places, in now what is Pakistan-occupied Kashmir, to stay put in the Valley. He drove them to Jammu. There were two reasons for his doing this. He did not want the non-Muslims to settle in the Muslim-dominated Valley in such large numbers that could offset his electoral calculations in the post-independence era. Moreover, these people came from the belt that was not the support base of Sheikh Abdullah. He also did not want any major change in the demographic character of the Valley.

Secondly, their resettlement in Kashmir would have resulted in sharing the land and resources of Kashmiri Muslims with them. Sheikh did not want that. The argument was that there was plenty of land in Jammu which would offer their inhabitants security and also provide them with enough resources for life. Moreover, a huge section of the Muslim population of the Jammu region had migrated to Pakistan and they had left behind their land and properties. These were occupied by refugees[14] who were more or less in permanent possession of these properties. There was the threat that once the descendants of the Muslims returned from Pakistan, they would lose possession of the same. That economic fear and also the fear of yet another displacement haunted them. They had very strong reasons to oppose the bill. And anybody who did so was perceived by them as a messiah.

They distrusted the National Conference and its leadership. Sheikh Abdullah had promised that these people would not be dispossessed of their land and homes, but there were no takers. That mattered little to Sheikh Abdullah because what he had done had strongly consolidated his Muslim constituency in the Valley. That mattered most to him. They, the Kashmiri-Hindus[15] on the other hand, were always a dispensable commodity as far as he was concerned. Farooq knew that equally well. Any tampering with the status quo of the bill would have been a political disaster for him. But he did not know that by getting the bill passed, he had also shown his defiance to the mighty Indira Gandhi, whose arrogance of style and action was legendary.

Defying Indira Gandhi

That was the first inkling of confrontation between Farooq Abdullah and Indira Gandhi. The Pradesh Congress Committee President, Mufti Mohammad Sayeed was there to stoke the fires. He projected Farooq Abdullah as a playboy running the state. 'At least Sheikh Abdullah knew Kashmir politics, this boy knows nothing,' he would comment in the most contemptuous manner while dismissing the political credibility of Farooq Abdullah. That Farooq had to learn many things in politics was obvious from the very day he took over. He would betray signs of nervousness quite frequently. He did not know what direction to follow. At a rally of the party workers at Iqbal Park, he announced the dismissal of all the ministers who he said were corrupt and incompetent. 'I will throw all corrupt ministers in to the deep waters of Dal lake.' He could not do it even later because his own proteges had constructed houses by filling the lake with mud and earth. His ministers were filling their coffers in the name of cleaning the waters of Dal lake which had turned murky due to weeds. Tens of thousands of dollars went down the drain or lined the pockets of corrupt politicians, some of whom were his ministers.

That was patent proof of his political inexperience. 'The people could have lynched us,' M. K. Tikoo, a minister in the Sheikh Abdullah cabinet between 1977 to 1982, had remarked over the dismissal of the whole cabinet in this cavalier manner, 'He should have done this at a proper forum. Though that was indisputable proof of his inexperience and impulsiveness, it enthralled the masses. They had wished for a leader who would rid them of corruption. For them Farooq had come as a fresh breeze wafting in the air. They were delighted. The street talk was that what Sheikh could not do his son had done. There were accolades for him. He represented a new generation. But that was to be only an illusion. This became clear as the years went by.

The old guard had accepted him because he was the son of the legendary Sheikh Abdullah and the young ones were fascinated by his ways of playing to the gallery. 'These *Jamaitis* (Jamait-i-Islami activists)[16] led by Syed Ali Shah Geelani 'do not know what the life is. There is life in *Lal Pari* (liquor),' he often commented.

Soon, the bitter realities of politics began to sink in on him. He knew the elections were coming and the life of the Assembly would end in June 1983. He had to decide which way to go. Indira through her emissaries was still trying to work on him. But Farooq was not willing to move beyond a point. The Congress Party wanted a 45:55 share of the seats. Ghulam Mohi-ud-Din Shah,[17] then NC General Secretary and other leaders prevailed upon him. And the deal was never struck.

There opened a new chapter of hostile confrontation between Indira's Congress and Farooq's National Conference. The National Conference had fought and won the crucial test of the electoral battle of the 1977 election by going to Pakistani voters in salt green uniforms. The 1983 election would be more crucial. The campaign slogans had to be different for Sheikh Abdullah was no longer around.

Choosing Farooq as his successor was Sheikh Abdullah's personal decision. That was where the Lion of Kashmir had fallen for the love for his son. It was called perpetuation of dynastic rule in Kashmir. Sheikh had made this choice even when there were many seasoned politicians around in the party and those who had a better claim to step into his shoes. Quite apart from the fact that the Sheikh himself was aware that his son was none too keen on politics, Farooq was obsessed with golf, beautiful women and dancing. He loved everything except serious matters like governance.

Fissures from Within

The test had come for Farooq to lead the party to victory in the elections. But the party was not fully behind him. There were conspirators within the party. Ghulam Mohammad Shah18 was sulking and Devi Dass Thakur[19] who was the Finance Minister in the Sheikh Abdullah Government was also nursing his wounds of being thrown out of the Government. Shah and Thakur were bitter enemies in the Sheikh Abdullah cabinet, but now they were drawing closer to each other to oppose Farooq Abdullah. Farooq Abdullah's younger brother, Tariq Abdullah , was also fretting and fuming. He felt that he had been marginalized by his father and shunned by the family. He developed an extreme hatred for his elder brother By feigning indifference to these developments within his party and his family, Farooq did not help matters for himself. There were complications from which he could disentangle himself. Sycophants swarmed around him, preventing him from developing greater insight into the complexities of the situation evolving before him.

The Congress Party sensed a victory for itself in the elections. It had all the money power coming through the coffers of the north block with the blessings of Indira Gandhi to make inroads into the bastions of the National Conference. Moulvi Iftikhar Hussain Ansari[20] was with Indira's party and Mufti headed the hate campaign against the Abdullah family and targeted Farooq, in whose hands, he alleged that Kashmir was not safe. Mufti's Congress described Farooq as a 'security risk.' Farooq was blissfully ignorant of the things that were happening in the opposition camps. He was never one who entered into details. Nor did he do so now.

Farooq was relying on his charisma. That he had excellent communication skills and that he knew how to strike an instant rapport with the people, was the envy of the opposition leaders. But that was probably not enough. Something more was needed to offset the opposition and consolidate the ground for the National Conference. He struck the card of Muslim unity in Kashmir.

A surprise was sprung on the people of Kashmir when the 'double Farooq alliance' came into being. Farooq Abdullah and Moulvi Farooq, head of the Awami Action Committee, held each other's hands afloat in Iqbal Park, marking an end to the bitter Sher-Bakra fights in the streets of Srinagar. Sheikh Abdullah's supporters were known as *Sher* or 'Lion' and because of the goatish beard of the supporters of the Moulvi, his supporters were nicknamed as *Bakras* (Goats). There were persistent clashes between the two sides over almost all issues. Moulvi was considered close to Pakistan. His uncle Moulvi Yusuf Shah had migrated to Pakistan-occupied Kashmir and settled there. The fight was over the political supremacy in the interior Srinagar. While Sheikh had made Hazratbal his political platform, Moulvi had converted Jamia Masjid into his political stage. The two would run each other down for ever. But Farooq Abdullah sprang a miracle when he brought Moulvi to his side. His Awami Action Committee agreed to contest the Assembly elections on the NC symbol of the plough, something that was an astounding political success. Though the Awami Action Committee had a specific and limited area of success, the fact of the matter was that his men were hardcore supporters willing to die for him and secondly the message of the Sher-Bakra truce gave a sense of Muslim unity all across the Valley and also in the Muslim-dominated parts of Jammu region. That was Farooq Abdullah's master stroke. He had checkmated his political adversaries by winning the Mirwaiz to his side. This prevented

Congress from wooing Mirwaiz Moulvi Farooq, the way the Janta Party had done in 1977. Farooq Abdullah had expanded his support base at the cost of rivals. He had killed two birds with one stone.

This move was watched with anxiety by Congress. It saw its tools slipping out of its hands. It had thought that it would capitalize on the differences between the two sides make a gain politically. Indira, a keen Kashmir watcher, lost no time in finding out what best could be done to counter the rising tide of Muslim unity if her party had to win the elections. The election victory was always a matter of great prestige for the Prime Minister. She hated losing. The Resettlement Bill was invoked to raise the anti-National Conference sentiment among Hindus in Jammu region and the themes of the corruption and other failures of the National Conference were made issues to pin it down in the Valley. The money was not a problem.

The Broadway Hotel of Srinagar had become the hub of political activity of the Congress Party, much more than that of the PCC headquarters at Maulana Azad Road that was just a stone's throw away from the hotel. The hotel, owned by capitalist Lala Tirath Ram Amla, knew how to use his financial clout to obtain positions within the party. Indira was lulled into the make- believe that Congress would sweep the polls. Indira Gandhi was a shrewd politician and had no appetite for such dream weavers. There were calculations that Congress might win more than 25 seats in the Jammu region and the rest as it needed just 14 more to have a majority in the Assembly of 76. Indira's campaign managers Arun Nehru and the likes of him who were bent upon digging out everything that would go against Farooq Abdullah were confident of securing that magic figure in the elections.

Congress' strategy was clear: work a pro-Hindu line and inject fears among the minorities in Jammu and Kashmir and somehow win the seats in the Valley to cobble together a majority. What came in handy to the Congress Party was the issue of the alliance between the National Conference and the BJP in the Jammu Municipality. The BJP had got its chairman elected simply on the basis of the support of the NC's councillors. The BJP had tried to shun this alliance and demonstrate that it had been compelled to promote the smooth functioning of the Municipality, but no one was convinced. Congress was able to draw political mileage out of it.

Farooq was attending a police function at Kathua, where the Information Department had brought in car loads of scribes from Jammu. I was part of that group. J. N. Sathu,[21] a senior journalist among us asked him when he was going to hold the Assembly elections, Farooq replied: June. That was the beginning of his dalliance with politics.

The campaign began with the themes that the Centre was trying to browbeat the National Conference, the champion of the cause of the people of Kashmir. This was a recurring theme of the party at all elections. This time it was more hyped and intensified and bitter. Mufti Sayeed was called a stooge of Indira Gandhi, who had tarnished the honour of the people of Kashmir in the eyes of the rest of the people in India. There were shrill voices that challenged Indira for visiting so many places. 'Look the Prime Minister is visiting every *mohalla* (locality) to campaign for removing Farooq Abdullah,' taunted Mohammad Shafi Uri,[22] a shrewd brain in Farooq's team to mock at Indira Gandhi. 'You may visit each and every home in Kashmir, but when it comes to voting, the people will vote for us,' Farooq would tell his audiences. There were religious slogans and such was the intensity of hatred in the atmosphere that the PCC President who was contesting from two constituencies also had no option but to allow his supporters to chant the same religious *'Naar'e Takbir, Allaho Akbar'* (Allah's greatest of all) slogans to counter the National Conference. Congress had placed all the national media on its side. Even newspapers that were critical of Indira Gandhi at the national level, sided with her and her party in Jammu and Kashmir. *The Indian Express* was one such newspaper. *The Indian Express* that had raked Indira Gandhi over the coals for her excesses during the Emergency, was seen to be on her side when it came to Kashmir. Its Resident Editor in Delhi, A. N. Dar arrived and wrote laudatory pieces about Congress and stopped just short of calling the National Conference and its leader anti-national. That was the theme and song of all the newspapers.

Farooq was not losing any sleep over this relentless media campaign against him. He was whipping up the sentiments of the Kashmiris against the Centre and he was assisted in this job by his colleagues who knew that their survival was in raising the anti-Delhi tone and tenor.

Indira Gandhi was at her most eloquent. She campaigned well past midnight. There were no terrorists around at that time. She went from place to place on the sole ticket that the National Conference and BJP were two sides of the same coin. It was something that her daughter-in-law Sonia Gandhi was to repeat in the 2002 polls.[23]

Indira took on the National Conference for making the Resettlement Bill the core issue of the whole campaign. 'Look, if you do not vote for change, there, just across this border, there are Pakistanis who would come and claim your land and homes and you would be refugees once again,'[24] she told a huge public gathering at Hira Nagar, a border town barely 12 kms from the Indo-Pak border, about 55 kms south of Jammu. This was her way of portraying the horrors of the continuance of NC rule to Hindus.

Her campaign was moving Hindus. She was playing the communal card to perfection just as Farooq was playing the Muslim unity card with finesse. But the two never reallized that their bitter campaign on communal lines was causing damage to the state and its edifice of secularism. The regional and religious divide was growing ever wider.

Congress took the campaign to extremes. Old files were dug out and Farooq Abdullah was shown in the company of the Jammu and Kashmir Liberation Front leaders in PoK where he had once gone and declared himself against the Indian rule in Kashmir. Those dusty photographs were splashed across the pages of the obliging newspapers in Jammu[25] where Farooq's association with separatists could show him in a poor light. Congress condemned Farooq as an anti-national. The damage was done.

'If you don't vote for me, go to hell. I will not spend even a single penny on your development,' Farooq would tell the election meetings in Hindu areas of Jammu region thereby providing ammunition against himself by confirming Congress' charges that he was being anti-Hindu and anti-Jammu. Back in the Valley, this was chalking up votes for him. The NC imprinted on the minds of Kashmiris that 'Hindu *sarkar'* (government) was anti-Muslim at the Centre. Farooq Abdullah was inflaming hatred towards Delhi. Tauntingly, Farooq Abdullah asked the Kashmiri Muslims: 'How many of you are in the Central Government services, how much share were you getting in the banks and other Central government departments?'[26] The bitter religious overtones were undeniable in his references to the Kashmiri Pandits, a miniscule minority with a lion's share in these services.

The germs of hate sown during this campaign would later develop into the full-blown militant secessionist movement. If Farooq is to be blamed for whipping up these sentiments of the masses, Indira Gandhi was no less guilty. She compelled Farooq to adopt an aggressive posture not realising that, though the initiation of the election campaign along communal lines might bring in a few more votes, it would cause incalculable harm in Kashmir for years to come. She was playing the Punjab game in Kashmir. Pakistan was watching with delight. Indira and the Sheikh's son were paving the ground for secessionist militancy.

Kashmir is not Uttar Pradesh or Bihar, two of India's most populous states. It is a place that is under international focus. Myopic politicians with eyes riveted solely on votes could not forsee that the rise of Islamic fundamentalism in this part of the world might have a pernicious effect on people in the rest of South Asia and even give cause for worldwide alarm.

Those who trace the root of militancy to the 1987Assembly elections reveal their ignorance of the history of Kashmir. The first step along that route was taken in the 1983 elections when Hindus were identified as Indians who wanted to subjugate Kashmiri Muslims. Indira Gandhi only aggravated matters by launching a communal campaign and provoking Farooq to respond with a matching game. The ill-effects of that campaign were felt everywhere.

Indira was the loser. Congress' defeat was not seen as the defeat of the party but that of the Prime Minister who had put her personal prestige at stake. It was also a defeat for India in Kashmir. She could not reconcile herself to the defeat. She had seen the big bad days when she had lost elections in 1977 for her Government's atrocities during the Emergency. She had jailed the opponents, gagged the press and ran the country as her personal fief. That was an era of *na daleel, na appeal, na vakeel-*

no argument or logic, no appeal and no legal aid. All cases were summarily dismissed and the only punishment prescribed for all those challenging her was 'jail.' But that she should be trounced by a man who was a novice in politics was something that she could never ever swallow.

Endnotes

1. *Kashmir Times,* a prominent English newspaper in Jammu and Kashmir published from Jammu.

2. Ved Bhasin is a politician-turned-journalist. He was editor of *Kashmir Times* and now he is Chairman of the *Kashmir Times* Group of publications. He is also known in Jammu and Kashmir's journalistic circles as father of professional journalism in the State.

3. UNI (United News of India) is one of the two main news agencies of India, the other being Press Trust of India (PTI).

4. Dogri is the native language of the Jammu region.

5. Mohammad Sayeed Malik, a prominent journalist of Kashmir who worked for *Patriot* and later retired as Editor of *Sunday Observer* published from Delhi. Mohammad Sayeed Malik and Ved (see note) form one of the best pairs of political analysts in Jammu and Kashmir. They have keen political insight; their predictions are generally accurate. Of the two, Malik is perhaps superior. He is objective, balanced and cool where Ved is impulsive and impassioned.

6. Zafar Meraj, a senior journalist in Kashmir who started his career with *Aina,* an Urdu newspaper and later became Chief of Bureau of *Kashmir Times* in Srinagar. Currently, he is editor of a Srinagar-based English newspaper *Kashmir Monitor.*

7. Indira Gandhi, daughter of India's first Prime Minister Jawaharlal Nehru, herself became Prime Minister in January 1966 after the death of Lal Bahadur Shastri who died of a heart attack immediately after signing an agreement with Pakistan's dictator Mohammad Ayub Khan in Tashkent then in the USSR. She was the first PM in India who imposed the Emergency in 1975 and her party Congress was

routed in the 1977 elections and the Janta Party formed the first non-Congress government in the country. She bounced back in 1980 and was assassinated by her Sikh bodyguards on October 31, 1984.

8. Giani Zail Singh was a Sikh leader of Punjab who became Chief Minister of Punjab and later was taken as India's Home Minister and then Indira rewarded him for his loyalties by getting him elected as President of India in the 1980s.

9. Hazratbal is the most revered Muslim shrine in Srinagar, located on the banks of the famous Dal Lake. It is a white-marbled structure that houses a holy relic, a hair of the Prophet Mohammad.

10. Girdhari Lal Dogra was an associate of Sheikh Abdullah who subsequently joined Bakshi Ghulam Mohammad and Congress. He was a popular figure in Hiranagar from where he was elected between 1957 and 1977. He was Finance Minister of the State until 1975. In 1980 he became a member of parliament from Jammu and in 1984 he was elected from Udhampur constituency. He died in 1988.

11. The Janta Party was formed by Jan Sangh, Congress for Democracy, Kranti Lal and Lok Dal. The Janta Party was the brain-child of Jayaprakash Narayan, one of India's greatest leaders who had started a movement against the dictatorial tendencies of Indira Gandhi and offered stiff resistance to the Emergency era of her rule. Emergency was imposed in India on June 25, 1975 and it lasted till March 1977. Janta Party's first and last government was headed by Morarji Desai. The government fell in 1979. Charan Singh, another leading light of the Janta Party, formed the government with the help of Indira Gandhi's Congress. However, Congress soon withdrew its support and the government fell, paving the way for fresh elections. That marked the end of the Janta Party. All its constituent parties have withdrawn, maintaining their distinctive bias and it is almost non-existent on the Indian political scene.

12. Abdul Rashid Kabuli, Awami Action Committee activist, after having quit the BJP, formed the Jammu and Kashmir National Democratic Front in 2003.

13. Charar-e-Sharief, a revered shrine of the Muslim saint Sheikh Noor-ud-Din Noorani who believed in mutual love and coexistence between Hindus and Muslims.

14. These were Sikh and Hindu refugees from the Mirpur, Muzzaffarabad and Kotli areas which are now in Pakistan-occupied Kashmir. They were pushed to Jammu and made to settle in the homes vacated by Muslims who had fled to Pakistan.

15. This is a reference to the refugees who came from what is now PoK and other Hindus living in the Valley at that time.

16. Jamait-I-Islami, the Muslim fundamentalist party in the Valley. Its leader was Syed Ali Shah Geelani. This fundamentalist organization is working for the merger of Kashmir with Pakistan.

17. Ghulam Mohi-ud-Din Shah, a senior leader of National Conference. He was General Secretary of the party during Sheikh Abdullah's time. He later became a minister in the Farooq Abdullah government (1982-84; 1986–87). He was leader of the opposition in the State Legislative Assembly and leader of the National Conference Legislative Party. He died in 2004.

18. Ghulam Mohammad Shah, son-in-law of Sheikh Mohammad Abdullah and brother-in-law of Farooq Abdullah. He is married to Khalida, the eldest daughter of Sheikh Abdullah and sister of Farooq Abdullah. He is an ambitious politician. He was active during the Plebiscite Front days and later became Transport Minister in the Sheikh Abdullah Government (1977–82).

19. Devi Dass Thakur was a leading lawyer and judge of Jammu and Kashmir High Court in 1975 when Sheikh picked him up as his Finance Minister. He remained in that position till September 1982. He could not continue with Farooq Abdullah. He joined hands with Ghulam Mohammad Shah and toppled the Farooq Abdullah government. He was Deputy Chief Minister and Finance Minister in that government. He is back in legal practice.

20. Moulvi Iftikhar Hussain Ansari is a senior Shia leader of Kashmir having a wide influence over his sect. He was in Congress, Janta

Party, now in National Conference. He was also a minister in the Farooq Abdullah Government (1996–2002).

21. J. N. Sathu, a senior journalist who worked for *The Telegraph*, London. Although he is a Kashmiri Hindu, he is deeply attached to Kashmiri Muslims.

22. Mohammad Shafi Uri, a Pahari leader who is quite popular in his constituency in Uri, a border town in the north of the Kashmir Valley. His suffix is derived from the name of his town. He was in the Congress and later joined NC. He has served as a Minister in Sheikh Abdullah's and Farooq Abdullah's governments. He lost the 2002 Assembly elections with a narrow margin of 70 votes to his Congress rival, Taj Mohi-ud-Din.

23. Arun Joshi, 'Sonia promises "better tomorrow" to people of J&K,' *Hindustan Times*, September 21, 2002, p.4.

24. 'Mrs. Gandhi attacks BJP, NC holy pact for elections', *Kashmir Times*, May 23, 1983.

25. The pictures of Farooq Abdullah with the JKLF were published in *Srinagar Times*, a Srinagar-based Urdu newspaper and *Kashmir Times*, Jammu in May 1983.

26. Farooq's speech was extensively reported in Srinagar newspapers, in particular *Aftab* and *Srinagar Times*, two Urdu newspapers of Srinagar between April–May 1983.

Part III

6

Egoistic Claims to Democracy

Farooq Dislodged

Farooq Abdullah might well have a very poor memory for dates but July 2, 1984 is one that will be forever etched on his mind. It marks the day when his government was dismissed and the installation of the government of his brother-in-law Ghulam Mohammad Shah, the day when all the antagonistic forces ranged against him, finally moved forward to oust him from the post of Chief Minister. For in Kashmir, as elsewhere, power and popularity are not always synonymous.

The truth of this had already been demonstrated back in August 9, 1953 when his father Sheikh Mohammad Abdullah was deposed. This time, the Centre did not repeat the mistake of levelling charges of sedition or conspiracy against Farooq Abdullah for times had changed and these charges would not stick. Nehru's daughter meted out a different treatment for Sheikh Abdullah's son.

Indira Gandhi was revengeful. She was outraged by and had never forgotten the spectacle of National Conference supporters who had stripped themselves naked at her rally in Srinagar, in 1983. Farooq was equally embarrassed by the incident. The newspapers were splashed with the photographs of demonstrators[1] who the Congress leaders had been quick to identify as National Conference activists. When, on his appointment as Chief Minister in 1983, Farooq went to see Indira urging her to let bygones be bygones, her first question was, 'Is Farooq properly dressed?' Indira Gandhi had nursed the bitter memories in order to take revenge.

Defections were engineered in the National Conference and Farooq was dislodged. It was a family coup. Ghulam

Mohammad Shah, the irrepressible son-in-law of Sheikh Abdullah, had always wanted to become Chief Minister. But he had no political support base among the masses. The PCC President Mufti Mohd. Sayeed had lost the elections in both the constituencies Bijbehara and Homshallibagh from where he contested in 1983 .Both the seats were won by the National Conference. The Shah knew that Mufti would never be elected. So he seized the opportunity to make peace with the sworn enemy of the Abdullah family: Mufti, whose single-minded ambition was to remove the Abdullah family from power. Mufti, for his part, was also aware of the fury which consumed Shah with the appointment of Farooq as Chief Minister.

Indira Gandhi had had a hand in the successful installation of Farooq on September 8, 1982. She knew what was in store for her country if the political earthquakes in the aftermath of the Sheikh's death went unchecked. Farooq was then her best bet. She thought Farooq was willing to play Delhi's game. He was a close friend of Sanjay Gandhi, younger son of Indira, who was killed in an air-crash in 1980. But Indira's patronage was quickly withdrawn when Farooq showed signs of rebellion in the 1983 elections. She asked Governor B. K. Nehru to dismiss Farooq's Government in January 1984. Nehru did not oblige his niece. Farooq had had an inkling of this. On the first day of the budget session of the state legislature in Jammu in 1984 even before the copy of the Governor's address could be tabled in the State Assembly, Farooq rose and sought a *suo motto* vote of confidence of the House. It was granted with a thumping of desks by the National Conference members. Farooq had won the vote. But there were many within the House who were waiting for a chance to undo him, despite their ingratiating smiles.

On July 2, 1984, Farooq was rudely woken by a call from Raj Bhavan. Jagmohan[2] had replaced B. K. Nehru. Jagmohan was Sanjay Gandhi's underling. His complete obedience to his masters had got him the job of Governor. He was somewhat of a departure from his predecessors who were men of great learning and unparalleled intellect. Jagmohan was a brash but relentless go-getter, nevertheless. Abdul Ghani Lone, the People's Conference leader had described Jagmohan as the 'thug of Turkman gate' in the Assembly and voiced apprehensions that Jagmohan had been sent to Kashmir on 'a mischief-making' mission. Lone was voicing the thoughts of the NC leadership, even though he was in the opposition. Farooq had somehow learnt the art of using political opponents to express his concerns.

By now twelve of Farooq's MLAs were to defect and his government had been reduced to a minority. Farooq could hardly believe his ears. He rushed to Raj Bhavan from his Gupkar road residence.

It was 8 in the morning. He took off to Raj Bhavan, which was hardly two kilometres from his residence. He was oblivious to everything, wondering who could have switched sides and for what consideration. Among them were the two nominated women MLAs, Khem Lata Wakhloo and Gurbachan Kaur Rana. Farooq was incredulous as he stared at the two ladies whom he had nominated as legislators. There were others—Mehboob Beg, Sheikh Abdul Jabbar, Hakim Mohammad Yasin, Ghulam Nabi Dar, Dillawar Mir, Rafiq Khan. All of them looked rather sheepish. They did not dare look him in the eye. Farooq walked away from Raj Bhavan, feeling bitterly betrayed. His popularity among the masses had become meaningless. Sheikh Abdullah Sher-e-Kashmir's son was close to breaking down at both the loss of job and the betrayal. He had been too trusting and had placed his trust in the wrong kind of people.

Farooq was blind to the resentment which he had created at his very first public rally when he had openly admonished and denounced members of his own party, accusing them of corruption and incompetence, adding that he would pick a new team of honest and competent people. His ego had been further inflated by self-seeking sycophants with neither political experience nor any goodwill towards him. Though this mattered little to Farooq whose own loyalties were constantly changing. One of his close confidants once remarked that 'he is (the) best friend of his enemies and (the) best enemy of his friends.' Nor did he have the gumption to stand up for his friends.

Rashid Baba, his security officer, who is also a sort of Man Friday to Farooq Abdullah once confided in me that the source of many problems was Farooq's dismissive attitude towards his party leaders. Rashid Baba recalled the times when party workers had full access to the government and when their word carried weight. 'Those were good times,' he reminisced, speaking of the era of Sheikh Abdullah when the people working for the National Conference commanded respect and recognition. That was essentially *'Kharpanch Raj'* or rule of the NC strongmen. These party strongmen, working in their respective areas were able to get things going, grab contracts and recruit people into the government services. In turn, they would get votes for the National Conference. These strongmen had invested their lives in the National Conference and enjoyed a place in the party and in society. That had vanished with the death of Sheikh Abdullah. These *kharpanch* no longer enjoyed the privileges that they had in the past. Farooq was surrounded by sycophants; his ministers had come to replace these strongmen. As a result, the party suffered. Farooq acknowledged that his men had a problem with him but was adamant that he was above political and party considerations and that while he gave due respect and recognition to his workers he had no intention of denying others his favours.[3]

But these were veterans who had tasted power and were familiar with the intricacies of Kashmir politics. He had alienated them and had now to pay the price for his negligence. But even more costly was the price that he had to pay for offending Delhi and its mandarins. He might love golf, but he was a novice when it came to holes in the game of politics. Masters of the political chess-board, like Mufti were skilfully using Ghulam Mohammad Shah to further their own political objective.

There were a number of options open to him. He would not compromise with the Centre and had been advised against doing so. There was tremendous support for Sheikh's son and he could not squander it away within a year after having forged the Muslim unity. The streets were calm. There were no TV satellite channels to keep tabs on the movement of their leaders. But there was sufficient strength in the Central Reserve Police Force and the contingents of the Madhya Pradesh Police Constabulary who had been specially airlifted two days before to the place where the political coup was actually to be staged. Farooq Abdullah, Chief Minister of the State had no idea what was happening in his own backyard. He was unaware of the landing of the paramilitary forces, and that summer in Srinagar, he had no inkling that conspirators were gathering outside his very front gates to oust him.

The other option he had was to take to the streets. His call would have brought thousands out on his side. But he was not a politician in the mould of his father. He had not lived street politics at close range. He was far away from it all. What he knew best were the whistling times outside the Girls Hostel in Jaipur city. He was a student of SMS Medical College, Jaipur. The people at Ajmeri Gate and Chora Rasta remembered him for his youthful pranks. He might have been a leader of sorts but he was no politician. He loved the company of the fair sex.'I admire the beauty of the rose. Don't you? What is the harm in that?' he asked Vir Sanghvi,[4] editor of *Hindustan Times* in a Star

Talk programme. Farooq tried to steel himself as he came out of Raj Bhavan.

The July 2, 1984 coup had been planned with clockwork precision by the political managers of Indira: Arun Nehru,[5] Mufti Mohammad Sayeed and Arif Khan. When his Government was dismissed, the Kashmiris fought on his behalf. They felt that whatever faults he might have they should stand by him. And they did. They resorted to protests and shutdowns and Ghulam Mohammad Shah's government came to be known as 'curfew sarkar' (curfew government meaning that government survives by imposing curfew). But Farooq did nothing. He could not take up the political challenge. He baulked at the thought of taking risks.

It was November 1984; he was in Jammu preparing to leave for Srinagar. One of his confidants, Ajay Sadhotra,[6] who later became a minister after the 1996 elections, called me urging me to go to the airport, as something big was about to happen. At the airport, I saw Farooq surrounded by partymen. I asked him what the matter was and he replied that they were going to put him away. It was obvious that he was afraid of the prospect. But he was not arrested. Perhaps the Shah Government realized that an arrest would make a hero of Farooq. The Shah had misgivings about Farooq. Though the Chief Minister knew that Farooq was not of the mettle of his father, he was sure that the people in the Valley were die-hard supporters of the NC and Farooq. Farooq had come to enjoy a degree of sympathy and support among the people of the Jammu region where the National Conference had never enjoyed popular support except for pockets of Muslim-dominated parts. The sympathy had come because he was seen as the victim of Indira Gandhi's machinations in the politics of Kashmir. Farooq was now out of power. That was the cold and bitter reality. It took some time for him to come to terms with this bitter fact. He sought solace in the opposition camp dominated by TDP (Telugu Desam Party)[7] leader N. T. Rama Rao and the likes of Harkrishen Singh Surjeet (CPI-M) and George Fernandes (then the Janta Dal, now Samta Party). They proved to be of little help to him.

Ghulam Mohammad Shah

But the unpopularity of the Shah regime was a factor going in Farooq's favour. Shah was losing favour for two reasons: he had been unmasked as a treacherous and disloyal son-in-law working against his wife's brother and this was perceived less as a betrayal to Farooq Abdullah than of Sheikh Abdullah. Secondly, his reconciliation with the Congress, the party which the Kashmiris had rejected at the hustings could not be stomached. How could Delhi have the audacity to negate the people's verdict by throwing its lot in with the power hungry son-in-law of Sheikh Abdullah, with the connivance of Mufti Mohammad Sayeed? For as events unfolded, it became clear that Mufti had helped Ghulam Mohammad Shah to power by poisoning the ears of Indira Gandhi against Farooq, in the pursuit of his own dream of becoming Chief Minister of Jammu and Kashmir. But it was to be another 19 years before his dream would be fulfilled.

Public protests against the Shah regime were growing. Victimized by the rampant corruption under his government, people revolted against the underling Delhi had imposed on them. Shah tried every trick in the book to remain in power. He knew that it was his final chance. Being a veteran politician, he had a keen insight into Mufti's ambitions. It was crucial for Shah to focus on building good relations with the Congress leadership in Delhi. As long as Indira Gandhi was alive, Shah had little to fear about the stability of his government. First, he had risen to become Chief Minister on her orders and secondly, it was difficult for anyone to make her change her mind. She was a lady of steel in politics. Shah might not have been the best choice. But once she had made it and as long as he was doing her bidding, he had no problems.

However, her assassination on October 31, 1984 at the hands of her own security guards in her Safdarjung residence, changed the scene of Kashmir politics as well. Her son Rajiv Gandhi succeeded her, thanks to Giani Zail Singh, who was repaying his gratitude to the deceased leader who had propelled him to the highest constitutional post in the country. President Zail Singh accepted Rajiv Gandhi[8] as the leader of the Congress Party. Rajiv was sworn in as Prime Minister when parts of the country, especially Delhi, were witnessing the worst ever communal frenzy. Sikhs were being killed mercilessly. They were being burnt and the whole nation was shaken by these events.

Rajiv did not inherit his family's penchant for politics. He had neither the temperament nor the interest for it. But destiny had vowed to throw him into the political arena. It was June 1981. Indira Gandhi was broken by the death of her younger son, Sanjay Gandhi, Rajiv's younger brother. In her grief, she turned to her eldest son Rajiv Gandhi for support. Rajiv was made to resign his job as a pilot in the Indian Airlines and join politics against the protestations of his wife Sonia, the girl from Italy, with whom he had fallen in love at Cambridge and subsequently married. Sonia Gandhi[9] was against her husband's joining politics. Up to then he had led the relatively sheltered life of a pilot. Sonia was unwilling that her husband should exchange this for the rough and tumble of political life. Indira was aware of all this. But she had no option other than to persuade Rajiv to shoulder some of the responsibility.

Overnight, everything changed. The pilot was thrown into the front seat of India's leading party. He contested elections from Amethi, the seat earlier held by Sanjay and became AICC General Secretary.

Mufti tried to secure Rajiv's favour. But Rajiv was a man of the modern era, surrounded by men like Mani Shankar Aiyar[10] and Arun Singh who had envisaged their computer version of India and who had little or no time for the in-depth discussions of the Muftis and these were further curtailed once Rajiv became Prime Minister. Shrewd politician that he was, Mufti could not reconcile himself to the fact that his party with twenty-six MLAs in the Assembly was actually supporting the National Conference, the party headed by Shah's wife Khalida, the eldest child of Sheikh Abdullah. He therefore started to plot for the removal of Shah. Smarting from the scant attention he received from the new leader, nonetheless Mufti decided to contest the by-election from R. S. Pura, a border town in the Jammu district, for the Assembly. The seat had fallen vacant due to the election of Janak Raj Gupta (who held this seat) to the Lok Sabha in December 1984. Mufti was able to prevail upon Rajiv Gandhi, somehow, that Girdhari Lal Dogra should be shifted to Udhampur and in his place Janak should contest the Jammu seat. Dogra had been very bitter about it as he was extremely worried about his chances of winning the hilly constituency where he expected a contest from Dr. Karan Singh, who had won that seat four times in a row since 1967. But the Jammu leaders lacked the courage to stand up against the Kashmiri leaders' wishes, especially when these were endorsed by the high command. Farooq was out of the picture. He suffered from depression and had momentarily lost interest in the Parliamentary elections.

Mufti's Machinations

Mufti who had been defeated in Bijbehra, his home town in the Kashmir Valley and Homshallibagh, the neighbouring constituency in 1983, won easily from R. S. Pura. He took advantage of the government machinery and Shah had no other option but to oblige him, to ensure his victory. Mufti's victory was the beginning of the woes of G. M. Shah. Stories started appearing in newspapers about the rampant corruption in the government. The same Shah who was hailed as a hero and saviour of the people of Kashmir from the irresponsible Farooq Abdullah, was now portrayed as incompetent in the newspapers loyal to Mufti. The moles in Shah's cabinet would leak everything to Mufti who in turn ensured their publication. It was an open secret that the PCC in Jammu and Kashmir was run on Union Home Ministry funds some of which was channelled to newspapers in the state. It was the duty of such newspapers to report on Mufti's comings and goings in and out of the state, similar to the way in which the Prime Minister's programme is chronicled by the newspapers in Delhi.

Mufti manoeuvring was not altogether lost on Shah. But his hands were tied as he did not have the adequate number of seats in the Assembly; this prevented him from taking any precipitous action that might throw him out of power.

Shah was increasingly becoming a pawn in the hands of the Congress Party and his image as a strong man of Kashmiri politics was being gradually tarnished. He was fast losing his grip over politics and the administration. His ministers, sensing the strength of Mufti's hand, transferred their loyalties to the latter. They were mere opportunists guided only by self-interest. After all, it was Congress that had sent them the money bags to buy support for Shah. The Chief Minister had closed his eyes to the looting.

Finally Shah resorted to what in Kashmir is known as *Gushtaba* politics.[11] With a number of chefs in tow, left for Delhi where he hosted a great feast for Rajiv Gandhi in Delhi. He attempted to sort out matters with Rajiv Gandhi and it was believed that he had obtained a reprieve and there was no immediate danger to his government. Shah returned from Delhi, a happy man. He thought his troubles were over. Shah, who had told Indira at the beginning of his innings as Chief Minister that having Congress ministers in the government would pose problems for his government making it a jumbo-sized ministry which might threaten his government, secretly and successfully conveyed the message to Rajiv that Kashmir politics would be far more tractable if Mufti were removed from the Kashmir political scene.

Mufti, however, had been the PCC chief since 1975 and had been an aggressive and successful party chief. He would never allow these successes to be wrested from his hand. He had earned the trust of Indira Gandhi. She had been consulting him on every development concerning Kashmir. She was in Madras, now Chennai, when she heard that Mirza Afzal Beg had parted ways with Sheikh Abdullah. She immediately rang up Mufti Sayeed and demanded to know what impact it would have on Kashmir politics and what gain Congress could make out of it. Such precision and specific questioning by Indira of Mufti showed his clout. Mufti had the abilities of a good organier. He was blessed with the friendship of politically astute journalists like Mohammad Sayeed Malik, Shyam Kaul and Ved Bhasin who were always there to explain the stratagems on the chessboard of politics for their friend. Mufti also sought political advice from Krishen Dev Sethi, a veteran in the politics of the State who would weigh every word and action of the contemporary politicians. Mufti valued the friendship of these men who were great assets to him. They had forewarned him that with Rajiv's arrival on the Indian political scene, his fortunes could fluctuate. That had indeed happened.

Shah's words and Farooq's growing friendship with Rajesh Pilot,[12] whom Rajiv trusted a lot were preparing the ground for Mufti's exit from Kashmir's political scene. Mufti got wind of it and let loose his foot soldiers. His first task was to get Shah removed. To remove him in the way he had removed Farooq Abdullah would have been a disaster. He knew this. He also knew that Rajiv would not approve of it. So he decided to take on Farooq later. That was the first political mistake which he made.

Shiv Sena: Sowing Ethnic Strife

In February 1986, Shiv Sena, a Hindu fundamentalist organization that champions the cause of Hindu supremacy, started a campaign to host a *bhandara* (big feast) in the civil secretariat premises in Jammu, the kind of which had no precedent. Shiv Sena had become quite active in 1983 and also played a role in organizing relief for stranded passengers and especially for the Shri Mata Vaishno Devi pilgrims when trains were stopped in the wake of Operation Blue Star in June 1984 and also after the assassination of Mrs. Gandhi in October-November 1984. It had emerged as a force in the city politics.

Shiv Sena's leader Ashok Gupta who had become one of the most powerful men in Jammu argued that if Muslim employees could offer *namaaz* on the lawns of the secretariat, there was no reason why Hindus could not worship their deity there. The argument was perfectly logical. However, the proposal generated a great deal of tension. Muslims resisted saying that the practice was unprecedented. Shiv Sena also had a ladies wing headed by Shanti Devi[13] who was in the forefront of organizing things. She played a very active role in seeking public support, particularly among women.

It is true that the lawns of the civil secretariat and for that matter all the government offices had become prayer sites for Muslims in Jammu and Kashmir. But then that had been the practice for many years and it had never occurred to Hindus to organize a *bhandara* ever before. Negotiations were initiated; the government finally succumbed and Hindu groups suddenly scored a victory for themselves. Just as things appeared to be reaching an amicable conclusion, a Muslim employee of the secretariat was stabbed, triggering off a spate of Hindu-Muslim strife. There were many reports of Hindu temples and houses being attacked in south Kashmir and communal tension in Jammu. The rumour mills were working overtime. 'Truckloads of bodies of Muslims are reaching Srinagar. Jammu Hindus have massacred Kashmiri Muslim employees.' Attempts to arrest Shiv Sena leader Ashok Gupta, were frustrated by his supporters. Jammu city began to echo with the clang of tin beating, to express Hindu unity. But the Muslims were also preparing their response. Hostility was more widespread in South Kashmir where temples were desecrated and Hindu- Kashmiri Pandits were hounded out. Kashmiri Hindus were gripped in fear. The Jamait-i-Islami saw through the game. Its activists who should have been the first to target Hindus (for they did not believe in making any concessions to non- Muslims), nonetheless came to the rescue of the Hindus. One of the Jamait-i-Islami activists stood with the holy Quran in his hands when a mob attempted to set ablaze a Hindu temple in Wanpoh village in Anantnag. He asked the hoodlums to quote the verse of the holy book which authorized Muslims to vandalize the places of worship of the minorities. 'They are under our protection,' he proclaimed. The mob melted away and the ray that Gandhi had seen at the time of the partition of the country in Kashmir still appeared to be shining.

The government was blamed for its failure to stem the first communal riots in Jammu and Kashmir in the post-independence period. At night, in the streets of Jammu women would bang *thalis* (steel plates) to show the solidarity while police action was termed as atrocities. Reports were exaggerated in the newspapers to incite the communal discord. Shah was at a loss. It was obviously the handiwork of vested interests who wanted to engineer large-scale communal riots. It later turned out that these communal riots were the contrivances of those who wanted to see Shah ousted in order to realize their own political ambitions. But the riots had done their damage. No one blamed Jammu Hindus. The Kashmiri Muslims were denounced in the national media as communal, rioters and rapists. Kashmir was never to be the same again. Delhi's politics of experimenting had made Muslims in the Valley feel that even if they did good they were entitled only to castigations. Though not a single rape had taken place, it was represented as if rapists were at large in the Valley.

These distortions were pernicious and particularly wouding to the Kashmiris. It was a vilification campaign against the Muslims in the Valley that was distancing them both from India and Hindu Indians. And even Indian Muslims were viewed with suspicion and mistrust. They were perceived as the part of an Indian system that was bent upon perpetuating its rule over Kashmir. Political distance soon led to religious alienation much to the delight of Islamic fundamentalists who were waiting in the wings for just such feelings to be manifested among the people. They needed to hear what had eluded them for decades in the Valley: an echo among Kashmiri Muslims of their alienation from India and the Indians.

End of Shah's Round: Trouncing of Mufti

The communal riots brought an end to the rule of Shah. S. B.

Chavan, the Home Minister who had made an on-the-spot assessment of the situation gave a disturbing report to Prime Minister Rajiv Gandhi. A message was flashed to Iftikhar Hussain Ansari, the Congress legislature party leader, requesting that he visit Raj Bhavan to withdraw support from the Shah government. Shah was in Delhi pleading his case with the Central Government. He revealed the conspiracy theory and blamed Mufti Mohammad Sayeed and his men for the orgy of violence in Kashmir. He was duly heard but when he returned to Jammu on the afternoon of March 7, 1986, the decision had already been taken by Jagmohan to dismiss the Shah Government and to impose Governor's rule.

Shah tried one last tactic: prior to his departure for Rajbahvan on March 7, 1986 he announced that he and his ministers would accept Farooq Abdullah as their leader. He asked the Governor to install Farooq as Chief Minister. Shah had foreseen the sequence of events and had spoken to Farooq. The mediatory role was played by Farooq's mother Begum Akbar Jehan between her son and son-in-law. Initially, Farooq agreed to the proposal. But he had developed such a distrust of Shah and his men, that he exposed Shah's cards at the last minute. He told Jagmohan on the phone from Delhi that he was not interested in power at the moment.

Shah's removal had proceeded according to the wishes of both Farooq and Mufti. But the imposition of Governor's rule was a setback for Mufti.

Mufti, whose ambition to replace Shah had been dashed to the grounds by Rajiv, received yet another setback when he was removed from State politics and made Union Minister for tourism. Mufti was unhappy. His chance of becoming Chief Minister had been snatched from him at the last minute. Besides, the Rajiv-Farooq friendship was flourishing and the key player in this was Rajesh Pilot, then Union Minister of State for Surface Transport. Rajesh was an astute politician. He knew that he had to work for the success of his party and this he did with amazing success.

Governor's Rule

It was Jagmohan's belief when he assumed leadership of the State in March 1986, upon the imposition of Governor's rule, that he would be there for all time. Instead of laying the groundwork for the development of the political process and creating the conditions for the hand-over of power to politicians, he initiated a campaign against the politicians targeting those belonging to the National Conference and the National Conference *(Khalida)*.[14] 'All of them were corrupt,' he would say. Divisional Commissioner, Kashmir, Hamidullah Khan, Deputy Inspector General police, Kashmir Watali figured prominently among those whom he consulted regularly. The first thing he did after assuming power was to give marching orders to the Chief Secretary R.K. Takkar,[15] a highly placed senior IAS officer, whom he did not trust by virtue of the fact that he had been Chief Secretary during Shah's regime. The Director General of Police, M. M. Khajuria[16] was also in his bad books for a similar reason. Raising the caste card Khajuria, a Brahmin appealed to Congress leader Mangat Ram Sharma,[17] a leading political figure of Jammu and Kashmir to save his job. Takkar also attempted some string-pulling, but to no avail. Jagmohan was intoxicated with power and he was there to do what he called a cleansing of the Augean stables.

Jagmohan was unpopular with the people, who had had their fill of politicians. Certain sections, however, were very happy with him. Engineers were getting a great deal of money, in laying roads and the construction of new buildings in urban areas. Rural development funds were being diverted to beautify the cities.

Jammu and Srinagar, the two capital cities were the chief beneficiaries. He invested in their development to showcase his skills in transforming unpaved roads into paved ones. In Jammu, he took over control of the Shri Mata Vaishno Devi shrine.[18] He created a trust and undertook massive development on the shrine and the roads leading to it. Pilgrims were happy and broadcast the message throughout north India that Jagmohan was doing a great job.It was a big achievement for him.

But the problem arose when Jagmohan started displaying his Hindu chauvinist thinking. He ordered a ban on the slaughter of animals on Janam Ashtami—the birthday of Hindu Lord Krishna. But Ummat-i-Islami chief Qazi Nissar Ahmad,[19] who was known as Mirwaiz of south Kashmir, challenged the ban. He was a doctorate in Arabic studies and he was a mesmerizing orator. He lived in a modest house in Acchabal Adda in Anantag but commanded great respect among his people for his knowledge of the holy books of Islam and his unparalleled rhetoric. Qazi Nissar took offence at the order that had both religious and political overtones in Kashmir. First, there had been no such ban in Kashmir ever since 1947 after the departure of the rule of Dogra kings. Furthermore, it was thought to be an onslaught on the religious rights of Muslims in the Valley. Secondly, it was pregnant with a political message. Since the practice of not slaughtering animals on Janam Ashtami was in vogue during Dogra rule, Muslims interpreted Jagmohan's order as a new attempt at subjugating them. 'He wants to make us slaves once again,' thundered Qazi Nissar at Lal Chowk, main square in Anantnag town and to the amazement of his admirers and supporters, he slit a goat there in sheer defiance of Jagmohan's order. Jagmohan had helped consolidate the Islamic forces by his ill-advised moves which completely ignored the complexities and sensitivities of Kashmir. His bulldozing[20] skills, glimpses of which had been displayed at Turkman Gate in Delhi, were fuelling fires that would prove unquenchable. Muslim fundamentalism developed strong roots and Jagmohan who either had no idea as to what he was doing or was bent on a deliberate course of action, was fanning the embers to flame. He might perhaps have been unaware that his acts of commission and omission would prove catastrophic for the State and the country.

Farooq Reinstated

Farooq was repeatedly plagued with the message that he would not survive without the help of Congress and that to ensure his political existence, he should do the bidding of Congress and Rajiv. Eventually, he accepted Congress' terms of sharing power with the Centre's ruling party in a bid to survive. That earned for him a brief return to power and the isolation of his sworn enemy in politics, Mufti Mohammad Sayeed, but in so doing he had betrayed his own people and caused irreparable damage to his political career. By now, Muslim fundamentalist groups under Muslim Mutehada Mahaaz or the Muslim United Front had secured their bases in the Valley.

That the return of Farooq Abdullah to power in November 1986 was not at all to Jagmohan's liking is an understatement. At Ladies Park, each word of Rajiv and Farooq spelt poison for him. He sponsored a series of demonstrations in the streets of Jammu the day Rajiv Gandhi and Farooq flew in from Srinagar announcing that from that day onwards they would work together for the welfare of the people of Kashmir. The sponsored demonstrators raised slogans urging the Prime Minister to continue with the President's rule in the state and also retain Jagmohan as Governor.

Farooq did little to improve matters for himself. Soon after the swearing- in ceremony on the lawns of Raj Bhavan on the night of November 7, 1986, Farooq declared that he would lose heavily if Jagmohan were to contest polls in the state.'His box would be full and mine perhaps empty. But he is like my elder brother and 'he can box my ears wherever and whenever and wherever I go wrong,' he announced.[21] It might have been an attempt to keep Jagmohan in good humour, to begin his innings afresh. But that was not to be. The two men had serious differences in approach and attitudes and could never see eye to eye. Having tasted absolute power, Jagmohan could not reconcile himself to its loss.

Dissolution of the Legislative Assembly

Farooq attempted to show his popularity and demonstrate his democratic credentials by announcing that he would seek a fresh mandate. The Assembly had been elected in June 1983 for a period of six years, ending in November 1989 was to be dissolved and fresh elections held in March 1987. That was his trump card. He did not consult Rajiv Gandhi on it. He simply informed him. Farooq had his own logic—both personal and political. He did not trust the members of the Assembly, whom he thought could let him down any time and secondly, he wanted to have the mandate of the people in favour of his confidants. 'We want to go to the people,' was his single one-line response when asked why he had dissolved the Assembly when the House had yet a further three years to go. There was no need for Farooq to go to the polls. Perhaps, he would not have called for elections, had he known that the polls in March 1987 would start a new trail of controversies and throw the Kashmir Valley into perpetual turmoil and the quagmire of unending bloodshed. But then he thought that people were with him and that they would once again vote him to power. He was certain of this fact, although he had to carry with him the unwanted baggage of the Congress Party which was to become a liability for him in the next three to four years.

Here, Farooq had missed out on the point that Mufti Sayeed had made time and time again. Reconciliation between the secular and mainstream parties in Kashmir meant the stifling of secular opposition. And the stifling of secular opposition had its corollary in the fanning of the fires of fundamentalism. A third force did not exist to maintain the equilibrium on Kashmir's political scene. And so it was that the MUF or Muslim United Front[22] was born.

But the ground had slipped and what happened thereafter is a story of the repetition of mistake upon mistake in the cauldron of turmoil that is now Kashmir.

Endnotes

1. *Srinagar Times, Aftab* (two Urdu dailies based in Srinagar), April 1983: *Srinagar Times, Aftab*—two Srinagar-based Urdu dailies.

2. Jagmohan, a civil servant, close to Sanjay Gandhi, younger son of Indira Gandhi, was appointed Governor of Jammu and Kashmir in 1984. He stayed on as Governor for a full five-year term. He was re-appointed Governor of the state in January 1990 but remained in office for less than half a year. He was recalled after the May 21 massacre of more than 50 people during the funeral procession of the assassinated Awami Action Committee chief, Mirwaiz Moulvi Farooq, who was also chief priest of Kashmir. Jagmohan became close to the BJP and became minister in the Atal Bihari Vajpayee Government from 1998 to 2004.

3. Farooq Abdullah told me this in February 2002 at a meeting at his official residence in Jammu.

4. Vir Sanghvi, editor of *Hindustan Times* (1999 to December 2003). He is now Editorial Director of *Hindustan Times* and a familiar figure on TV channels interviewing celebrities.

5. Arun Nehru, a cousin of Rajiv Gandhi, who fell out with him and later joined the National Front Government headed by V. P. Singh.

6. Ajay Sadhotra, a National Conference leader from Jammu, who became a minister in the Farooq Abdullah Government (1996 to 2002). He is now provincial president of NC (Jammu Province).

7. Telugu Desam Party, a regional Party of the south Indian state of Andhra Pradesh founded by film actor N. T. Rama Rao. He was outsted by his own son-in-law Chandra Babu Naidu in the 1990s. Naidu introduced technological revolution to the state. He was routed in the 2004 Assembly Elections held simultaneously with the Lok Sabha Elections.

8. Rajiv Gandhi, eldest son of Indira Gandhi, who became Prime Minister after his mother's assassination on October 31,1984. He ruled till 1989 but was routed in the elections in December 1989. He was assassinated by a suicide bomber in the south Indian state of Tamil Nadu on May 21, 1991.

9. Sonia Gandhi, Italian-born widow of Rajiv Gandhi. She became the President of the Congress in 1997. She was leader of the opposition in the Indian parliament from 1999 to 2004. In 2004, she was elected leader of the Congress Parliamentary Party and allies asked her to stake claim for the Prime Minister's post. She declined.

10. Mani Shankar Aiyar, a close friend of Rajiv Gandhi and loyalist of Sonia Gandhi.

11. Gushtaba politics: Gustabha consists of mutton balls cooked in milk. It is considered to be a Kashmiri delicacy. This term has been specially coined in Kashmir where it refers to the practice of currying favour.

12. Rajesh Pilot, a pilot in the Indian Air Force who quit the job to join politics. He was close to Rajiv Gandhi and served as a minister in his government (1984 to 1989) and worked behind the scenes for rapprochement between Farooq Abdullah and Rajiv paving the way for Farooq to return to power in November 1986. Pilot was killed in a road accident in 2000.

13. Shanti Devi: She had unsuccessfully contested the Assembly Elections on the Shiv Sena ticket in 1987. She became a nominated MLA in the Jammu and Kashmir Legislative Assembly when Mufti became Chief Minister in November 2002.

14. The National Conference was headed by Farooq Abdullah and NC (Khalida) by his eldest sister Khalida Shah. This later got rechristened as the Awami National Conference headed by Ghulam Mohammad Shah.

15. R. K. Takkar, a senior civil servant, who became Chief Secretary of the state.He is considered very close to Mufti Mohammad Sayeed.

16. M. M. Khajuria: He retired as Director General of Police in Jammu and Kashmir.

17. Mangat Ram Sharma, a senior Congress leader who became Deputy Chief Minister in the multi-party-coalition government in 2002.

18. Mata Vaishno Devi, the revered goddess of Hindus. Her shrine is in the foothills of the Himalayas and it attracts five million pilgrims every year.

19. Qazi Nissar, a religious scholar who founded Ummat-i-Islami in Anantnag in south Kashmir, which became part of MUF. He was an eloquent orator. He also called himself Mirwaiz (chief priest) of South Kashmir. He was in jail for two years (1990-1992). But he was assassinated by suspected militants of Hizb-ul-Mujahideen in June 1994.

20. Bulldoze-Jagmohan was Vice Chairman of the Delhi Development Authority in 1975-77– the Emergency period. He cleared a Muslim-dominated area of Turkman gate by running bulldozers, which no one had earlier dared to. He was known as the bulldozer of the Turkman gate.

21. 'You can box my ears-Farooq,' *Kashmir Times*, November 8, 1986.

22. Muslim United Front or MUF, an alliance of Muslim Fundamentalist groups that started the fight for the rights of Muslims in Kashmir and also contested in the March 1987 Assembly elections and lost. The MUF attributed the defeat to large-scale rigging by the NC-Congress coalition government headed by Farooq Abdullah.

7

Democracy Enacted with Fraud

The air was pulsating with frenzy. Everyone was ecstatic at the sight of their leader, they were singing *'wanwun,'* a Kashmiri song of welcome for heroes. Never had I witnessed such an outpouring of emotion.

Farooq Abdullah was in the driving seat and the crowds of men and women jostled to reach him in the torrential rains. They seemed to be intoxicated with love for their leader. The unrelenting February rains lashed Ganderbal, hardly 25 kms. north of Srinagar. But that was no dampener. People were soaked through, swinging in rhythm and raising their arms to the chant of *'Aawaaawa sooh ha aaw'* (Come everyone look, the big lion has come) they sang, first in Kashmiri and then in Urdu: *'Aa Gaya Aya Gaya, Sher-e-Babbar Aagaya.'* These chants had been made up by the loyalists of Sheikh Abdullah. I remember first hearing them in the streets of Anantnag.

Farooq was clearly moved by the shower of love and affection and this was apparent to all of us watching him that day as he arrived to file his nomination papers for the March 1987 Assembly elections.

I had seen people lining up in neat queues with garlands waiting for hours on end for the arrival of Dr. Karan Singh in Kathua. He was revered as *'Yuv Raj,'* the prince out of awe and gratitude. Karan would acknowledge the greeting by waving hands. Farooq did so by shaking hands and accepting the affectionate kisses on his forehead. Farooq was indeed deeply cherished by his constituents.

At the office of Tehsildar Ganderbal, there was a big crowd

and hundreds were there chasing after his jeep. His trusted lieutenant P. L. Handoo,[1] a brillant Kashmiri Pandit from Anantag who had risen to become a minister in Farooq's Cabinet, was with him. It used to be said in Kashmir that no Muslim can work in the Valley without the help of Kashmiri Pandits. Pandits are reputed to be highly intelligent and shrewd; they are accurate in their observations and work out things to the minutest detail, leaving nothing to chance.

Farooq is poor at details. He doesn't have the patience to read beyond the length of a page, leaving it to his aides (of whom Handoo was the most trusted) to read and make the necessary propositions. But, on occasion, Farooq could be extremely adroit: As Tehsildhar rose from his chair on seeing the Chief Minister walking in, Farooq motioned to him to resume his seat saying, 'Sir, you are the returning officer, I am a candidate at the moment.' Tehsildar was nonplussed.

When the formalities were over—the cavalcade moved to Khir Bhawani temple—one of the most revered shrines of Kashmiri Hindus in the ganderbal area where Muslims sell *'puja samgiri'* (articles for prayers such as flower petals and milk). Legend has it that the waters of the shrine pond turn red when bad things are in the air. The goddess is pleased with *'kheer'*—a sweetish pudding made of rice and milk.

'Shall I also join you?' I asked my friend Meraj-ud-Din, a gifted photographer and now a cameraman with APTV. 'Why not, but have you eaten egg or mutton in the morning?' he asked. I recalled having eaten an egg for breakfast. 'Then you better stay out,' he advised. To satisfy my curiosity, I asked Meraj, about himself. 'I knew that Farooq would visit the shrine, so I have not taken anything.' He and Mushtaq Ali, another friend of mine, who was killed by a parcel bomb at BBC office in Srinagar in September 1995, followed Farooq into the temple.

Fundamentalists used to vilify Farooq as an infidel, who had no respect for Islamic laws. One of the charges against him was that he visited Hindu temples and applied *tilak* (vermilion mark) on his forehead, the way Hindus do. Farooq was conscious of this virulent campaign but visited the shrine nonetheless. The priest applied *'tilak'* and the cameras clicked. Farooq requested the photographers not to print this photograph as opponents would go around town reporting that he was not a Muslim. He knew that the political consequences in the Valley where fundamentalism had begun to take root, could be disastrous. Some thought he was being hypocritical like all other politicians. Hypocrisy is regarded as a qualification for the politicians adept at the art of survival. But others say he was being honest. This curious combination of his personality was always mystifying. At times, he spoke his heart to me as if I alone enjoyed his confidence, and on other occasions, he would ignore me as if I was a man from some other planet. This trait has hurt many of his friends and contributed a great deal to distancing him from friends or worse yet, from turning friends into his foes.

At a seminar on spiritualism in Jammu University, he reflected on this episode. He is also a regular visitor to the Shri Mata Vaishno Devi Shrine nestled in the Trikuta Hills about 60 kms. north of Jammu. But he questioned his detractors about this 'I can wipe out *tilak* applied by a priest in the temple but what about the natural *'tilak'* I have on my forehead. How can I remove that?'

Farooq has a natural reddish sign like *tilak* on his forehead. Those having this mark, in Hindu mythology are regarded as being blessed with *rajyog*–and are destined to rule. His next destination was the home of a National Conference activist who was hosting lunch for the Chief Minister. We were waiting outside when word came from inside that Farooq wanted all the media men inside. The message came from Najma Heptullah, while we were having lunch. She was a familiar figure as the Vice Chairman of the Rajya Sabha. Then she was in charge of Congress affairs in Jammu and Kashmir. Congress was willing to cede the Ranbirsinghpora seat, a border constituency in Jammu, to the NC in lieu of Kargil. It wanted to retain full control in the Ladakh region. It already had the Leh seat in a sharing arrangement with the NC. Farooq would have no such change in the arrangement. He did not want Congress to have control of Kargil and there were no benefits involved in taking the overwhelmingly Hindu majority seat of Ranbirsinghpora where his then Forest Minister R. S. Chib, an ex-serviceman, was interested in contesting. No, he said to himself. The wireless message scribbled on the paper was rolled like a used paper napkin and thrown away. 'As if we have never received it,' he smiled.

Roots of Islamic Fundamentalism in Kashmir

In the meantime, a new generation had grown up in Kashmir that did not feel any obligation either towards Sheikh Abdullah or the National Conference. This generation was not aware of the restoration of 'land-to-the-tiller' reforms initiated by Sheikh Abdullah which freed thousands of poor landless farmers from the yoke of feudalism. The National Conference flag's emblem—the plough—symbolized the power of the peasantry. The generation, born in the 1950s and 60s had witnessed the transformation of the National Conference turned into the Plebiscite Front in the 1950s. It advocated the right of self-determination for the people of Jammu and Kashmir, to choose between India and Pakistan as their future nation. This showed the growing grip which Pakistan was having on Kashmiri minds. To them, Pakistan had come to represent something akin to a messiah. While this was happening, Sheikh Abdullah was in jail and the influence which the NC wielded over the people in the Valley convinced them that India was not a country to be trusted. Kashmiris felt betrayed as the man who had sided with India in rejecting the two-nation theory, was now implicated in a conspiracy case.

Then came February 1975 when Sheikh Abdullah was back in power not as Prime Minister but as Chief Minister. It was a crushing let-down. His people were disillusioned and bemused by this 'taming'of the 'Lion of Kashmir.' From their stand-point, it was obvious that there must have been a deal of some kind. The new generation refused to accept that it was the most pragmatic thing to do in the circumstances. Disillusionment was growing. The younger generation felt that the National Conference and its leaders were self-seekers. Though this section was small, it was highly articulate. And those among it, who were silent on the issue, were nursing wounds of betrayal. These potential rebels were far more dangerous. They had started a silent campaign against the National Conference. Since they were denigrating the National Conference for siding with Congress, the ruling party of India, they were in effect nursing an anti-India constituency in Kashmir that was later to prove a big problem for India. The silent majority joined forces with the articulate minority in launching a scathing campaign against India and Indians and provided the mass support that the armed rebels needed in their violent campaign against India.

Some analysts have interpreted events as of the National Conference's own making, as they had betrayed the people and created an anti-India segment in the Valley that was then taken over by Pakistan and its agents. Committed Jamait-i-Islami cadres were already there who did not look beyond Pakistan and aggressively pursued its Islamic fundamentalist and staunch pro-Pakistan agenda through its network of *madrasas* which had been set up with petro-dollars from the Gulf nations and also some support that it regularly received from Pakistan.

The Gulf nations had been sponsoring the cause of religious education and Islamic fundamentalism in Kashmir since the 1970s after the dismemberment of Pakistan in the aftermath of the 1971 Indo-Pak conflict. These oil rich nations were not enamoured of India being a secular and democratic state where Muslims could rise to the highest political positions. Democracy was anathema for them as none of the Gulf nations had a history of democracy. They were and still continue to be ruled by dictatorial regimes. To divert domestic attention from the freedom required in the modern world, their rulers focused on religious fundamentalism pouring hundreds of thousands of petro-dollars to promote the cause of Islamic fundamentalism elsewhere. That was a strategic way to distract the masses in their own countries from nurturing any ideas or aspirations towards democracy. They were pushed to the paradoxical obscurity and glamour of religious fundamentalism. It was in much more the same way that Iraqi ruler Saddam Hussein had starved his own people in order to fund Palestinians and their suicide bombers to win support in the Islamic world. The Kashmir Valley offered an ideal location for them. The Valley is almost exclusively Muslim but it was part, at least geographically of India and India, despite having the second largest Muslim population after Indonesia, was viewed with suspicion by the Gulf nations. Firstly, India was not an Islamic country and secondly, Pakistan—an Islamic republic had always viewed India as an enemy nation because of the bitter history of the partition. This view was further propagated across the Islamic world and no matter what stand India might take in favouring the Arab world or supporting Palestinians irrespective of its consequences on the Kashmiri psyche, the Gulf nations never trusted India. Kashmir offered them the best investment for their petro-dollars for the religious causes achieving the twin objectives of weakening India and at the same time serving their own religion in the eyes of the people of their own nations. Now,

Kashmiri Muslims are graduating as *'jihadis'* in the global Islamic network to fight against infidels.

These petro-dollars were targeting students. Youths can be easily stirred emotionally and can quickly fill the streets holding anti-American and anti-Israel demonstrations, clashing with the police over the issue of the suppression of Muslims in Palestine. That has indirectly provided a platform for the consolidation of anti-India sentiments in the Valley. The clashes with the police are usually coloured by anti-India overtones. Demonstrators have been incited to raise anti-India slogans even as they declared the supremacy of Islam.

People were caught in the grip of religious fervour. I vividly remember that while passing by the famous Hanuman temple at Hari Singh High Street, when I was in Kashmir covering the March 1987 Assembly elections, my photographer colleague Meraj-ud-Din folded his hands in reverence as we Hindus customarily do. 'Don't do this,' a stern voice sitting in a minibus warned him. It was Meraj's friend Mushtaq. I looked towards him. Ignoring me, Mushtaq told Meraj, 'this is sin, we, Muslims are not supposed to bow our heads before temples.' Meraj kept quiet.

Mushtaq then turned towards me and said, 'Don't mind. Islam doesn't permit that.' I too kept quiet.

But it did cross my mind that fundamentalism had taken a hold. The following day, it was visible on the streets. Hundreds of youths wearing green bands on their heads were moving in front of a jeep carrying Mohammad Yusuf, a bearded man who was passionately shouting slogans; *'Yahan Kya Chalega- Nizam-e-Mustafa'* (What sort of governance will function here, Islamic governance). That very Mohammad Yusuf is now Syed Salahauddin, Supreme Commander of the Hizb-ul-Mujahideen which is based in Pakistan and also chief of the United Jehad Council, the top body of a dozen militant outfits that directs military operations in Jammu and Kashmir. He figures on the top of the list of the most wanted men in India. While the petro-dollars and Pakistan's support was laying the network of '*madrasas*' (religious Islamic schools) across the Valley where anti-India feelings were being injected and promoted, the political leadership was embroiled in intrigues. To neutralize the opposition directed at him, from within the Congress Party, Chief Minister Syed Mir Qasim (December 1971 to February 1975) had entered into a secret agreement with the Jamait-i-Islami and helped the Islamic fundamentalist party to win five Assembly seats in the 1972 Assembly elections which were boycotted by the Plebiscite Front of Sheikh Mohammad Abdullah, who was then in the political wilderness and trying to resurrect his political fortunes by undertaking the reconstruction of the revered Hazratbal shrine. These themes converged on the Islamic fundamentalism in the Valley and in subsequent years it was increasingly apparent that the Kashmiri psyche was getting more and more imbued with Islamic values and virtues. The Islamists drew their support from the conservative quarters as well as the older generation both of whom were embittered by the influence of the west on the minds of the younger generation. Beauty parlours, cinemas, and theatres had mushroomed everywhere and Kashmiris were beginning to enjoy English adult movies which they did not find in the Indian movies. Islamists were quick to point out that the western influences were eroding the core values of the Islamic way of life. Parents and teachers were imparting more religious education to their children to keep them away from the 'evil influence' of the West. It was almost mandatory for the children to have religious education from the Moulvi. Children who excelled in the recitation of Quranic verses received awards. Fundamentalism was taking its hold in the Valley but it was overlaid with political connotations as the religious education and the money that came from the oil rich Arab world were also preparing the ground for a political set-up that favoured the Islamic way of life. *Nizam-e-Mustafa* was the catch-word; it signified that the ideal way of governance would be through Islamic rules.

This process was gradually capturing the imagination of the people. The political leadership of the Valley was aware of it. India was helping their cause by showing itself in an anti-Muslim and anti-Kashmiri light.

Islamic Fundamentalism Enters Politics

It was at this point that the various Muslim groups saw a chance for themselves to unite. They joined to form the Muslim United Front. It first appeared on the scene in 1986 and soon became the voice of the Islamic fundamentalists. The leading lights were Syed Ali Shah Geelani of Jamait-i-Islạmi, Prof. Abdul Ghani Bhat, a college professor of Persian at Sopore, a north Kashmir town, once known for its rich apple crops, and now for being the epicentre of Islamic fundamentalism. Bhat was dismissed from service by Jagmohan. Others included Moulvi Abbas Ansari, a Shia cleric and Qazi Nissar Ahmad. The mission of the MUF as pronounced by its leaders was to set up *Nizam-e-Mustafa* in Kashmir—this was an indirect way of saying that they did not accept Indian rule over Kashmir and also appealing to the religious sentiments of the Kashmiri Muslims. It was a grand design to have a separate rule in Jammu and Kashmir without having to wage war. If the MUF could win a majority, this would be a negation of the Indian claim on Kashmir.

The MUF had also gained ground because, with the establishment of the Rajiv-Farooq accord of November 1986, there was no longer a legitimate channel, in Kashmir, through which the voice of opposition or dissent might be channelled or make itself heard. People were disorientated. The National Conference was not only guilty of having struck an agreement with Congress but had also failed in its responsibility to fulfil the role of the opposition after July 1984 with the dismissal of its government. It had cocooned itself and the field was left open for the fundamentalists to take over.

Farooq Abdullah was oblivious to the damage that he had wreaked upon the Kashmir political scene. His inertia in Kashmir had served to consolidate the Islamic fundamentalist forces which were sweeping aside the secular forces and also doing away with the Sufi cult of the Valley. This failure was all the more disturbing because the consolidation of the fundamentalist forces also gave momentum to the secessionist voices. Where he should have stood up and demanded silence, he looked the other way. 'I promise you that I will close all Jamat-run schools, once I return to power,' he thundered. But it slipped from his mind once he was back in power.

When, in November 1986, he again took over as Chief Minister, he was too overwhelmed by the taste of power to take heed of the signs on the ground. He thought that he had overcome the political threats of Mufti Mohammad Sayeed through Congress' power-sharing scheme. His political calculations were wide off the mark. He realized this only when it came to facing the elections of 1987. Mufti, who had been sidelined by Rajiv Gandhi could not bear the humiliation. He supported the MUF clandestinely and even when he came to campaign for the NC-Congress alliance candidates, he would give enough indications by taking up a pen from his pocket and hold it to his chin- symbolic of the beard to indicate that he favoured the candidates of MUF whose symbol was the pen and ink pot. Later, he chose the same symbol for his party—the People's Democratic Party in the 2002 elections. The MUF rallies would attract huge crowds. The star speaker was often Qazi Nissar. His speeches in Kashmiri calling for Islamic revolution used to enthuse his audience no end.

Surprisingly, there was no mention of Pakistan in any of the speeches of the MUF leaders. But, Abdul Ghani Bhat, former chairman of the grievously fractured, and now divided, combination of secessionist groups All Parties Hurriyat Conference (APHC), did violate the code. 'I love Pakistan,' he said and stunned the audience of over 30,000 people in Iqbal Park in February 1987 before they erupted into wild cheers. He raised his finger and then continued, 'but that doesn't mean I hate India.' He had cleverly drawn a distinction between love and just not hating others. The inference was more than clear. The whole idea seemed to work for Pakistan's agenda in India-ruled Kashmir.

The words were very well chosen. The MUF was willing to taste power. That it was a do or die battle was dramatized by the MUF leaders. They wore white shrouds while presenting themselves before the people at the dais. 'We are willing to sacrifice our lives for the cause of the people in Kashmir,' Syed Ali Shah Geelani proclaimed and journalists from the national media were scribbling fast. The rally had shown that Kashmir would never be the same again.

Another equally strong voice rose from Maisuma, a congested locality in Srinagar—notorious for what the people in Kashmir call *kane jung* (battles of stone-throwing). Youngsters in the locality were perfect in the art of stone-throwing. They manipulated stones as if they were missiles and aimed them in the way pace and spin bowlers do making it difficult for the opposition to judge the direction from which they were coming. Invariably it was the police who were targeted. It was here that the JKLF Jammu Kashmir Liberation Front leader Mohammad

Yasin Malik was born and brought up. He was not a good stone thrower but a great motivator. His powerful speeches inspired the young people to wage war against the Indian rule in Kashmir. Later on he earned a place for himself, in the folk lore of the people when the secessionist movement culminated under the HAJY—Hamid, Ashfaq, Javed and Yasin group. Yasin can jump from a four-storey building and can shoot for miles and even hundreds of soldiers running in pursuit of him are unable to arrest him. This myth was woven around him and his associates, who were the first to bring guns to Kashmir. Yasin Malik, is a thin, frail man who has a heart problem complicated by a kidney condition. Yasin and his associates were sent to Pakistan by Abdul Ghani Lone, the assassinated leader of the People's Conference. Lone himself was a great motivator. Lone had his own reasons for fuelling Kashmir anger against India. He was cheated in the 1987 polls in Handwara. Lone was defeated with a small margin in Handwara, a small township in Kupwara close to LoC where he was regarded as invincible. Lone was prevented from visiting the counting centre. He was not allowed under orders of the government. But a Kashmiri Pandit deputy superintendent of police allowed him to do so, at the risk of his job. Even before Lone could reach the counting centre in Kupwara, the district headquarters where the counting was on, he was told that he had lost and no details for his loss were available. No arguments, he was told and a strong posse of police removed him from the scene.

But he was not part of the MUF because he could not reconcile himself to the agenda of the '*mullahs*' or clerics. Lone was a politician to the core.

If one had seen the MUF rallies in 1987, the obvious conclusion one would have drawn was that the MUF was winning. Farooq informed Rajiv of his fears that the MUF was gaining ground, whereas the National Conference- Congress alliance were on a sticky wicket as a result of the religious onslaught on the political themes of the two parties in power. Farooq Abdullah sought to project the development of the state to counteract the religious influence. But the people were wary of these obsolete slogans. Farooq stood discredited. Rajiv Gandhi gave Farooq Abdullah the go ahead to deal with the situation in the Valley in whatever manner he chose and wherever he felt that there was a threat to the candidates of the Alliance.

Yasin saw how the Indians and pro-Indian politicians in Kashmir had bungled the polling process in the 1987 elections and it deepened his hatred towards India.

The Amira Kadal constituency in Srinagar from where Mohammad Yusuf had been contesting was certain of his victory. He had mass support especially from the youth. But he was still losing to Ghulam Mohi-ud-Din Shah, a minister in the Sheikh Abdullah and Farooq Abdullah governments. I had seen him campaigning with his Karakulli and speaking into the megaphone seeking votes in the name of *'Nizam-e-Mustafa'* the number of those who attended his rallies and processions was countless. Hundreds of supporters walked behind the huge banners and green flags emblazoned with the pen and the inkpot, pledging their support to the MUF nominee. Voters defied all odds and voted for him.

But when the counting started, the message from above did the trick. Mohammad Yusuf and his supporters sensed this and demanded that counting be held in a transparent manner. But the police had its own way. It arrested the supporters. Hamid Sheikh, who later became the JKLF leader, was picked up and locked in Kothibagh, a police station at Residency Road in Srinagar where Ghulam Mohi-ud-Din Shah himself beat him with his belt and demanded to know whether he would ever try to defy him. Yasin had heard of everything that was happening and when Mohammad Yusuf protested he also found himself behind bars. So it was then that rebels were born. Mohammad Yusuf too was defeated in the polls, marking a turning point in his life.

Zafar Meraj, a senior journalist of Kashmir who profiled him as the 'Most wanted profiles of terror,' recounts Mohammad Yusuf's journey to the new name of Syed Salahauddin.

'After nine months, following a High Court verdict that proclaimed their (Mohammad Yusuf and his supporters) detention illegal, the government freed Salahauddin and other leaders. Upon his release, Salahauddin resumed his office as chief of Jamait-I-Islami in Srinagar district. He also started the new practice of propagating *jihad* in his addresses to congregations at Jamia Masjid (Mosque) in the city's central market. The official authorities found this unbearable. So in early 1989, he was again arrested and sent to jail. But he was no longer helpless. Outside the jail, his companions, disciples and devotees had started a *jihad* for freedom. He was still in jail when the Hizb-ul-Mujahadeen was established.

Farooq had won the polls in alliance with Congress. His party, the National Conference could have won without its support as well. But the alliance had been forced on him by the Congress leadership under Rajiv Gandhi in the spirit of the November 7, 1986 Rajiv-Farooq accord which restored government to Farooq.

The MUF lost the elections. Large-scale rigging was alleged. The National Conference maintained that the results were fair. Farooq argued that if the elections had been rigged, his Law Minister Abdul Ahad Vakil[2] would not have lost. Vakil had lost to Syed Ali Shah Geelani in the northern Kashmir constituency of Sopore, one of the strongholds of the Jamait-i-Islami.

But the MUF had achieved its objectives. It had once again shown that Indian democracy was a farce and that the genuine winners were shown up as losers in the elections. This was a clear message to the youth that India was taking Kashmir for granted and a cue for the youth to rise up in revolt. And they did. When Pakistan started the proxy war—the first casualties were the MUF members of the Assembly who then resigned. Political combat was replaced by guns—these had travelled from Kabul to Kashmir via Islamabad.

The modern history of Kashmir would have been scripted differently if Farooq had not aligned himself with Congress in the first place and also not allowed his overwhelming desire to prove his democratic credentials and teach the 'defectors a lesson' to prevail over him. The Valley had to pay a heavy price for satisfying his love for power and to prove that he deserved that power because they the people had willed it.

Terror Centre

It was the afternoon of March 10, 1988; the overcast sky cast a gloomy spell over everything. The drizzle was fast turning into a torrential downpour. It was in Jammu—the city founded by Dogra kings, where legend has it that Jambulochan—the founder of the city had been struck by the sight of a lion and a goat drinking water from the same river. This symbol of harmony had prompted him to set up a kingdom there. Jammu was later to become the seat of government of the Dogra kings, who ruled the state for nearly a century before the last Dogra king the Maharaja Hari Singh relinquished it to Indian sovereignty.

Chief Minister Farooq Abdullah allowed himself to be drenched as he walked from his chamber in the State Legislative Assembly to his room in the imposing building of the Civil Secretariat.

He appeared to be lost in thought. Syed Ali Shah Geelani, had refused to answer the question that he had pointedly asked him: 'Do you condemn terrorism?' Farooq Abdullah had repeatedly asked the MUF member, who was later idolized as *Rehbar-e-Inquilab* (leader of the revolution). Geelani had remained impassive.

As Farooq Abdullah worriedly took his seat, I was escorted into his office chambers by Sati Sahni, the Director General of Information. I saw how anxious Farooq was. He indicated that I should commence the interview. I was representing *Amrit Bazar Patrika,* a reputed Eastern India daily published in Calcutta. His replies were crisp and brief.

Farooq replies in this fashion, whenever he is tense. I had known him since 1975 and did not need anyone to tell me that he was not feeling in good spirits. Farooq is a miser. He rarely offers reporters or interviewers a cup of tea. I was trying to get something extra out of him that could enrich my article. But nothing came of it. Sati Sahni was casting glances at the wall clock time and again. It was a broad hint for me to end the interview. A few questions here and there. On being reminded that he had promised in the widely talked about March 1987 elections that he would close the Jamait-i-Islami run schools, a sort of helplessness showed up. 'What can I do, those schools are better run than government schools. Their results are far better.'

What will be the outcome of this helplessness, I asked myself. Farooq suddenly erupted. 'You know what is going to happen,' he mused and then what he told me was startling. 'Once Pakistan is free of this Afghan business, Kashmir is going to have the guns and militants coming to Jammu and Kashmir. I know it for certain.' I was shocked.

The militancy in the neighbouring state of Punjab, where Sikhs wanted to set up *Khalistan*—or the land of the pure—had been in the headlines of the local newspapers in Jammu too. Everyone knew the dread of the people of Punjab. I could imagine the horror Farooq was talking about. For once, I felt that Farooq was serious.

'Pakistan will divert the guns to Kashmir We are in for a bad time. Terrorism is knocking at doors. We have got to be cautious.'

The reporter within me told me that the lead was there. My heart was thumping. No one had ever heard Farooq saying this. Sati sat quietly. He could not gather the courage to interrupt his boss. But then came a word of caution. 'Arun, for God's sake don't publish this,' the Chief Minister said with added seriousness. All my hopes of getting the interview to the front page collapsed like a deflated balloon. I tried to protest.

'It is in the national interest,' he said to which I had no answer.

The interview was published without these details. But whenever I am reminded of that rainy day I remember Farooq Abdullah, in his immaculately ironed sherwani, with the Karakuli cap, the seriousness of the expression on his face and his sombre thoughts; at the same time I recall his father Sheikh Mohammad Abdullah who, at the inauguration of a bridge across river Tawi in 1982 had predicted that 'Kashmir would be a battlefield of the Indo-Pak war games.' Those were prophetic words.

The war had indeed travelled from Kabul to Kashmir. It was terrorism that has once again connected the historic cities in the region. One has been hit by America and another is waiting for redemption from terrorism. Both Kabul and Kashmir are victims of the same set of problems and the source of the problem is the same: Pakistan.

Is Pakistan really the problem? Or is the problem in Kashmir purely because of Pakistan. The subject has often been debated in endless discussions. But there has never been a unanimous answer. India, a nation of one billion people remains as confused today as on that day when Jawaharlal Nehru decided to move the United Nations to ask for a cease-fire. What is called Pakistan-occupied Kashmir by India and what Pakistan fondly terms *'Azad Kashmir'* (Free Kashmir), remains an eye-sore for India. For Pakistan which casts eyes of greed and lust upon this part of Jammu and Kashmir, it is part of the 'unfinished agenda' of the partition of the subcontinent in 1947.

And forty years later, the 1987 polls have only helped to confirm this theory.

Endnotes

1. P. L. Handoo was a Kashmiri Pandit, who became a trusted aide of Farooq Abdullah. He was a minister in the Farooq Abdullah government from 1987 to 1989 and from 1996 to 2000. He died in 2000.

2. Abdul Ahad Vakil was a close associate of Sheikh Abdullah. He hails from Sopore, the north Kashmir town, also the home-town of Syed Ali Shah Geelani. He was Law Minister in Farooq Abdullah's government from 1986 to 1987 and was defeated in the March 1987 elections by Geelani. He was elected in the 1996 elections and became Revenue Minister and later Speaker of the Jammu and Kashmir Legislative Assembly. He lost in the 2002 Assembly elections.

8

The Long Shadow of Militancy

A shadowy blanket was cast over everything. The Valley was enveloped in darkness except for a few celebration lights flickering in government buildings. These lights were a reminder that there were officials who were keen to demonstrate Indian presence in Kashmir on this night of August 15, which marks India's independence day. During the day, the Valley had observed a complete general strike on the call of the JKLF. Its word was final. No one would dare to defy the group that was gradually emerging as the symbol of the compulsion for independence of the people of Kashmir.

Mohammad Yusuf Halwai was the exception. He blatantly defied the call of the JKLF to observe a complete blackout on India's independence day. He kept the lights on at his house—deliberately signalling himself out as a defiant soul to the militants, perhaps unmindful of the dangers that awaited him. The local youth of the JKLF shouted in the direction of his house, demanding that the lights be put out. He shouted back in chaste Kashmiri and dared them to action. He was a leader of the National Conference, the ruling party.

The shadow of terror cast its long shadow over the whole Valley. The JKLF had started bombing targeted Central Government buildings. The first of such explosions had been heard at the Central Telegraph Office facing Partap Park on Maulana Azad Road and the Srinagar Club in July 1988.

They heralded the arrival of bombs, detonations, explosions and terror.

The campaign generated waves of fear. Gunfire was aimed at tourist buses and the killings of VIPs were being planned.

Ghulam Geelani Pandit,[1] Director General of Police was a boastful but worried man. He believed that he had thwarted the plans of the terrorists to fire rockets at the Bakshi stadium in Srinagar during the course of the Independence Day parade. 'There were plans of massive explosions and killing of a number of people,' he said as he underlined how dangerous the situation was and how the government and particularly the state police had averted all these disasters. But Pandit himself was responsible for having allowed the situation to have come to such a pass.

He had ignored a series of intelligence agencies messages that infiltration was takıng place and that the men were coming with arms.These reports had been presented to him daily. Instead of taking cognizance of these alarming reports, he would dismiss those as 'flights of imagination of the intelligence gatherers.' At one such meeting, he had scolded a non-Muslim officer for spreading canards about the Muslim youths of the Valley. Anyone suggesting this was dubbed as an Intelligence Bureau (IB) agent. The IB in Kashmir was viewed as the CIA of India, perpetually engaged in weaving conspiracies to cause problems in the Valley.

Farooq Abdullah was alternatively alarmed and casual about these reports. Things began to go seriously wrong. From time to time, Governor Jagmohan would send notes to the government about the worst case scenario emerging within the state. But Prime Minister Rajiv Gandhi also failed to recognize the seriousness of the situation. The militants were emboldened.

The Valley was in the throes of a psychosis of fear. It was at this point that the government decided to do something; they started arresting militants and their supporters. The people, as yet were not fully prepared to back the militancy as a movement, though their sympathies were with them. At one point of time, the top brass of the JKLF had decided to surrender. The People's Conference leader Abdul Ghani Lone[2] who had played a pivotal role in motivating these youths to go across the border and train themselves in handling arms and ammunition to launch an aggressive and violent movement, dissuaded them from nurturing any thoughts of surrender. He warned them that it would be suicidal and also played on the fears of Pakistan and the ISI not sparing them and their families if they happened to give up arms at the initial stage of the movement. He was able to prevail upon them. He did not know that this persuasion would be his undoing a decade later. He had not imagined that the situation could go out of control in this fashion. For the moment he was convinced that by pressuring the youth to launch a violent struggle, he would be able to create the conditions for fresh elections and then win the polls. His eyes were fixed on power. Lone had been uncomfortable ever since he was out of power after his exit from Congress. He had joined the National Conference only to leave it again to form his own party the People's Conference on the platform of regaining autonomy for the state. He had made his intentions clear when he became the first leader in the Valley to call for shutdown on February 11, 1984, the day the founder of JKLF Mohammad Maqbool Butt was hanged to death. Butt was convicted of having killed a CID officer.

Maqbool Butt hailed from a sleepy hamlet Tregham in Kupwara in north Kashmir, close to the Line of Control (LoC). He was a born motivator. He had been influenced by the anti-India sentiment in the Valley since his childhood. He had planned many things and set up the Jammu and Kashmir National Liberation Front (JKNLF). Faced with the prospect of being charged with the killing of a CID official, he crossed over to Pakistan. He was also instrumental in planning the hijacking of Fokker Friendship in March 1971. The event escalated Indo-

Pak tensions and finally led to the war between the two countries in December that year.

What Bhat had done was to sow seeds of the concept of an independent Kashmir. It was to flower again during the late 1980s, after the 1987 elections. The new crop included Yasin Malik, Ashfaq Wani, Javed Mir and Sheikh Hamid, who came to be known as the HAJY group of the JKLF. Ashfaq was the think tank of the JKLF. He was infuriated by reports from his boys that Mohamad Yusuf Halwai had called the JKLF names labelling them as 'stooges of Pakistan.' Halwai's execution was ordered and on the afternoon of August 20, 1989 he was killed. This was the first political assassination in the Valley. The murder shook the whole Valley. Could this have happened in the Valley where even normal murders were unheard of? Questions appeared on the fear-stricken faces of Kashmiris. The Valley, an abode of peace, was beginning its downward tryst with blood and this was unacceptable. Even the bitterest critics of the National Conference and its rule in Kashmir and even those who loathed Indian suzerainty over Kashmir condemned the murder. The streets were alive with whispers and loud noises denouncing the murder. Did he deserve to be killed simply because he had not observed the blackout? Terrorists had snuffed out his life for his audacity to keep the lights on in his house. This was to happen to many more in the days to come.

His body lay in the pool of blood in Khankah Mohalla surrounded by wailing members of his family. Chief Minister Farooq Abdullah received this message while he was in the Legislative Assembly. He swore revenge, which he never took.

I was sitting in the press gallery when I heard an emotional Farooq shout: 'These are Pakistani terrorists who have killed Mohammad Yusuf Halwai. I swear by the blood of Yusuf Halwai that I would see to it that his killers don't go unpunished.' He also asked the Government of India to 'wake up to the bitter realities. Pakistan is bleeding us and you are extending your hand of friendship towards Islamabad. But please don't foster this friendship on our bodies,' he said while trying to fight back his tears. Farooq called for the bombing of terrorist camps across the border to root out terrorism from Jammu and Kashmir. 'The problem is there—across the border smash it or otherwise we would have to live with this terrorism for several generations. That is the only revenge that can be taken to end the bloodshed in this state,' Farooq spoke the truth. But his words lacked conviction..

Tensions began to build up and the MUF legislators had resigned from the Assembly under threat from the militants. The only exception was Abdul Razaq Mir of Kulgam. He did not oblige the militants and later paid with his life. He was also killed in the same fashion as were the leaders of the National Conference. Three other MUF leaders who had been to the Assembly and obeyed the militants were spared. They were Syed Ali Shah Geelani, Ghulam Nabi Sumji and Mohammad Sayeed Shah, brother of Shabir Shah.

Shabir Shah, himself a prominent separatist leader, spent more than 20 years in prison sloganeering for independence for Kashmir. His supporters even called him the 'Nelson Mandela of Kashmir,' Amnesty International has classified him as a 'prisoner of conscience.'

A difficult situation was in the making. Very few people had any clue as to what was happening in the Kashmir Valley. The Farooq Abdullah Government vacillated between harsh treatment for the militants and on occasions, and a more lenient attitude towards them. It was soft on them.

It set free more than 70 militants, much to the annoyance of the police who had intercepted them and arrested them at great risks. The Centre too was not happy. Many of those who were set free, disappeared to emerge as high profile militant leaders. The police was losing faith in itself. The administration was at a complete loss, not knowing what to do and how to tackle the situation.

Militant Intimidation at the Polls

Wheels within wheels were in operation, impelling the militancy forward. The nexus between militants and politicians was tightening. Those who were aware of this were spreading word down the line and as a result the government authority was being undermined. The Chief Minister was the least bothered about the situation, or so it appeared from his actions. He continued to keep his date with London. He lived under the illusion that Congress would continue to rule at the Centre and there would be no danger to his government. That was more than enough solace for a man who vacillated most of the time. But the 1989 parliamentary elections proved to be a great psychological boost for the militants. That kind of victory they were never again to repeat afterwards. Militants placed colour TV sets at the main crossings as a reward for those who would dare to vote. No one came forward to claim those rewards. That was a big success. Even though the National Conference and Congress combined had won all the parliamentary seats: P. L. Handoo from Anantnag, Abdul Rashid Kabuli from Srinagar and Saif-ud-Din Soz from Baramullah, P. Namgyal from Leh, Janak Raj Gupta from Jammu and Dharm Pal Sharma from Udhampur, the defeat by the people was written large on the faces of these parties, especially for the three seats in the Valley where the boycott was almost complete. The voter turn-out was less than 2 per cent. The moral high ground of Farooq Abdullah and his government that they had not rigged the March 1987 Assembly elections had been rudely shaken.

Backed by gun-power, the militants had brought out the popular resentment against the Government in Kashmir and, more so, against India. They demonstrated that they had no faith in the Indian democratic system as far as the Valley was concerned. Abdul Ghani Lone used to say that the Indian democracy never travelled beyond Lakhanpur (the gateway to Jammu and Kashmir) towards the north.

'It stops there.'

It was in these elections, that Farooq's worst political enemy Mufti Mohammad Sayeed had taken to national politics. Having deserted Congress he had joined V. P. Singh[3] and when he contested for election from Muzzaffar Nagar in Uttar Pradesh on the Jan Morcha ticket, he won. Then the Abdullahs were opened to the grim reality that Rajiv Gandhi and Congress had lost the government. It was the National Front government headed by V. P. Singh who was returned to power. Farooq tried to strike a chord with the new government but without much success. His first test came on December 8, 1989.

It was Friday afternoon when a young medico Rubiya Sayeed, the youngest daughter of India's first Muslim Home Minister Mufti Mohammad Sayeed, who was travelling in a mini bus (something unusual for the family members of the country's second most important man, after Prime Minister, to make the journey home in such a casual manner). But so it was. Rubiya with apron in her hands, smilingly boarded the mini-bus from her college without any clue, so it seemed, that her journey to her home would be cut and she would be redirected to some unknown place. She had been kidnapped by the young men who had stopped the vehicle and taken her into a waiting Maruti car.

Zafar Meraj, bureau chief of the *Kashmir Times* was sitting in his office when his phone rang and the voice at the other end told him that JKLF had abducted Rubiya. It was strange that Rubiya's abduction should have been conveyed to a journalist rather than to the police or some other agency. Moreover, Zafar was a print journalist who could not have aired the news as the BBC or Voice of America, might have done. The objective was clear: Zafar was a close family friend of Mufti Mohammad Sayeed and worked for the newspaper *Kashmir Times* run by Mufti's friend Ved Bhasin.

Zafar called Mufti in Delhi and informed him about the abduction. The demands were not immediately known. Mufti was shaken by the fact that his daughter should have been abducted by the youths towards whom he had always been soft. The Chief Minister was in London and Geelani Pandit had no clue what to do. He came to know about the abduction at least three hours after the incident. It was a complete failure on the part of the police and the intelligence agencies.

Immediately, the alarm was sounded in Delhi. Arun Nehru, who was Internal Security Minister in the Rajiv Gandhi government, had changed sides and become Power Minister in the V. P. Singh Government. He advised Mufti to send NSG[4] commandos to Kashmir to launch rescue operations to free Rubiya from her abductors. Mufti did not like the idea. But he had no other choice. He was keen on trying other channels.

I was serving on the *Kashmir Times* at that point of time. Ved Bhasin and Mohammad Sayeed Malik—both friends of Mufti heard the news while they and their families were preparing for the wedding party of their common friend Baldev

Kalra's son. It was Zafar who called Bhasin to his place at Wazarat Road in Jammu and broke the news to him. Bhasin turned to Sayeed Malik and recounted what Zafar had told him. His voice was fraught with anxiety. 'Who has done that?' It was Rukaiya's, Sayeed Malik's wife's turn to ask. Bhasin replied: 'The JKLF.'

'I don't think that our *mujahid* would ever kidnap a girl,' was Rukaiya's conclusion. For common Kashmiris the militants were the epitome of religious purity and had a clear sense of purpose.

Both Bhasin and Malik rushed to the office, to make a few phone calls here and there. One of them was made to Mufti Mohammad Sayeed; he was reassured that he should have nothing to worry about. 'I am sure Zafar will find a way out,' Malik said. The two friends and their families then left for the wedding party. Malik seethed with anger on his return. It was the very first time that the words 'JKLF terrorists' were used in the *Kashmir Times*. And in the story linked to Rubiya's kidnapping.

The next day the JKLF was again simply JKLF because the militant group's leadership had strongly objected to the terrorist label and as far as I can remember there was no mention of this word again in any of the *KT* reports until Rubiya was set free in exchange for five top militant leaders of the JKLF, one of whom was a Pakistani national, Sher Khan. The soft tone was meant to ensure that the hostage was not harmed.

Who was behind the abduction? There were no straight answers to the question. One theory was that Dr. Abdul Ahad Guru, a leading cardiologist at Sher-e-Kashmir Institute of Medical Sciences who was treating Sheikh Hamid, and himself a strong votary of Kashmir's independence, had stage- managed the whole show to get the JKLF men, including Hamid, released. He was part of the JKLF's think-tank and had been in the forefront for guiding the line of action of this group which had the unqualified support of a number of journalists, intellectuals and lawyers. The slogan of independence for Kashmir was a rallying cry for the Kashmiris who felt that they were lost in the desert of slavery under the Indian rule. For tactical reasons they were not critical of Pakistan despite Islamabad's controlling one-third of the territory of Jammu and Kashmir, for the JKLF needed the support of Pakistan to launch what it called its 'war against Indian occupation of Jammu and Kashmir.'

On December 8, 1989 after the copy was written and sent for print, Ved Bhasin called me to his chamber and asked me to get Abdul Ghani Lone from his home. Lone did not have a phone at his Jammu residence in those days. It was walking distance. I wondered what Lone could possibly do, on my way to Bawe wali Ghali where his house was located. What could these two friends want from him at that odd hour? It was already 11.30 at night and in half an hour's time it would be midnight, I thought as I hurried towards Lone's residence. Lone himself came out in response to my persistent knocking.

'Joshi, you here at this hour?' he wondered when he saw me giving him a look of recognition. I told him that Vedji and Malik sahib wanted him to be in office.

'At this hour, what is the urgency?' he enquired.

'You know Mufti Sayeed's daughter has been kidnapped,' I told him hinting at what he could expect in the discussions that Malik and Bhasin were waiting to have with him.

'What can I do?' he half-asked himself.

He followed me in silence to the *KT* office. The trio sat for over two hours, making a number of phone calls. At least half a dozen were meant for Mufti Sayeed and a few to Zafar Meraj. Lone spoke at length to Mufti and assured him that 'no harm would come to Rubiya.' I guessed that these words were far more reassuring to Mufti, the country's Home Minister than reliance on the National Security Guards or even the Prime Minister V.P. Singh.

Lone's relations with the JKLF were unknown to me until then. The stories unfolded and Zafar became mediator.

Farooq Abdullah was summoned from London. But he put his foot down on the freeing of any militant in exchange for Mufti's daughter. He believed, like all Kashmiris did, that the JKLF would have to set the girl free, under pressure from public opinion. The public was aghast. There were no demonstrations because that would have amounted to sympathy for India's Home Minister after the people had effectively boycotted the November 1989 parliamentary elections. V. P. Singh sensing trouble phoned Farooq and asked him to release the five militants that the JKLF was asking for. 'You come yourself and release them, I am not going to do it. That would be a great setback to our fight against terrorism,' Farooq was blunt. He had the full support of Governor Gen. K. V. Krishna Rao[5] in this matter. Moreover, he knew that his stand was politically right and morally correct. But the V. P. Singh Government would have nothing of it. Inder Kumar Gujral and Mohammad Arif Khan, the country's Foreign Minister and Coal Minister respectively flew to Srinagar and asked Farooq to release all the five militants under threat of dismissal of his government.

Mufti Mohammad Syed and his family saw Farooq's opposition to the release of the militants in exchange for Rubiya as 'a political opponent's attempts to settle scores.' Mufti not only believed it personally, but also told the Prime Minister that the state government saw in the kidnapping of his daughter a political opening to settle scores with him. Justice Moti Lal Bhat, a friend of Mufti Mohammad Syed's was sent to Srinagar to establish contact with the JKLF militants. Bhat engaged the services of a couple of local journalists to establish rapport with the JKLF leaders. Rubiya's release in exchange for the jailbirds demanded by the JKLF was agreed upon and thus the release of the Indian Home Minister's daughter was secured. The cost paid in terms of Indian authority in Kashmir and the subsequent upsurge in public support for the JKLF was phenomenal. From the point that Rubiya reached home that winter and the moment the jailed militants reached downtown Srinagar after release from jail, there would be no turning back. The morale of the abductors and their supporters was high. So also was the public belief that India could be forced to negotiate unpleasant and disagreeable settlements provided the screws were sufficiently tightened.

The JKLF began calling all the shots after this event. Their support on the ground and among the local officials working for the state government grew to an unbelievable level. Doctors, engineers, bureaucrats and police officers used influence and connections to come close to the JKLF. Its militants became the darlings of the locals whose support conferred a new-found social status for these people.

Believing seriously that Indian authority over the state was fast loosening its grip and that the future governance in the state would naturally be in the hands of the JKLF even highly placed businessmen vied with each other for proximity to the new heroes. Talking in terms of the insurgents' capacity to wage military battles one can say with hindsight that the JKLF firepower was more cosmetic than real. Emboldened by the Rubiya experience the JKLF started targeting social and political opposition ruthlessly.

Farooq Abandoned

His anger was uncontrollable. He could not stand the sight of a reporter at the most crucial juncture of his life. I did not know that within the next few hours he would be submitting his resignation. Mufti had played his game and he had got Jagmohan re-appointed as Governor of Jammu and Kashmir. The bitterness between Jagmohan and Farooq's relationship was an open secret. That was a way of easing out Farooq, who had refused to kowtow to the Delhi government. Threadbare discussions followed between Farooq and Rajiv. Indira's son was sulking after his defeat in the elections at the hands of the party that was headed by his one time cabinet colleague Vishwanath Pratap Singh. The Rajiv-Farooq discussions were held at 7 Race Course, the house that Rajiv had still retained. The talks were veering around the next course of action. Rajiv was a political novice. For him what counted most at that point was urging his friend and Congress ally Farooq to resign; it seemed to him to be the best option. That would put matters in a spot as the elections were not possible; neither was any attempt at installing any other government So the V.P. Singh Government would suffer loss of face internationally. This was typical of the political subterfuges that the rival Indian politicians would play against each other.

For Rajiv the real target was not Jagmohan, whom Farooq disliked, but V.P. Singh and for V.P. Singh, the whole thing was targeted at Rajiv with Farooq being used as a pawn. Such chess games are not uncommon in Indian politics. Later, Singh was to play the same game with his own allies Tau, the grand old man of Haryana politics—Devi Lal, who had rallied behind him and was Deputy Prime Minister in the Jan Morcha Government. V. P. Singh had uncorked the genie of the Mandal Commission which wanted to reserve more seats in schools and colleges as well as jobs for the low castes and the high caste students were out on streets—burning themselves at the main crossings. The nation was inflamed and the high caste party—the Bhartiya Janta Party that had come to epitomize the upper class invoked the issue of the construction of the Lord Rama temple in Ayodhya, presumably the Lord's birthplace which the BJP sponsored. Hindu saints have identified the site where the Mughal Emperor Babur had constructed a mosque by dismantling a temple. Hindu sentiments were inflamed. That led to the clash of egos and then the BJP withdrew their support after having precipitated and brought the country to the brink of war. The disaster had taken place. And one such political game was being played by Rajiv and V.P. Rajiv was trying to kill two birds with one stone. By making Farooq resign, he was making the V.P. Government suffer internationally and at the same time convincing Farooq that he would be able to save himself from the pressures of Delhi.

Jagmohan also could not see the game. He came to know it later when Mufti Mohammad Sayeed dubbed him 'communal' and 'anti-Muslim' and leaked a story to *The Times of India* that he was being recalled. Jagmohan was angry over this betrayal. He had no idea why it was happening to him. He has recorded these moments of extreme anxieties in his book, *My Frozen Turbulence*, a title that many mock as being a reflection of his rigid mindset.

Farooq landed in a special AICC aircraft in Jammu on the night of January 18, 1990. He saw me and became extremely furious. Two officers—the Divisional Commissioner Vijay Bakaya and DIG Gopal Sharma were nervous. What if Farooq were to turn to them and demand to know how a scribe and a photographer Raju Kerni had found their way to the airport at such an odd hour? Farooq could be extremely touchy at times. He told me that he suspected there was a mole in his cabinet. I mentioned that I had heard he was about to resign. He was outraged; I insisted, however, and he confirmed that he was going to resign as he was being driven away: Farooq's retort 'Do you want the state to burn?' in reply to my query about his imminent resignation sounded boisterous to me. His capacity for governance is more often expressed in negative terms. How could his resignation possibly unleash the fiery forces that would set the state afire? I thought Farooq had too high an opinion of himself. He didn't have the guts to quit. He loves power, so I thought, and he was making himself appear indispensable.

But in that I was wrong. I was to find out within the next few hours. Farooq had convened a meeting of his cabinet. Most of the ministers were present. They had been preparing to hear the worst. Though Farooq's brother and Works Minister Sheikh Mustafa Kamal had said that Mufti's becoming the country's Home Minister was a rare honour to Kashmir, yet matters were not smooth. This was becoming quite obvious. Farooq, as I was told by Mohammad Sayeed Malik, had tried to mend fences with Mufti to smooth things out for Kashmir.

It was 10 at night. We were drinking when a call arrived from Farooq that he was coming to see Mufti. Mufti was perplexed. This is not the time for him to come, he had murmured but Farooq was insistent. Mufti Sahib suggested that he come in the morning and have breakfast, but finally gave in at the insistence of the Chief Minister. We were just finishing our drinks as Farooq walked in.

Farooq tried to explain to Mufti that the volatile situation was wiping out the essence of Kashmiri life and peace in the Valley. But Mufti understood otherwise. He thought that Farooq had come to see him in order to save his seat. His aides like Malik and Ved had only confirmed his thinking. Mufti was guided more by his friends rather than by the political correctness of things. When Farooq left, Mufti remarked derisively, 'He had come to canvass for the safety of his chair.' He was to find out within the next two weeks how terribly wrong he had been.

'After having made all calculations, it has been decided that we should quit,' Farooq announced to his cabinet colleagues, some of whom were trembling at the prospect. But they could not gather the courage to challenge their leader's decision. It is also no secret that some of them were, at best sympathetic, to the separatists and, at worst, were mixed up with them. There were authentic reports from the intelligence agencies that the vehicles of high functionaries were being used by the terrorists for ferrying arms. The Cabinet meeting did not last for more than 15 minutes. After that it was the turn of these people to prepare a resignation letter and alert Raj Bhavan that Farooq was going to meet the Governor. The stage was set for Farooq's departure. There was a striking similarity and two differences between this, the 1984, and the 1987 episodes. Farooq was once again the victim of political intrigues connived in Delhi; and in this instance too, Mufti was the key player on Delhi's side.

However, it was now winter in Jammu and this time the situation was not brought about by any defections. Rather, it was Farooq himself who had chosen to leave. Gen. Rao had developed a sense of extreme gratitude for the Chief Minister, who had resigned to protest against the removal of General Rao. Three years later, on March 12, 1993, Gen. Rao was again brought back to the state as Governor; it is the day which India remembers better as the day when serial blasts in Bombay devastated the city and placed the names of Dawood Ibrahim and Chotta Shakeel on the list of terrorists operating at the behest of Pakistan.

Endnotes

1. Ghulam Geelani Pandit retired as Director General of Police. It was during his days as Police Chief that the militancy grew in Kashmir.

2. Abdul Ghani Lone, founder of People's Conference, a regional political group having influence in north Kashmir. He was assassinated by suspected militants on May 21, 2002 at the memorial rally of Moulvi Mirwaiz Farooq at Idgah in Srinagar. He was suspected of hobnobbing with the Government of India for separatists' participation in the elections of 2002.'

3. NSG, National Security Guards, who are specially trained for major rescue operations particularly during hijacking of planes and abductions.

4. Gen. K. V. Krishna Rao has retired as chief of the Indian army. He was first appointed as Governor of Jammu and Kashmir in July 1989 succeeding Jagmohan on the latter's completion of his five-year term. He was removed from the post in January 1990 and Jagmohan was appointed Governor for a second time. Farooq Abdullah had protested against Jagmohan's re-appointment and resigned. Gen. Rao was again appointed Governor on March 12, 1993. He stayed on till May 1998.

9

The Flight of the Kashmiri Hindus: Collapse of the Kashmiriyat

The summer of 1989 was a portent of the times ahead. Blasts were becoming routine. Bullets were aimed at bars, cinemas, theatres and beauty parlours. These were patent signs that the religious fundamentalists were forcing their agenda on Kashmiris who had adopted the ways of the modern world and whose changing lifestyles were drawing them closer to the Global Village with all its alluring by-products. The fundamentalists, however, were bent on reversing this trend for their own ends. Putting back the clock meant, on the face of it, forcing the veil on women and beards on men and dispensing with worship at the Sufi shrines. All this was synonymous with a greater plan. The exploitation of patent religious symbols was only part of a wider stratagem in the expansion of their political agenda. Pakistan was behind it all; seeking to demolish the secular character that India had endeavoured to maintain in the Valley.

While it is true that Kashmiri Hindus were Indians, Kashmiri Muslims were different, at that point in time, from their co-religionists living in fundamentalist societies elsewhere in the world. They were born and brought up in the land of Lal Ded[1] and Nund Rishi,[2] where Hindus and Muslims were what sugar is to milk. This *douceur* in their relations was not approved of by the forces of fundamentalism. Kashmir Valley was to be purged of these errant 'infidels' who were, doubly guilty on account of being Indians. Targeting the Kashmiri Pandit community served several ends at the same time. The community was considered the last bastion of India in the predominantly Kashmiri Muslim Valley.

The Pandit Community: Death and Humiliation

This was a community which had the potential to turn the situation around. It could have shown the population the disastrous consequences that would befall them if they continued in the self-destructive path of secessionist violence. Kashmiri Pandits could have pointed out how it was not only ripping apart the existing fabric of Kashmiri society but also spawning a generation of youths who were more akin to the 'warriors' of Afghanistan than the coveted fruits of civilized society: engineers, doctors and scientists. They had the potential to turn people's interest towards India once again. So they had to be exterminated.

For the first time, perhaps, the Kashmiri Pandits who formed a miniscule minority of the population in the Valley were living in a mode of misplaced self-confidence. They were Kashmiris first. This fact had been overlooked by those who saw them as Indian agents. Pakistan stoked hatred towards India by perpetually reminding Kashmiri Muslims that they were slaves in Hindu India and persuaded them that their rule was personified by the Kashmiri Pandits. That the latter far outnumbered other communities in the various Civil Service departments of the State was exploited by Paksitan to substantiate this anti-India thrust. It was further claimed that Judge Neel Kanth Ganjoo had convicted and sentenced the JKLF founder Maqbool Butt to death purely on religio-ethnic grounds, the judge being both a Hindu and Indian while Maqbool was a separatist Muslim. Next on the firing line would be Tikka Lal Taploo, a BJP leader who was shot dead in September; then came the turn of Prem Nath Bhat, a renowned lawyer from the southern Kashmir town of Anantnag. These murders were being executed to widen the divide between Hindus and Muslims. Hindus were dubbed as IB or RAW agents.

The motives were obvious. IB and RAW were seen as the most potent saboteurs of the cause of Kashmir and so they had to be dealt with in the same fashion. The media proclaimed that any Kashmiri Pandit youth—unemployed or serving in any department—was an agent of one or other of the two Indian intelligence agencies. The IB or RAW Agent tag was used to repress the sense of revulsion that these murders might evoke in the majority community, which despite its sympathies for freedom, was against violence and especially acts of violence committed against fellow Kashmiris, notwithstanding their being of a different religion with a different place of worship.

The result of all this was to force the Kashmiri Pandit community to take stock of its options and all the more so as the number of killings increased. It also instilled fear in the majority community. Kashmiri Muslims were simultaneously enthralled by the spectre of freedom and repulsed by the military prowess of the militants. Life had become a downward spiral of mayhem murder and humiliation. Hindu girls were accosted by *goondas* (goons) asking for *khushi dikha* (sexual favours). The Pandits were taunted as *dhale batta*, i.e. dal eaters who, by implication, could not match the masculine prowess of the mutton eaters. It was also a contemptuous way of telling them that they were cowards. Word went round that the community was full of traitors to the cause and had therefore to be wiped out or weeded out of the Valley. The whispers gradually became blatant clamours as the militants secured the support of the ruffians and other such elements to hold demonstrations and processions, filling the air with their strident cries *'Ase gasi Kasheer, Battav rous, Batnaiv saan'* (We will make Kashmir part of Pakistan by driving out Kashmiri Pandits but keeping their women here). Kashmiri Pandit girls silently put up with the molestation and other physical advances, knowing that their protests would be of no avail. Furthermore, if these were reported to their male relatives and friends, the resultant provocation and subsequent clashes would only spell the loss of more male members of their community rather than ridding themselves of their perpetrators. Threatening posters were pinned on the doors of the Kashmiri Pandit families; they taunted at markets and other public places with questions like: Are you still here? Doesn't the situation worry you? 'Pack up and go,' they were advised. Kashmiri Pandits knew that their overwhelming presence in the Central Government and the key positions they held in the Civil Service and other important sectors was anathema to many and those who found this galling now came forward to support the militants in the campaign to remove the Kashmiri Pandits or help in killing them. Fear and terror reigned in the community. Movement became restricted; young boys were forbidden from venturing out. Girls stopped going to schools and colleges. Government employees dreaded turning up for work. Shopkeepers would offer extra prayers for their safety.

The community gradually understood the deeper meaning of each murder. If the judge's murder was to avenge the death of the 'freedom fighter' Maqbool Butt, Tikka Lal Taploo's execution was a statement, written in blood, to say that Kashmir politics had no room for non-Muslims. Prem Nath Bhat was an intellectual and his influence in countering terrorism was the last thing fundamentalists wanted to see in the Valley while Lassa Kaul, Director Doordarshan had no business directing the Indian electronic media in Muslim Kashmir. Those who planned the executions of the Pandits followed a carefully executed plan. These were not the widescreen massacres of its members seen in the late 1990s and early 21st century. The targets were well and deliberately chosen to convey specific political and religious messages. The game was perfectly planned. The icons of the community would be decapitated before the ordinary members were put on the firing line. Realization dawned on the Pandit community when they found that they had lost even the right to protest.

Angry protesters had taken to the streets in Srinagar denouncing the militancy for the assassination of Tikka Lal Taploo. Among the frontline protestors was Ashok Khazanchi, a youth who had carved a niche for himself in the community for his social work. He was shot dead a few days later. Anyone who raised his voice against the militancy was dispatched. Many others like him were gunned down. Nor was the community allowed to mourn their dead for long. Public mourning was interpreted as defiance and carried the ultimate punishment: nothing short of death.

The re-run of the tribal invasion of 1947 was on the anvil. Fear was palpable in the elders of the community who had seen what had transpired at the time of the partition. Those horrors had come to re-visit them once again. They had not forgotten that Kashmiri Pandits had been the first targets of the invaders. Their homes had been looted, their women raped; they had no choice but to flee to other parts of India.

Something similar, though on a much wider scale was imminent. It had to be prevented. How? The question haunted the community. There were striking similarities in both situations with minor variations. Pakistan was once again out to 'Islamize' the Valley leaving non-Muslims bruised and humiliated or compelling them to move out of the Valley. It was part of a dangerous play scripted by Pakistan. Anti-India forces were on the rise and the sentiment of the majority community was clearly with them. The Jammu and Kashmir Liberation Front had lured Kashmiri Muslims with its slogan of *Azadi* or freedom. This had become a rallying point for the people who were keen on maintaining the distinctive identity, culture, ethos and traditions of the land. Taking advantage of India's failures, Pakistan backed this effort, seizing the opportunity which it had so painstakingly created for itself and for the secessionists. Later, however, when Pakistan realized that the JKLF slogans threatened to wipe out pro-Pakistan sentiment as well, it forced the creation of the Hizb-ul-Mujahadeen and started, itself, to neutralize JKLF cadres. Though there were severe ideological differences between the Hizb-ul-Mujahadeen and the JKLF at the political level, they were indistinguishable when it came to hounding down of Kashmiri Pandits. All talk of 'Kashmiriyat' was hollow on their part. They didn't believe in it. Hizb openly demanded the departure of the Pandits from the Valley, through advertisements placed in newspapers. *Al-Safa*,[3] one of the Urdu dailies published in Srinagar asked the Kashmiri Pandits to 'leave the Valley,' because they had been 'oppressors of Muslims.' This advertisement on April 14, 1990 was a clarion call to the community to pack up and leave their native homes for good.

Until then, Kashmiri Pandits had clung to the hope that they might stay on in the Valley. They were convinced that the protests were coming only from fringe elements and that things would subside and the situation return to normal. I remember my conversations with Kashmiri Pandit friends in those days. Kakji was a government employee. He was a resident of Bhanmohalla in Habba Kadal and had more Muslim friends than Hindu ones. He would always argue in favour of Muslims, sharing his cigarettes with them. Kakaji's house was in the heart of a Hindu district and he believed in the fairness of the Muslims more than that of his community. When the situation turned hostile against the community, he cautioned his family against making any move to leave the Valley. 'It is our home, our place, where will we go?' His family took his advice. Kakaji's proximity to journalists was regarded as his asset. The family believed that he had access to better information about the coming events.

There was firing in Bhanmohalla in March 1990. No one was hurt. The firing was meant to scare the community. Kakaji clung adamantly to the belief that it was not. I rang him up at his home to find out whether he was safe. 'Absolutely. Don't worry; these things are not going to continue for long,' he reassured me, in confident tones.

When posters appeared on the temple walls asking Kashmiri Pandits to pack up, he ignored them, taking them for the work of mischief makers. The posters would re-appear at regular intervals. Still he did not take any of it seriously. There were grenade explosions and then finally posters appeared in individual homes and one of them was that of Kakaji. He knew then that the time had come to say goodbye to the Valley. His Muslim friends offered him help in migrating but none dared to stop him from leaving. Some of his friends were themselves active in the militancy.

Lacking the force to resist, the tiny minority which moreover had no weapons with which to defend itself, was compelled to seek the protection of the government.

Kashmiri Pandits Abandoned on All Sides

Farooq Abdullah's government had already disappointed the community. Farooq was stuck with the image of a casual administrator. He never trusted the community nor did the community have faith in his government. He thought that he had served the community adequately by giving a ministerial berth to Kashmiri Pandit P. L. Handoo whom he later fielded as a candidate for the Lok Sabha seat from Anantnag in the elections which turned out to be a farce with less than 2 per cent participation. His other tool was H. N. Jattoo, a Kashmiri Pandit leader, who was close to him and whom he took to be the voice of the community, though, in fact, his influence in the community was minimal. They turned to him because of his proximity to the government in the same manner as they would visit Handoo. Though Handoo had been an influential minister in the Farooq Abdullah cabinet, yet he never stuck his neck out for the community or fought on their behalf over issues of vital concern to them. He was more comfortable with Kashmiri Muslims rather than with the members of his own community.

Handoo knew that he owed his position to Farooq Abdullah rather than the community, so as a pragmatic politician, he displayed his loyalty to the leader rather than to the community. Jattoo was no different. Farooq for his part, suspected the community of siding with Congress in the 1983 elections and this had deepened his distrust of them. The Pandits were opposed to Farooq as they had been, by tradition, against Sheikh Abdullah and his dynasty. The community is believed to have turned Nehru against Sheikh Abdullah and this had resulted in his deposition and arrest in 1953. Their protection came from the Congress leadership: first from Jawaharlal Nehru and then his daughter Indira Gandhi. Kashmiri Pandits had the ears of Nehru and Indira possibly because of their Kashmiri Pandit origin. Right up until the assassination of Indira Gandhi they had been directly entrusted with big assignments in the state by the kitchen cabinet of the Congress Prime Minister. The National Conference leaders had never trusted the Kashmiri Pandit community as a whole. The chief weapon in the possession of the Kashmiri Pandits was their complete control over the media: P. N. Jalali of PTI, and J. N. Raina of the UNI—the two premier news agencies of India. Influential newspapers like *The Indian Express*, *The Hindu*, *The Statesman* and *The Tribune* were represented by Kashmiri Pandits and their reports were perceived to be twisted and prejudiced against the organizations of the Kashmiri Muslim leadership. Moreover, the Kashmiri Pandits had a strong presence in central government organizations and they were also the beneficiaries of the patronage from Delhi.

It was true that, with the assassination of Indira Gandhi, the Kashmiri Pandits had lost their godmother. They were orphaned politically. Indira's son Rajiv Gandhi was hardly as politically astute or attached to his roots in Kashmir as his mother had been. Kashmiri Pandits tried to exercise their influence over him but Rajiv had little or no time for them. Rajiv who ignored the alarming signals in the reports of Governor Jagmohan on the situation that was developing in the state, was even less likely to take note of the reports of the Kashmiri Pandits. So the community had lost direct access to the Prime Minister of the day.

Farooq knew this better than anyone else. He gave up on them. Neither Farooq nor any of his representatives ever visited the homes of the Kashmiri Pandits who were killed. That, however, only created greater mistrust.

Governor Jagmohan had his own failures. He believed in his own self-aggrandizement. He thought that good roads and buildings were the only means of winning the hearts and minds of the people. He sought to play the role of 'nursing orderly' when he became Governor of Jammu and Kashmir for a second term on January 19, 1990. He showed inexplicable cowardice over the assassination of 52 Kashmiri Muslims on May 21, 1990. He did not step out of Raj Bhavan to see what was happening. He could not protect Mirwaiz Moulvi Farooq.

He alienated the Muslims by his tough action against them, wielded through the security forces. To Hindus he promised protection but failed to live up to his promises. He could win neither Hindus nor Muslims. Hindus, who saw a ray of hope in Jagmohan, were to be disappointed. Jagmohan, whom the

Muslims in Kashmir accused of engineering the migration, can be easily acquitted of this charge. The absence of the luxury residential blocks belie the charge that Jagmohan had intended to replicate Tiananmen Square in Srinigar, promising land and five star comforts to Hindus to move out of the Valley. The Pandits are unanimous in their assertion that Jagmohan could neither protect them nor offer practical help in the aftermath of migration. Their sole reward was tattered tents and hissing serpents.

Flight

In the absence of a strong governing hand and general indifference to the plight of the community, the militants took full advantage to deal a hard blow against the Kashmiri Pandits.

They were enmeshed in helpless fear. Their confidence in the Indian security forces had been misplaced. Fundamentalist forces had infiltrated the various government departments, institutions and the police itself and these elements were perhaps keener than even the militants to see the backs of Kashmiri Pandits. The Kashmiri Pandits were a tiny minority, devoted to studies and white collar jobs. They had no answer to the guns of the militants. Their numbers were nowhere close to the street-filling power of the majority. They began reluctantly to pack up. Their efforts were half-hearted because they persisted in the belief that this land belonged to them[4] and that their neighbours were with them. But their neighbours were equally helpless. It took some time for them to realize that if they were vulnerable, the neighbours who took their side were even more galling to the militants.

Finally, when the murders became rife, when the militants began gunning down Pandits in their homes; when no one came forward to lift the bodies of the slain, the Pandit community knew that the time had come to leave the Valley. This they did, with sorrow gripping at their hearts, in the darkness of the freezing nights of the Kashmir winter. The road to Jammu was the only way out of the labyrinth of death, despair and humiliation.

They entrusted the keys of their homes to Muslim neighbours, hoping to return, soon. How could they live in the hot plains for long? They did not know what was in store for them and how the Government of India was going to bungle time and again and their return would remain as elusive as ever.

Apologia

The massacres of Nadimarg,[5] Wandhama[6] and Sangrampora[7] have proven that there was a definite conspiracy to annihilate the community. Their decision to leave was probably the best option, all things considered. There have been accusations that the community had acted out of cowardice. If they were true Indians, so the speculation goes, they should have stayed on, for the interests of India, in the Valley, were under attack from Islamic fundamentalists, pro-Pakistan and pro-independence forces armed with guns and bombs. Or, had they been true Kashmiris, they should have shared in the pain and agony of the rest of the Kashmiris. Those who advance such arguments forget that when the storms of religious fundamentalism strike, they sweep away everything in their wake. All defences fall. And its victims cast about for protection. Those who accuse them of not standing up to the storm have not known the pangs of leaving home, maintaining that every storm soon blows over. But the storm leaves behind it only a trail of death and destruction and those who are foolhardy enough to confront it are inevitably wiped out by it. There were no storm-proof structures in place to save Kashmiri Pandits from the onslaught of the fanatics bent upon killing them and forcing them out of the Valley. It is better to run to safety than perish for nothing or for a failed cause as the Kashmir Pandits did. The security of hell is often preferable to people, to a heaven of uncertainties. It is however, debatable whether the migration, has not brought the same catastrophic consequences for the community that it had attempted to avert by migrating.

How could the tiny community become cannon fodder for India which lacked the political will to assert itself in Kashmir, the pathetic spectacle of which has been repeated time and time again. Those who maintain that Kashmiris are an inseparable part of Kashmiri culture and ethos forget that they themselves have come from the Valley. Muslims too have migrated from the Valley. They too have become victims of the terrorist campaigns launched against them by Pakistan— sponsored terrorists. Those who remained had to make compromises. Some (of the Muslims) were asked to give up their daughters others to dole out funds. Things have come to the point where people are harassed by militant groups just for the skin of the sacrificial lambs on *Id-ul-Zuha*.[8]

In these circumstances, how could they be expected to stay on in the Valley? Those who did, have had to face the massacres that followed. The survivors then regretted that they had remained. When the Kashmiri Pandits fled, seeking safety in migration those who remained would pour scorn on them only to find out, in their turn, how vulnerable they themselves were and took flight in their turn.

It is clear now that even if the Pandits took the risk of going back, the dark forces that threw them from the Valley, would not allow this to happen. Massacres have followed, each time that the government has announced its plans to restore Kashmiri Pandits to their homes in the Valley. When Farooq Abdullah said it in 1997, Sangrampora took place. The landscape was bloodied by the Wandhama massacre when he raised the pitch again in 1998, Mufti followed in Farooq's footsteps, and Nadimarg resounded with wails. Even the whole effort by the government is now suspect. Whether it was a deliberate strategy to provoke the militants to force the community to flee rather than to effect its return history alone will be judge. What is now more uncertain is whether the funds allotted for the reconstruction of homes for the Kashmiri Pandits is being utilized in Kashmir to build assets that would never be used by those for whom they were intended. It is another way of grabbing Central funds.

The Dubiosity of Returning

It is legitimate to ask how a community so devastated by violence and hostility can expect itself to return to the Valley where it has lost all prospects of livelihood. If the government, under pressure from the Centre, were to create jobs, this is likely to create more animosity and bad blood.

If the community were to stay outside the Valley, the vacant jobs would be given to local residents. Why should the latter then be made to share the economic benefits thereof? The prevalent distrust has been aggravated by the government. Talk of the return of Kashmiri Pandits is just a mirage to fool the world. The rhetoric of Kashmir being incomplete without them is just a means of blinding world opinion.

Endnotes

1. Lal Ded, a woman saint in Kashmir. For Hindus, she was Laleshwari and Muslims call her Lala Arifa. She is revered by both communities equally and intensely. She breast-fed Nund Rishi. Nund was not taking milk from his mother, but did so when Laleshwari, revered as a saint offered to breast-feed him.

2. This is Sheikh Noor-ud-Din Noorani, a Muslim saint, whose shrine is in Charar-e-Sharief in the central Kashmir district of Budgam. He was a strong believer in communal brotherhood.

3. *Al Safa* is an Urdu daily published from Srinagar. At the start of the militancy the newspaper was seen as being close to militants. However, its founder and editor Shaban Vakil was killed in his office on April 23, 1991 by suspected militants. Now the newspaper is being run by his son Ashraf Shaban.

4. Kashmiri Pandits believe that they are the original natives of Kashmir, so the land belongs to them.

5. Nadimarg is a sleepy village in the south Kashmir district of Pulwama. Militants massacred 24 Kashmiri Pandits there on the intervening night of March 23 and 24, 2003.

6. Wandhama-Militants massacred Kashmiri Pandits and burnt the houses in this village in the Ganderbal area of Srinagar district on the night of January 25, 1998.

7. Seven Kashmiri Pandits were massacred in March 1997 in Sangrampora village in the central Kashmir district of Budgam.

8. Muslims slaughter lambs on Id-ul-Zuha, a Muslim festival, as a symbol of sacrifice.

Part IV

10

Dateline Srinagar

August 16, 1990

Srinagar dateline[1] has its own charm and traps. A cool breeze greeted visitors at Srinagar airport on their arrival. But a strange fear appeared to have gripped them. They walked in silence to taxis as if they were part of some funeral procession. It was a different Kashmir where even the chirping birds appeared to have fallen silent.

The scene in the markets was different. Here there were crowds and everything appeared uncannily normal, apart from the ubiquitous bunkers and gun-snouts. There was the usual giggling of young girls and the cries of hawkers in Lal Chowk.

Only two days ago, on August 14—Pakistan's independence day, Pak flags had gone up and the various militant outfits had held special parades before the photographers. These celebrations were pregnant with as much meaning as the observance of 'black day,' the following day—August 15—India's independence day. Kashmiris were expressing defiance towards India rather than love for Pakistan. The dream of a free and independent Kashmir was more cherished than the prospect of being part of theocratic Pakistan. The protests on August 15 were just an extension of that feeling which Kashmiris sought to manifest in black flags or civil curfew—a term that would become ominous in the coming days. The militant elements flaunted their might in the enforcement of civil curfew—people were confined to their homes and the streets were deserted, without the presence of foot soldiers. But the civil curfew call was accompanied by the threat of reprisal in the event of defiance. The lessons of the assassination of Mohammad Yusuf Halwai were already there.

My arrival came soon after the assassination of Mirwaiz Moulvi Farooq, Chief of the Awami Action Committee. The chief's assassination occurred at his home at Nageen, close to the Hazratbal shrine on May 21, 1990. The forces were hell-bent upon eliminating those seen as a possible rallying point for the people were gradually coming to the realization that they had been trapped into supporting the movement. The silent majority mistrusted and hated the movement where brother had been led to kill brother, where fathers were afraid of saying anything against the *tanzeems* or militant groups or *tehreek* (movement) in front of their children. No one knew who might be a militant among them. Teachers were apprehensive of scolding errant students and mothers of boxing the ears of their sons. The place was rampant with rumours and horrendous reports. A girl was killed on suspicion of having links with the security forces. She was denied a grave in the community graveyard, cursed for being a traitor. There was no priest willing to perform her last rites. Her brother took her on his shoulders and started digging a grave for her in the veranda. Even as his shovel struck the earth to find a resting place for his sister, he was hit by a barrage of bullets; and he fell dead over the body of his sister.

Assassination of Mirwaiz Moulvi Farooq

The story of Mirwaiz's assassination was also one enmeshed in betrayal and political intrigue. The Mirwaiz was sitting in his study when he heard the voices of two men inquiring from his gardener about him in the lawns. Within minutes he found himself greeting the two young men. Gun shots were heard, immediately afterwards. As everyone rushed to the study both the assassins were seen making their escape from it. Mirwaiz's hands were extended as if in the gesture of a handshake before he was shot in his chest, resulting in instant death. Though the two men whom the CBI (Central Bureau of Investigation) claimed as assassins, were duly arrested no one has, to date, come forward with new evidence against them. Even the gardener has not identified them. That is the nature of the fear that still holds the minds of the people. Immediately after the assassination, a press note was prepared by Hizb-ul-Mujahadeen claiming responsibility for the murder. It was then an honour to make such claims. It was a feather in the cap of the militants. They had done it in the case of Mir Mustafa[2] and at Hizbullah after murdering Maulana Masoodi, a veteran leader of the National Conference. But when those drafting the press note heard of the mob fury of the fiercely loyal *Bakras*—the followers of the Mirwaiz—against Jamait-i-Islami and the Hizb-ul-Mujahadeen, the Jamait cadres feared the worst. Soon the press note was torn and the word was spread that Shiv Sena[3] activists had killed the Mirwaiz—a piece of fiction that the Kashmiris themselves did not believe, but could not deny for fear of the gun. The rest of the job was done for them by the CRPF which opened fire on the crowd carrying the body of the Mirwaiz Moulvi Farooq at Hawal and which left 52 people dead and many more wounded. As I was mulling over the complexities of the situation looking forward to the days ahead in Kashmir, I found myself at the MLA hostel, in the room of *The Indian Express* correspondent George Joseph—a great human being—waiting to tell me the dos and don'ts of reporting in Kashmir in the terribly alarming situation. Never take the same route every day, never tell anyone on the phone in advance about your movements, keep your thoughts to yourself and never display any anger over your feelings about the militancy. Ironically, he was to fall victim to the same 'dos and don'ts' when he was placed on the list of reporters banned by the Hizb-ul-Mujahadeen from 1992 onwards. George and I were colleagues in *The Times* (now closed) in Jaipur in 1985. We had one thing in common: both of us were outside reporters in Kashmir, which had its pros and cons. The security forces would trust us more though the militants had their doubts.

The difficulty of the assignment dawned on me that very evening. The militants had fired two rocket launchers. One of them hit the fourth-storey of Broadway Hotel.[4] The rocket launchers exploded with a big bang, missing their intended target: the MLAs' hostel. It was reported to house the IB–intelligence bureau and policemen. Surprisingly, I never found any IB man in the building where I had lived for almost 11 years.

All inmates of the hostel, mostly security personnel came out of their rooms. The CRPF guards were on the alert. I remember them challenging even the car of DGP J. N. Sakesena.[5] *Halt, Kon Aaata Hai* (Stop, who is coming?), the sentry on guard duty shouted with his gun pointed towards the DGP's car. Even while this was happening, I heard a rattle of bullets being fired all over and light tracers going up in the sky throwing light all around. Everyone was rushing about.

The DGP had come to see whether the MLA hostel was hit. George was very keen on filing the story. He didn't have a telephone in his room. He rushed to the room of Ashraf Sahil, Deputy Director, Doordarshan, Kendra, Srinagar, a charming and helpful person. He offered George his telephone. But the moment George started dialling, the phone went dead. The process went on repeatedly and we spent almost two hours in struggling to get connected only to give up in the end. True to Kashmiri traditions, Ashraf was extremely hospitable. He served us several rounds of tea in those two hours and shared his views about the Kashmir situation. That was when I first realized that I had to devise my own ways of obtaining and sending news. The communication system was extremely unreliable in those days.

I learnt to 'beg, borrow, and steal' to communicate news

and I must say that my colleagues in Delhi were extremely helpful. At times they would hate my stories because these did not match their patriotic ideals especially when these were critical of the human rights violations on the part of security forces. But still they would not tamper with the spirit of the stories. That I think is the strength of the Indian press where a reporter can report what he feels and it is accepted by editors.

It would not be an exaggeration to say that I lived on the trust of the locals and security forces because they discovered that though I was Indian at heart, when it came to reporting, I simply reported the facts. Even militants, occasionally criticized or blamed for acts of rapes, extortion and harassment, would not protest when I asked inconvenient questions like:''What will you do, if the majority of the people decide to side with India in the plebiscite, why is militancy acting criminally or what justification does Jamait-i-Islami have in censuring mainstream parties, when it had, itself, contested in the polls which the erstwhile Plebiscite Front of Sheikh Abdullah boycotted it in 1972?' One press conference that I would never forget was in Amargarh, a village near Sopore in northern Kashmir in January 1991; guns were to be seen everywhere. The press conference was addressed by Hizb chief Master Ahsan Dar,[6] who was on top of the list of the most wanted militants. Hizb was and still is militarily the strongest group in Kashmir. It was here I saw Imran Rahi[7] and Majid Dar.[8] I did not know how important they were. The army was out on the road; the link road was four to five feet deep in snow. We all boarded the *tonga* (horse cart) and then walked to the place where the militants were resting. As far as I could see there were more than 300 armed, gun-carrying militants with fearless eyes. I asked a few acid questions and one of my colleagues Mohammad Shaban Vakil, who edited the Urdu daily *Al Safa* (he was assassinated in his office in Sarai Bala in

Srinagar in April that year) nudged me-signalling that I should be discreet. But Ahsan Dar answered all the questions and when he found it difficult to answer, he would turn to Majid Dar. Later, I was told Majid Dar was the real strategist and brain of the group.

After the press conference we were treated to *wazwan* during which several courses of mutton were served. It was during this press conference that Ahsan Dar said that if plebiscite was not in Pakistan's favour then 'we would go in for *Hijrat* (migration) as envisaged by Islam in such situations.' The criminality of the militancy was due to the indiscriminate recruitment of the youth, some with a criminal mindset. 'These are the people defaming the movement. We are taking action against them,' He vowed that in future no criminal would be found in the ranks of the militancy. But that was not to be—as the torture and murder of the innocent people, extortion and excesses of the militants would reveal.

The Widening Muslim-Hindu Divide

The face of the security forces was also turning harsh in retaliation. My photographer colleague Meraj-ud-Din and I were on our way to curfew-bound downtown Srinagar where 200 houses had been gutted. The security forces put the blame on the militants and the militants on the security forces. Our taxi-car had the sticker PRESS pasted on it and our ID cards were to serve as curfew passes. Curfews had become such a regular feature in Kashmir that issuing passes for facilitating movement in curfew bound areas was simply impractical. Besides, there was no civil administrative system in place that could undertake such a massive exercise. We were stopped by a Major of the army.

The conversation went somewhat along these lines:

'Are you from the press?'

'Yes,' I replied.

'Can I see your ID card?' he demanded.

'Sure,' I said as I pulled out my I D card from my pocket.

'Hum.'

He inspected the ID card closely and then said, 'You are Arun Joshi from the *Hindustan Times* and you are a Hindu.'

I thought that the mention of my religion by the officer of the Indian army acclaimed for its discipline and secular character, was something unexpected. Meraj was piqued.

'I am Meraj-ud-Din and I am a Muslim.'

The officer allowed us to move on but I could not help but reflect for many days to come of how far matters had gone when even soldiers were talking in terms of Hindus and Muslims. The gap was widening every day.

Ordinary Kashmiris were alienated and beginning to lose hope. Their land was being transformed into a veritable killing field. The people had watched their Hindu neighbours run, under cover of night, to Jammu and other safer places. They were helpless; they had seen their own children coming home dead. There was no love lost for anything Indian. Kashmiris would take to the streets in thousands over a single death and every procession tried to reach the office of the United Nations Military Observer Group[9] for India and Pakistan at Sonawar braving bullets, baton charges and tear-smoke.

An unprecedented snowfall in the winter of 1990-91 saw no letup in the militant activities. The attacks on security personnel, particularly the Central Reserve Police Force and the Border Security Force were intensified.

In 1991, militants, once again resorted to kidnappings. Many sensational abductions were made that year, beginning with the abduction of Nahid Soz, daughter of Saif-ud-Din Soz,[10] the former National Conference leader and MP. He is now in the Congress.

I had not known Soz when he was an officer in the Board of School Education. He was picked up by the National Conference to contest the Lok Sabha polls in 1989. He had promised to split the National Conference in 1995 if he were given the Rajya Sabha nomination by the Narsimha Rao Government. His daughter Nahid Soz was kidnapped by Ikhwan-ul-Muslimeen[11]–Muslim Brotherhood. In February 1991, she was released in exchange for three militants. Soz had demanded to know if his daughter was less important than that of Mufti Mohammad Sayeed. That was a legitimate argument. In between, the government had learnt how disastrous things might turn out if the demands of the militants were not met. This had occurred in the brutal assassination of Kashmir University Vice-Chancellor Mushir-ul-Haq, his private secretary, and Hindustan Machine Tools (HMT) General Manager H. L. Khera.

It was dark at night. The Kashmir Divisional Commissioner Wajahat Habibullah and several other officers were sitting at Soz's Tulsi Bagh residence waiting for the girl to come. With me was Meraj-ud-Din. We were travelling in a taxi run by Abdul Majid, an affable figure, who always took us to places. Besides, I always felt secure in his company. He was also a treasure-trove of information on Kashmir. His mind was replete with details of times and events. He was like a reference book to me while I was travelling in Kashmir.

The word went round that Nahid would be brought to her in-laws' home in Chaanpora. We drove there, only to find that the wait was endless. It was past 2 at night and there were no lights of any car bringing the girl. We gave up the hope of her arrival for that night. We drove back to our place through the deserted streets of Srinagar, occasionally stopped by security personnel. Early next morning the telephones rang; Nahid was back home. This is part of the trauma of reporting in Kashmir where any number of hours could just go waste like this.

Nahid's abduction and subsequent release in exchange for militants was a big boost to their morale. They started kidnapping people. The most sensational abduction was that of K. Doraiswamy, an executive of the Indian Oil Corporation, who also happened to be a relative of then President R. Venkatraman. The way his abduction was handled, the government ended releasing 14 militants, whereas they had originally demanded only five and they were willing to settle for Javed Shalla, a notorious character who was a rapist, extortionist and brutal killer. The government succumbed in one case after another as a matter of strategy. It released militants, keeping track of them and thereafter finishing them off 'in encounters.'

The year also witnessed fresh fissures between pro-Pakistan and pro-Independence groups and the first anti-Pakistan demonstration in Srinagar. But that was the end of it. It was April 1991. Differences had been patched up and bonhomie restored in the overall interest of the movement. JKLF and Hizb were involved in clashes and then in reconciliation.

If 1991 was the year of abductions and massacres, the following year in Kashmir would be remembered for the *yatras* or marches. The announcement of the Bharatiya Janata Party President Murli Manohar Joshi lead a march to Srinagar to unfurl the national tricolour at the historic Lal Chowk[12] on January 26 Republic Day, made the militant groups submerge their differences to form a united front to foil the BJP's plan. Joshi had planned the *yatra* to raise his profile within the party and emerge as a stronger force than Advani and Vajpayee. Neither of them liked the idea of the *yatra*. But they were forced to lend their support as it was such an emotional issue.

On the morning of January 24 even as the *Ekta yatra* led by Joshi entered Jammu and Kashmir from Punjab, the office of the Director General of Police in Srinagar was blown up in a bomb blast leaving two dead and all the senior officers of the State police including the DGP himself, and the paramilitary police force chiefs in Kashmir, critically wounded.

Nevertheless, Murli Manohar Joshi was brought in by aircraft to Srinagar and made to stay in Badami Bagh Cantonment. The unfurling of the national tricolour duly took place and the ceremony at Lal Chowk lasted for a mere 17 minutes. Even during this short span, militants managed to fire rockets tcwards Lal Chowk; fortunately none exploded near the site of the ceremony.

That marked the beginning of the phase of marches. Hardly had the government recovered from the *Ekta Yatra*, then it was confronted with another march announced by the PoK-based JKLF Chairman Amanullah Khan to cross the Line of Control (LOC) to reach the Indian administered side as the LOC was an 'artificial barrier.' The day chosen was February 11, coinciding with the death anniversary of the co-founder of the JKLF, Mohammad Maqbool Butt. The entire Valley was placed under curfew and, once again, media teams descended on Kashmir. However, the march was suspended and the next march announced for March 30, this time coinciding with the death anniversary of Ashfaq Majid Wani. The march met the same fate because of stiff security arrangements made by the governments on both sides of the border.

The marches announced by the JKLF had sharpened the differences between itself and the pro-Pakistan groups. The pro-Pakistan groups described these marches as machinations which diverted attention from the real issues confronting Kashmir.

The year 1993 began with a tragedy in January itself, in Sopore when 45 people were burnt alive or killed and more than 300 houses and shops were set on fire by the security forces. It had been provoked by a militant attack in which two soldiers were killed. G. Saxena was shocked. April proved to be even more cruel.

The Police Rebellion

On April 10 Lal Chowk was in flames, on April 22 the police went on strike following the''custodial death' of a police constable, Riyaz Ahmed. The police strike and the subsequent processions on the streets including one to the office of the United Nations exposed the helplessness of the government. Finally, the Army was called in to help disarm the distraught policemen. A hundred and thirty of them were arrested and subsequently dismissed. Eventually, they were released and transferred to other departments, such as the fire services.

Police constable Riyaz had returned from a game of volley ball in which he had hurt his left hand. He had turned up to report for duty at the bunkers at Hazratbal to which the army had laid siege on April 21, 1993. In one of the ensuing encounters, a soldier had been left dead and the columns of the 10th Gharwal were seeking permission to enter the shrine complex to flush out the militants, who were firing at them from the old portion of the complex. Permission was denied and there were even orders to lift the siege.

Riyaz was arrested on the suspicion of being sympathetic towards the militants. Two photographers Meraj-ud-Din and Mushtaq Ali had seen him being escorted away by army officials. Mushtaq Ali who worked for Asia News International (ANI) TV had captured the moments when Riyaz was taken in the army vehicle, on his video camera.

Late in the evening, Riyaz's body was brought to the Police Control Room (PCR) building in Batmalloo. Anger mounted as several of Riyaz's colleagues demanded that the killers be punished. They suspected that it was Senior Superintendent of Police (SSP) K. Rajendra, who had been responsible for handing Riyaz over to the army in whose custody, he had died. The police association: the Jammu and Kashmir Police Association which had been disbanded in the 1980s was revived and its spokesman Ashraf claimed that Rajendra had refused to intervene when urged by the police post officer of Nageen which has jurisdiction over the Hazratbal area. On the morning of April 22, news of Riyaz's death was spread throughout Srinagar. Trouble was brewing up at the PCR. The distraught policemen demonstrated against SSP Srinagar demanding his dismissal. The SSP was kept hostage in the PCR building for almost six hours. The body of Riyaz, with flowers strewn all over it, was lying in the PCR premises. Riyaz's colleagues refused to remove the body for burial till the SSP was arrested and action taken against him under Sections 302 RPC (Ranbir Penal Code); the RPC is equivalent to the Indian Penal Code (IPC). Section 302 is invoked for those responsible for murder. Governor Rao, who had taken over his current assignment on March 12, was informed about the ferment brewing in the police force over the killing of the constable. He, without making any comment on the tumult, immediately flew to Gurez, a verdant Valley close to the Line of Control (LOC) to trumpet his well- known theme of holding elections.

There was an exchange of fire between Rajendra's guards and the JKAP men. The JKAP men had attempted to reach the SSP who was sitting in the first storey of the PCR building.

M. N. Sabharwal,[13] Additional Director General of Police (Law and Order) appeared on the scene. He was joined by S. S. Ali, I. G. of Armed Police and Ashok Kumar Suri,[14] I.G. Kashmir range, to pacify the policemen. The distraught policemen were assured that an inquiry would be held into the killing of Riyaz and the guilty punished. With this assurance, the matter appeared to have been resolved. The Director General of Police B. S. Bedi[15] who was in Lucknow, was asked to rush back. Another message was flashed to M. A. Nomani, a senior police officer of the State police on deputation at the Centre, requesting his return. It was expected that he would be able to utilize his contacts with the police force to bring things under control. His return was perceived as a threat by all the senior police officers in the state. He was viewed as the obvious successor to Bedi as DGP.

Bedi, who was on extension, was to complete his term in November 1993. Nomani, a Muslim (from UP) and a Jammu and Kashmir cadre officer with a frank style of working and informal relations with his colleagues at all levels, was presumed to be the de facto DGP.

His return was not a happy development for either Amar Kapoor, the Additional Director General of Police (CID) or Sabharwal, both of whom were aspirants to the post of DGP. Both lacked the dynamism and also the additional qualification that Nomani had—both of them were Hindus and the Governor was more than keen on having Muslims in key positions. He had on so many occasions expressed the desire that he would prefer a team of Muslims officers with him to work with rather than Hindus and Sikhs. His premise was that Muslims in important positions would be able to strike a better rapport with the alienated Kashmiri Muslims.

Just as everything seemed to have been resolved, the daily police bulletin which covers events of the previous 24 hours sent out shockwaves. It was reported that three persons including a policeman had been killed in an 'exchange of fire in different parts of Srinagar City.' Fuel was being added to the flames. The police bulletin issued from the CID office put paid to Sabharwal's conciliatory efforts. He was flabbergasted. But as was his nature, he would not comment on anything. He did, however, make a feeble attempt to speak to the Governor who, after the visit to Gurez, had flown back to Jammu. However, once again, Gen. Rao was not available on the telephone. The official version of the killing, in both the Kashmiri and Urdu bulletins of Radio Kashmir and Doordarshan were immediately construed as a betrayal by the agitating policemen. They were intensely angry and in the minutes which followed, the policemen living in PCR and the Bemina police colony sat down to work out a plan, late into the night, to avenge what they perceived to be a betrayal. A number of aggrieved policemen who had been dismissed from time to time either for negligence in duty or their links with subversive elements also brought their grouses to bear upon the situation. They wanted to aggravate matters for the government and take advantage of the commotion to get back their jobs as well.

The Hizb-ul-Mujahadeen also exerted its influence on them. It wanted a full-fledged revolt in the state police force. Hizb was an extension of Pakistan. This became evident when it issued a statement asking the policemen to join its ranks and also offered to give them weapons and money. There were also elements within the state police force who wanted to bring to the notice of the world the shabby treatment which they had received at the hands of both the army and the paramilitary police forces.

Above all, it was the personal enmity and irrepressible ambitions of the top men in the state police force which helped the subversives and the men in the police force who were bent on revolt. They were playing one against another. Kapoor did not want either Sabharwal or Nomani to succeed.

Nomani had reactivated his old contacts in the police force and ensured that things remained boiling for as long as he wanted. Bedi was looking for more extensions. And Nomani had described the CID office bulletin on April 22 evening as a mischief-making act. Sabharwal told his confidants that it was a clear attempt to sabotage his efforts to silence the voices of dissent in the police force. The accumulated impact of the conniving of the top police officers against one another, the growing resentment of the police force and the instigation of the militants were apparent the next day on the streets of Srinagar. Even to Kashmiris who were used to witnessing massive pro-independence processions and marches of journalists, lawyers, and women to the office of the military observation group of the United Nations at Sonawar, it was an unusual procession. Policemen perched on the roof top of police buses, sporting black arm-bands and brandishing their service weapons—self-loading Rifles and 303, were shouting slogans against 'State terrorism.' They were also calling for the punishment of the 'killers of Riyaz.' Suddenly, the entire city of Srinagar echoed with these slogans.

There was not only the anger over the killing of Riyaz while in the custody of the army. It was more than that. Ever since the eruption of secessionist violence in Kashmir in late 1989, the Jammu and Kashmir police was gradually being reduced to a force with no or little role to play. First the CRPF which had been inducted to check the militancy, had clashed with the local policemen, openly dubbing them as Pakistanis or *ugarvadi police*, i.e. militants' police. This was not the fault of the CRPF because they were brought with a firm impression imprinted on their minds that all Kashmiri Muslims were anti-nationals, a euphemism for being Pakistanis or sympathizers of Pakistan. And, first the CRPF men, and later, the BSF and army units assumed that they were in the Valley to set these Pakistanis right. They acted as if they were teaching errant children a lesson.

This attitude had completely alienated the police force. Their identify cards were torn in public and they were subjected to all sorts of humiliation. Nor were they spared during notorious crackdowns or from cordon and search operations. Their families were treated without any consideration. At times they were meted out worse treatment. During curfew they were not allowed to come out of their houses. Living with such a disgrace was becoming intolerable for the policemen. The death of Riyaz had acted as a spark.

Reporters who followed these processions found that they were all converging to form a rally at the Police Control Room. Some assumed that it would be a repeat of the events of the previous day. These predictions proved to be incorrect as the massive procession of policemen, some armed, others in plain clothes, trooped out of the PCR building. The CRPF, the BSF and the army had been alerted. A clash now seemed inevitable. The marchers were joined by their colleagues, moving from the nearby police headquarters building towards Shaheedgunj. The journalists formed teams deciding how they would report on the procession, which threatened to be giving a new turn to the Kashmir imbroglio. All of a sudden, the procession made its way towards the United Nations Office. Will they be allowed to march towards the UN office? Since June 3, 1990 no procession had been allowed in the direction of the United Nations office. At that demonstration, journalists had demanded to know the whereabouts of Yusuf Jameel, who had been picked up by the army from his office-cum-residence at Partap Park, on the morning of June 1st. Any procession that had attempted to march towards the UN office had been broken up, sometimes with persuasion, on other occasions by force, often brutal.

Sabharwal and Suri were the only officers to be seen. Suri with his guards threw a road blockade at Poloview. That was immediately lifted as well. The blockade was a one-ton vehicle which was parked near the Tourist Reception Centre (TRC) crossing on Maulana Azad Road. The angry shouts were drawing closer and Suri's guards requested him to withdraw from the scene. He brushed them aside and stood firm. He tried to persuade the policemen to return to the barracks promising that he would redress their grievances. Those who were trying to listen to the I.G were pushed aside and the militant elements among them, pushed forward, shouting '*Khoon ke badla khoon se leange*' (blood would be avenged with blood). One of them snatched the rifle from one of Suri's guards, others cocked their guns. It was a personal affront to Suri, who had not expected this audacity from his subordinates. But despite this, he made yet another attempt to persuade marching policemen not to move to the UN office. It was the dream of dare-devil photographers of the Kashmiri press to join a procession in the full knowledge that anything might happen any moment. I admired their courage as my other colleagues Altaf Hussain of *The Times of India* (now with BBC) were watching the procession reaching the UN office from a safe distance. The trouble could flare up opposite. At the UN office several hundred were offering Friday prayers. Policemen, riding on the crest of euphoria, delivered speeches and read out the eleven-point memorandum which condemned the 'State terrorism' unleashed by the 'Indian security forces in Kashmir.' It sought immediate intervention of the United Nations in bringing to an end the 'state terrorism in Kashmir' and bring to book the 'culprits responsible for the murder of Riyaz.'

The memorandum was a direct challenge to the government's authority. It was a mutiny. After submitting the memorandum to the UN representatives, the policemen returned to the column of protestors, chanting similar slogans. The whole government machinery was looking miserably helpless. Kashmiris enjoyed every moment of this helplessness of the government. Anything that symbolizes defiance of Indian authority is heartening for them. This was an occasion which, they felt, would perpetuate a crisis for the Indian government and may bring more international attention to the Kashmir crisis. Internationalizing the Kashmir issue is an obsession in the Valley. One and all are in it.

A Canadian tourist was raped by National Security Guards (NSG) in Srinagar in October 1990. I wanted to speak to her. She had refused. But she was persuaded to break her silence, because the owner of the houseboat was persuaded by his fellow houseboat owners of the importance of for *tehreek* (the movement for freedom) if a foreigner were to say she had been criminally assaulted by Indian army men.

The whole decision to take the procession up to the UN office was a sponsored one. It later became clear that the policemen had no intention of doing so. But a message came to them from Hizb-ul-Mujahadeen and they obliged. As many policemen have their families in the villages, they were worried about possible reprisals. They knew the might of the militants and the power they possessed to kill. At the end of the procession, the government might have been expected to crackdown on the leaders of the policemen. But nothing of the sort happened. The following day, all things remained unchanged.

Bedi announced ex-gratia relief of Rs. 1.75 lakh to Riyaz's next of kin and employment to one of the eligible members of his family. A joint inquiry by the army and police was also announced. He also ordered the transfer of SSP Srinagar. It was hoped that this would help tempers to subside. Bedi was being naive if he expected that these concessions would evoke a positive response from the agitating policemen. He was clearly oblivious to conspiracies being hatched by his colleagues nor could he guess that it was the militants who were pulling the strings from behind.

Saturday, April 24, after holding a rally at the PCR premises and reiterating their demand for the arrest of the SSP Srinagar on murder charges, reinstatement of all the dismissed policemen, the agitating policemen dispersed. The following day, a Sunday, was Riyaz's fourth day ceremony and the State police Chief, as a gesture of goodwill allowed the policemen to participate in the ceremony at Riyaz's native village, Sumbal in the Baramulla district. On Monday, the rally was held again. By now, Station House Officers (SHOs) had deserted their positions. They had joined the strike. Traffic policemen had disappeared from their beats and the JKAP men moved from their guard duties. This was a complete revolt. Bedi tried to address the rallies giving details of what he had done for them during his tenure. He reeled off figures as to how he had got them better payscales, effected over 6,000 promotions at all ranks. But his audience was restive. A section owing loyalty to Nomani shouted him down and even snatched the microphone from him.

The rallyists marched out in a procession and dispersed on to the yards outside the PCR building.

Not to be outdone by this, Bedi, who had learned the art of organizing stage-managed shows, sent messages to the newsmen for an important press conference. Newsmen rushed to the PCR hoping that Bedi was going to make some startling announcements. There was something different which Bedi wanted newsmen to see. About 400 policemen who had gathered at the premises were made an audience for the DGP's speech along old themes. He repeated what he had attempted to say in the morning. At regular intervals, Bedi wanted his audience to respond with a thundering 'Yes' to what he was saying. 'Didn't I get you the promotions?' 'Haven't your families been given accommodation?' Bedi was saying all this to the amusement of the newsmen who were the least interested of all in the stage-managed show. The newsmen, however, suddenly found things turning 'newsy' for them. They stopped muttering in each other's ear when a man in civvies got up and identified himself as Ghulam Mohammad Constable, who had accompanied the DGP during his tour of Kishtwar, about 280 kms to the south of Srinagar, to remind him of what he had said during that visit, quoting DGP's words, the Constable said: 'You are my real and trustworthy defence. These National Security Guards (NSG) would not protect me if I am attacked.' Then the Constable went on to say, 'We were willing to lay down our lives for you. But do you know what is happening to us and our families?' Pointing towards the CRPF men forming the outer fringe of the audience, he said,"When I was in a crackdown, the CRPF men to whom I showed my identity card (which he pulled out of his pocket), asked me to "fold it and insert it into your ..." (three-letter word). Others cried "shame, shame."' When TV cameras zoomed in towards the audience, it strongly protested and Bedi had to ask the TV crew to stop filming. The show had obviously failed. But Bedi would not give up. He then addressed the press conference and served an ultimatum on the policemen taking part in the agitation. They were to report back to their duties by

Tuesday 1.30 p.m. and their strike period would be treated as leave. Failing which, the striking policemen would be dealt with under the law and they could even face dismissal. Now, the wait started for 1.30 p.m. April 27.

On April 27, evening when the army had cordoned the PCR, Rajesh Pilot flew in from Delhi and drove straight to Rajbhavan. Within less than half an hour the Governor, who had left the whole affair in the hands of the police bosses, also landed after he was reprimanded by the Prime Minister for staying out of Srinagar, when the situation warranted his stay there.

Both of them were constantly in touch with Delhi. While the Governor was opposed to the army operation, Pilot did not want matters to be prolonged further. Finally around midnight, the Prime Minister's office approved Pilot's line of action and Lt. Gen. Surinder Nath, Corps Commander was asked to order the storming of the PCR before Wednesday morning. It was from here onwards that the rift between Pilot and Gen. Rao began and continued to widen.

The following day, the policemen's procession was fired at from a CRPF bunker at Shaheedgunj. Five of them were injured. The entire Srinagar city was shut down as tension was running high.

My instinct took me to Partap Park. Naquash Habibullah, a brilliant photographer with *The Asian Age* and Noor-ul-Qamrain, a leading journalist and political commentator were willing to join me on a trip to PCR. We took a lift from Fayaz Ahmed Kaloo, reporter for *The Pioneer* and now editor of the English daily *Greater Kashmir*. Our car was stopped at the Exhibition crossing by BSF personnel. When they had examined our identity cards, we were allowed to proceed further. On the road opposite, was a fire brigade station and the passage to the PCR was blocked by the BSF. We did not succeed in getting to the PCR. The BSF kept forcing us back.

There was no point in starting an argument. We returned disappointed as we would not be able to witness the action. But, what was hurting us more was that some of our colleagues were inside and they would be watching the unfolding of the entire drama before their own eyes and we would have to rely on a second hand version. Professional jealousy was driving at least me to extreme anger and I was making all efforts to control it. As if trying to console myself, I told my colleagues that in a way it was good that we were barred, as we could at least submit our report in time. Naqash, who was always very frank said bluntly, 'but the action is here.' I had no answer.

Enraged by the firing upon their procession, the policemen returned to the PCR building, and in fits of anger they smashed window panes, deflated the tyres of the parked vehicles. They, however, did not attempt to storm into the first floor where Home Secretary Mehmood-ur-Rehman, Bedi, Sabharwal, Nomani were holed in. They were protected by their guards and under orders to open fire if any attempt was made to harm them.

Sensing more trouble, Bedi sought help from the Army. Everything else was organized by Patel[16] and Vijay Shanker, I.G. BSF. Suri was the only officer who was allowed in and out of the PCR building. Appeals to the striking policemen to lay down their arms were repeatedly made. But these were rejected. The striking policemen maintained that they were peaceful and did not want to create an 'ugly situation.'

It became clear after a few hours that the fire issuing from the bunker at Shaheedgunj was caused by a group of half a dozen men who were panic-stricken when they heard gun shots being fired from a distance They presumed that the shots were fired by members of the procession who were armed. Since the shots were aimed at them, the policemen concluded that they had been deliberately fired upon. The situation was obviously the result of some misunderstanding.

Izhar Ahmed Wani, who worked for *Saudi Gazette* and AFP, was one of those journalists, who was ever keen to be on the spot. He had a wealth of sources even at the young age of 23 in 1993 and was among those who had been holed-up and had therefore witnessed the entire drama. At 4.35 a.m., Wednesday morning, he phoned from PCR, informing me that the (army) operation was over. In typical agency reporter's style he said that in a swift operation the army had stormed into the PCR and disarmed the agitating policemen. Not a single shot had been fired. I heard the shouts of *Ho Ha, Oh Mar gaya* (I am dying) in the darkness outside. The DGP was lying flat on the floor with both his hands covering his ears. Other officers were almost in a similar condition. Silence engulfed the complex and the stomping of the boots of an officer, a colonel of the army, drew closer and Bedi got up to hear, 'Sir the operation is over,' Bedi beckoned Sabharwal to get up and they congratulated each other. Recalling the night of April 27-28 at the PCR, Izhar later told me that the chants '*Awaz Do Hum Ek Hai,*' '*Khabardar, Hoshiar*' (we are united, be aware, stay alert) were heard throughout night, before the pre-dawn operation was accomplished. Izhar recalled that, prior to the ending of the drama, several attempts had been made to resolve the crisis. At one stage, Nomani was taken to the roof of the microphone fitted bus. He had also repeated his appeal for the laying down of arms. Throughout this nightmarish period a clash between the army and the armed policemen, who had taken up positions, seemed inevitable. But when the army stormed into the PCR, there was no resistance.

The senior officers were to be removed from the bathroom of the first floor. A ladder was kept ready for them in case there was any violence. Izhar had done what even many veteran war reporters might have failed to do in the kind of situation, he was in. The moment he was woken from his sleep by the shouts of '*Ho ha*,' he picked up the phone, pressed the buttons to dial his Delhi AFP office number. He gave a full account of what he had heard and seen. During the night, he had shared three biscuits with all those present in the room. Since I had nothing to report at that hour, I tried to reconstruct the whole series of events. I rang Brig. Pandey responded. I gave my identity and asked, 'How was the operation?' 'Excellent' came the answer at the other end, without the least hint of excitement. Curfew was imposed on Srinagar and I knew that Vijay Shankar was coordinating the operations of disarming the JKAP battalions at other places. He added 'our jawans have disarmed JKAP men at Manigam and Zewan.' 'There was no resistance,' he had added as if anticipating what might be my next question.

The policemen had surrendered without offering any resistance. This was a collapse of their rebellion. They did not offer resistance, although they had arms because they were mortally afraid of taking on the professional army. They were outnumbered several times by the soldiers. They knew that if they resisted, they would be accused of being militant and their families would suffer harassment and torture. These thoughts were not far from their minds. They had not anticipated that things would ever come to such a pass.

In Kashmir, events often reach a dangerous and dramatic climax which no individual or group has sought. The individuals work in excitement and only to be confronted by the totally unexpected. This is precisely what had happened to the policemen who had gone on strike. They were looking for an exit strategy and that they saw in allowing themselves to be disarmed, humiliated. And somewhere at the back of their mind was their love for the job they were doing. It was a sad thing to have happened for the Kashmiris. The surrender by the policemen was a defeat to which Kashmiris would never be reconciled. When they saw policemen hustled into army trucks and being taken to PCR where they were paraded before hooded informers like militants, they were left in no doubt that this phase had been lost. 'They could have at least offered some resistance. Had they fired one shot, we would have said that they did not surrender,' was the common refrain of the Kashmiris. In the end 139 policemen were dismissed from service and arrested for instigating and causing the police strike. The impact of the army operation was visible on April 29, when the coordination committee of the Jammu and Kashmir Police gave the call for the general strike. While everything else was closed, policemen were back on duty in police stations, vital installations and even traffic policemen were manning their beats on the deserted roads. At Batmalloo, the residents, who were also witness to the whole drama, had beaten five policemen on duty questioning them about their ethics of asking others to observe strike, when they themselves were on duty. That the militants did not want the policemen to resume their duties became the evident when a grenade was hurled at a police vehicle injuring 14 of them at Nowhalta, downtown Srinagar. But gradually everything subsided.

When the police strike was resolved, the government took a major decision—that of handing overall major anti- militancy operations to the Army. A unified command was set up. While the Government of India was closing its ranks, so was Pakistan.

Endnotes

1. Srinagar dateline is so-called because of the disputed nature of Kashmir and international focus has a charm for reporters. Anything reported from Srinagar dateline carries more attraction than anywhere else in Jammu and Kashmir or even Pakistan, occupied Kashmir. In India, it is called a pressure cooker (of news) dateline.

2. Mir Mustafa, a respected political leader of Chadoora area of Budgam. He was elected as an independent member to the Legislative Assembly in 1987.

3. Shiv Sena is a party of Hindu fundamentalists in India which calls for the setting up of pure Hindu rule in India.

4. Broadway Hotel is a nerve-centre of political activities and also a favourite with visiting journalists.

5. J. N. Sakesana is a senior IPS officer from Madhya Pradesh who was appointed as state police chief in December 1989.

6. Master Ahsan Dar was the first Commander-in-chief of Hizb-ul-Mujahadeen. He later parted ways with the group in 1992 and formed his own group Muslim Mujahadeen.

7. Imran Rahi, a divisional commander of Hizb, who was arrested and on his release in 1995, turned anti-Hizb and favoured dialogue with the government for resolution of the Kashmir crisis.

8. Majid Dar, think-tank of Hizb. He migrated to Pakistan and on his return in July 2000, announced unilateral cease-fire for three months. He developed serious differences with his supreme commander Syed Salahauddin and was assassinated in 2003.

9. United Nations Military Observers group for India and Pakistan has an office in Sonawar in Srinagar. It comes into attention whenever the anti-India protesters want to make their point internationally or register their protest to the world body.

10. Saif-ud-Din Soz, a professor turned politician. He was with the National Conference. He was a minister in the United Front

government from 1997 to 1998. But he defied the party in 1998, and voted against the government at the centre as a member of the Lok Sabha. The Lok Sabha, the lower House of the Indian parliament was dissolved. Ironically, Vajpayee had lost by one vote. He is now with Congress and a member of the Rajya Sabha, upper House of the Indian parliament.

11. Ikhwan-ul-Muslimeen was originally the Students' Liberation Front or SLF, the student wing of the JKLF. But late in 1990 it parted ways with JKLF and its leader Hilal Ahmad renamed it Ikhwan-ul-Muslimeen.

12. Lal Chowk, the main square in the heart of Srinagar city. It is named Lal (Red) Chowk (Square) because Sheikh Abdullah and his colleagues who launched the revolt against Maharaja Hari Singh used to hold their rallies there. The term 'Lal' (red) is inspired by the Russian Revolution.

13. M. N. Sabharwal, a senior police officer who rose to the rank of Director General of Police (October 15, 1993) and later retired as DG CPPF.

14. Ashok Suri, a senior police officer who became DGP in Jammu and Kashmir in November 2000. He was shifted out as he resisted Chief Minister Mufti Mohammad Sayeed's attempts to placate militants by releasing them from jails.

15. B.S. Bedi, a Sikh police officer from Uttar Pradesh. He took over as DGP in January 1992 and remained in the post till his retirement in October 1993.

16. Ashok Patel was an IPS officer who became the Inspector General and later Additional Director General BSF. He was considered as one of the most brilliant brains in intelligence gathering.

11

Factions within the Separatist Movement

Nascent Distrust

The spring of 1993 saw the first ever bold attempt by the separatist leadership to relegate guns to the background as part of a political strategy designed and executed by Pakistan. The separatist leadership was fragmented, embroiled in personality clashes of its own. At the same time it was mortally afraid of the guns of the militants. The militants whom they had propped up were growing too big for their boots, refusing to toe the line of the political leadership.

The separatist leaders who had been set free by the Government of India received a silent welcome in the Valley in April 1992. Representatives from the media far outnumbered the supporters of these leaders who were gathered at Srinagar airport. Syed Ali Shah Geelani, Abdul Ghani Bhat, Abdul Ghani Lone, Ghulam Nabi Sumji and Qazi Nissar emerged from the airport and the oppressive air seemed to portend something ominous. This did not, however, turn out to be the case.

The distrust and lack of unity among them was immediately perceptible when they refused to speak to the media. Instead, it took them more than two hours of discussion before issuing a statement. The other four were suspicious of Qazi Nissar. Though Qazi had, by his oratory and the depth of his knowledge of Islam, been instrumental in the 1980s and particularly during the 1987 elections in making the MUF acceptable, this time round, he was viewed with deep distrust by his colleagues, who were convinced that Qazi had developed a hatred for guns and the atrocities of gunmen. He was suspected of writing anonymous commentaries for Radio Kashmir, condemning the acts of the militancy. He abhorred the aimlessness of the movement and the way in which it was drifting towards the cycle of bloodshed and violence.

I had visited him after his release at his residence in a narrow winding lane at Acchabal Adda in Anantnag in the summer of 1992. Qazi had effectively distanced himself from the rest of the Separatist leadership and re-entered the world of books and religion. He made some significant comments: 'We have to understand religion and its teachings in the real manner rather than misuse it.' He was emphatic in asserting his views. He could do so because he commanded the respect and had a strong following among the people of Anantnag.

The other Separatists were still trying to seek a foothold but were being repeatedly defied. The fissures between the Jammu and Kashmir Liberation Front and Hizb were deepening. Syed Ali Shah Geelani whom Hizb-ul-Mujahideen revered as *Rehbar-e-Inquilab* (Leader of the Revolution) was abducted by the JKLF men immediately after the assassination of Dr. Abdul Ahad Guru.[1] When confronted by the press over this soon after his release at the Sher-e-Kashmir Institute of Medical Sciences in Srinagar in the summer of 1993, he said, 'The JKLF boys are my children, I was never kidnapped.' A minute later, a slip was passed to him. He read it. And suddenly went back on what he had just said. 'Yes I was abducted by the JKLF boys. They were trying to kill me before I was rescued.'

The chit had come from Hizb and the 'leader of the revolution' could not continue with his version of the events and mouthed instead the script which the Hizb wanted to relay to the world.

Militant Excesses

Pakistan was getting shaky. The violence was directly

traced to youths who had become militants, armed and trained by Pakistan and sent back to Kashmir to cause trouble. Pakistan's argument that it was offering only 'political, diplomatic and moral support' was beginning to sound increasingly hollow, and it was becoming difficult for Pakistan to sustain this fiction. India proclaimed to the wider world that it was a terrorist movement and Pakistan was behind it. Pakistan saw that public support for militancy in Kashmir was on the decline by 1992. Militant atrocities were on the rise. They were forcibly seeking food and shelter in the homes of poor Kashmiris, raping and violating their women. There was no count of those who had become unwed mothers. The affluent had shifted out of the Valley. The new localities in the outskirts of Jammu were proof of the fear that impelled the migration of Muslims from the Valley to protect the honour of their women. Others bought peace with militants by bribing them. Only the poor suffered and they bore the full brunt of militant ire.

Anger against the militants was translating into emotions against Pakistan much in the same fashion as excesses by soldiers were intensifying anger against India. People started giving information to the police and security forces and there were successful raids in which the militants were being eliminated.

The internal squabble of militant outfits fighting for supremacy was also causing general disillusionment. The Hizb-ul-Mujahideen was fighting the JKLF in Srinagar. Al-Barq was embroiled in skirmishes with Hizb and the JKLF in north Kashmir, particularly in the Kupwara district close to the borders with Pakistan occupied Kashmir. In South Kashmir the JKLF, Al-Jehad and Hizb-ul-Mujahideen were trying to settle scores with one another.

On the international scene a mood of reconciliation was surfacing. The voice of peace was making itself heard in Ireland

and in the Norwegian capital Oslo, the Palestinian and Israeli leadership were attempting to work out a peace agreement. That was in September 1993. But Kashmir continued to be a major conflict zone. There was not the equivalent of a Yasir Arafat in Kashmir's separatist leadership even though Indian Prime Minister P. V. Narasimha Rao was willing to take on the role of a Yitzhak Rabin. The message was flashed to the capitals of the world. Pakistan became aware of the pitfalls of having solely to depend on the militants for achieving its objective.

Pakistan's Volte-Face: Discarding the Militant Mask

It wanted the separatist leaders to sink their differences and form a forum involving all political, religious and social groups committed to the objective of right for self-determination for the people of Kashmir. Ultimately, that was tantamount to preparing the stage, by moulding and shaping public opinion, for Kashmir's merger with Pakistan. Pakistan demanded that the leaders unite to give a political facade to the movement, which was increasingly assuming a terrorist face.

The setting up of a political platform was of acute importance to Islamabad. It did not want to be seen backing a terrorist movement 'morally, politically and diplomatically.' It was keen that this movement should have a political face as well. A political movement set on the course of achieving the right to self-determination—its long-time slogan to attract Kashmiris to its stand-point that Pakistan was the only credible and honourable option for the people of Kashmir. Pakistan had always lived in the belief that given the choice, Kashmiri Muslims would opt for Pakistan. It was only seeking to brighten its prospects by floating the new forum. It was worried by the increasing acceptance of the pro-freedom call 'We want freedom' which was drowning out the muted slogan: 'We want Pakistan.'

Pakistan's tendency to live in a make-believe world is legendary. So also is India's claim that Kashmir is an integral part of her territory. Both Delhi and Islamabad are woefully far distanced from the ground realities. Neither the slaughtering of Indian icons in Kashmir nor regular *fidayeen* attacks on army camps have won the day for Pakistan. Indian security forces may have killed more than 15,000 militants; still it remains hundreds of miles away from effecting any change. The Indian and Pakistani contest over Kashmir have a striking similarity of strategy. India created unified headquarters to counter militancy, Pakistan responded by launching the Hurriyat Conference to sustain its pursuit of objectives, politically.

As the events in 1993 unfolded, Pakistan was trying to consolidate its hold on the minds and hands of Kashmiris. It had given guns to young Kashmiris, exploited their passions and emotions. The familiar faces of the MUF were still there. But there were two remarkable additions this time. Abdul Ghani Lone of the People's Conference and Mirwaiz Umar Farooq of the Awami Action Committee. Mirwaiz Umar Farooq's father Moulvi Mirwaiz Farooq had been assassinated on May 21, 1990. The suspected killers were men of the Hizb-ul-Mujahadeen. They could not be convicted because no one had come forward to testify against those men. They are still facing trial with what seems to be an unending trial.

Pakistan forced the squabbling parties to confront each other across the conference table. Pakistan's message was thinly veiled: behave or else they might meet the fate meted out to the pro-India politicians. Syed Ali Shah Geelani and Abdul Ghani Lone who had never seen eye to eye with each other were also seen sitting and discussing how to put up a joint front. The Mirwaiz was made to sit with the leaders of groups who patronised the Hizb-ul-Mujahadeen, which was said to be behind his father's assassination. Umar Farooq has himself never addressed these questions.[2]

They were able to muster the support of more than 30 other groups and then came the announcement: the Hurriyat is born. The Hurriyat started showing itself on the political scene only after the Hazratbal[3] crisis.

Hazratbal 1993

I was about to switch off the transistor at my bedside, when the strident call of the telephone woke me from my sleep on October, 15. Out of habit before picking up the receiver, I switched on the bed light and glanced at my wrist-watch: It was 00.15 a.m. 'Who could it be?' I wondered as I picked up the receiver. Before I could even say hello, the voice at the other end announced, 'Operation Hazratbal has begun.' It did not take me even a fraction of a second to recognize the voice which went on, 'Don't ask questions. I am in a hurry.' It was clear enough that I should not try to ring him up again, at least for the night. Moments later, I was still staring at the receiver. My mind was flooded with incessant questions. What is this operation? Are troops going to storm the shrine? Have special contingents of troops landed in Kashmir? And why Hazratbal? Would it mean a scoop for me?

By the time I dropped the telephone, all I could hear was the howling of dogs piercing the silence of the dark night. The telephone did not have an STD[4] facility. How was I to inform my office? Booking a trunk call would mean wasting at least one more hour and by that time everyone would have gone home. Then it dawned on me that I could book a lightning call. I decided to make the call but also wanted to make a few verifications.

Wherever I rang, no one answered my desperate calls. There was not even an orderly to say *Sahib bahir gaya hai* (Sahib, is out). It was 2.00 a.m. before I decided to call off my efforts and wait till morning. As soon as I tried to sleep fresh thoughts occurred to me. 'Perhaps one of the colleagues has the story.' But, what was I to do? Filled with these anxious thoughts, I finally fell asleep. The phone rang again. The familiar voice, sounding slightly more relaxed this time, announced, 'The army has laid a cordon around Hazratbal. A curfew has been imposed downtown.'

'Are they going to storm the shrine?' I found myself asking, trying to conceal my irritation that he had not given me the exact details during his previous call. 'I don't know. May be.' 'How many militants are inside (the Shrine)?' 'Not more than 40,' was the reply.

The telephone line went dead. This happened often to my telephone as it was constantly bugged. There was little point in wasting time. I spent the next three hours trying to re-construct the whole thing. What became clear after that effort, was that the Border Security Force (BSF) which had first conducted cordon and search operations at the Regional Engineering College and Kashmir University campus on October 10, had information that several top militants were hiding in the Hazratbal shrine and they had recovered a sizeable quantity of arms and ammunition.

Then the government had received information that militants had broken the locks of two doors leading to the safe where a relic (a hair of the beard) of Prophet Muhammad was kept. They intended to create some mischief with the relic. The argument sounded plausible to some. Others dismissed it as pure fabrication. 'It was a ploy to enter the shrine,' Prof. Abdul Ghani Bhat, a senior leader of the Hurriyat Conference, said. How can a Muslim attempt to do such an irresponsible thing? It was unimaginable.

There were many objections to the theory put forward by

the government. Who had informed the authorities of all this and while militants were carrying out their operations, why did the Jammu and Kashmir Armed Police (JKAP) men on duty at the shrine not prevent it?

There were no convincing answers. But those who asked these questions knew full well, themselves, that in the given situation, the JKAP men could not have done anything nor tell the whole truth.

Curfew Imposed

The next morning, October 16, brought news that curfew had been imposed in eight of the 19 police station areas in Srinagar, which meant the entire downtown area was under curfew. Suddenly, the telephone sprang back to life and I was reminded that I had to be at the Raj Bhawan, on time, to witness the swearing-in ceremony of the new Chief Justice Satish Chandra Mathur, who had been brought from Allahabad High Court for the post. This appointment had caused some resentment in the local judiciary, particularly S. S. Rizvi, who had been acting as Chief Justice ever since the retirement of the Chief Justice S.S. Keng.

Justice Rizvi's supporters at the Kashmir Bar Association maintained that non-confirmation of the posting was the result of Rizvi's letter to the Chairman of the Law Commission in which he had highlighted the violation of human rights in Kashmir.

At the ceremony, the chief talk was about Hazratbal. The visitors, senior police officers at Raj Bhawan were keen on knowing whether there were any 'top' (militants) inside the shrine. But the Border Security Force (BSF) and senior army officers and even the newly appointed Director General of Jammu and Kashmir Police, Mahendra Nath Sabharwal were conspicuous by their absence. Even Mehmood-ur-Rehman, the additional Chief Secretary (Home), the man who was later to play a crucial role in the whole turn of events was also not there. Neither was Divisional Commissioner Wajahat Habibullah anywhere to be seen. Nor was there any need to ask also where they were.

The Governor Gen. K. V. Krishna Rao[5] looked glum as he administered the oath of office to the new Chief Justice. He seemed to be in an unusual hurry, which was not exactly characteristic of him. He exchanged pleasantries with a few of the civil administration officials present at the function. Speculation was rife. Kuldip Khuda, a young bright IPS Officer, DIG Security, who was a composite of Kashmiri intelligence and the inquisitiveness of a typical cop, came up to me asking, 'Who is in?' The question had more than one meaning. I refused to venture a guess. We were trying to sift truth from chaff. Was it Ahsan Dar,[6] once the most wanted militant of Kashmir? But at that time he was 'commander-in-chief' of Hizbul-Mujahadeen; he had since parted company with the group following a charge that he had swindled Rs. 3 crore from the organizational funds, a point also held against him by the Muslim fundamentalists and those undying faith towards Pakistan was that he was trying to strike a deal with the pro-independence 'Jammu Kashmir Liberation Front' (JKLF). Hizb and the JKLF despite their repeated proclamations of commitment to unity and singleness of purpose in 'forcing Indian occupation forces out of Kashmir ... ,' could never reconcile their ideological differences. The JKLF was convinced that the independence of Kashmir was the only solution as the people of the state detested India and Pakistan in equal measure. Hizb was not convinced. It always believed that the Muslim majority character of Jammu and Kashmir had only one option: to become a part of Pakistan.

Or could it be Syed Salahauddin, whose real name

Mohammad Yousuf Shah, who had succeeded Ahsan Dar at the top position in the Hizb-ul-Mujahadeen? But then the sources close to H.M., the abbreviation of 'Hizb-ul-Mujahadeen' had told me that their chief was not in the Valley. Salahauddin suffered from a number of diseases. Since it was difficult for him to obtain treatment in Kashmir with the entire array of security forces behind him, he had shifted to PoK. Others maintained that he was afraid and was using his ill health as an excuse to move out of the Valley. One could read anything into it.

But the Voice of America, which was little trusted in Kashmir at that time, because its reports which were often more imaginative than factual, revealed that the Mammon brothers were inside the mosque shrine. In fact, it even claimed that the shrine had been cordoned off in order to flush out the Mammon brothers, the principal miscreants of the March 12, 1993, Bombay blasts.

Reporters in Srinagar were summoned to a press conference on Thursday, October 15 by *Ikhwan-ul-Muslimeen* or the Muslim brotherhood, the group which had got into the headlines for a number of sensational abductions including that of President R. Venkataraman's relative, K. Doraiswamy in 1992. They took it to be a routine press meeting but were told from the very outset, that the Tiger Mammon was to hold the press conference. Immediately, the air was electrified. Had Tiger Mammon, who was being sought by the entire Indian police force, surfaced in Srinagar?

But the excitement evaporated, when, instead of Tiger Mammon in person, it was a video recording which was shown to the reporters. He was pleading his innocence.

The day was significant in another way for the police administration in Jammu and Kashmir. The exuberant

Balwinder Singh Bedi, had handed office over to Sabharwal who was now the new state police chief.

Incidentally, it was almost at the time when Bedi was handing over office to Sabharwal, that the latter received a call from Gen. M. A. Zaki's office asking him to make his way there. Gen. Zaki had been re-appointed Advisor (Home) when the police strike was over and the army was given control of all the anti-terrorist operations in Kashmir.

At the Raj Bhawan, itself I was informed that there was a press conference at the Tourist Reception Centre (TRC) at 12.30 p.m. Gen. Zaki was addressing the press conference, some of my colleagues told me. Knowing well the publicity shy nature of the Advisor Home Affairs, I did not attach much credence to it.

Siege of the Hazratbal

Since word about the siege of the shrine had already gone around, the Kashmir press corps which consisted of almost everyone, who was anyone in the Kashmir media, attended the press conference. A statement was circulated justifying the army cordon around the shrine and that it was imperative for the safety of the holy relic and the shrine itself.

To show that the matters were transparent journalists were being invited to the shrine.

The Hazratbal Shrine complex was on fire. Smoke was billowing out of it and we all rushed impulsively forward. We were stopped by Rehman, who wanted to speak to the Brigadier in charge of the operation. The patience of the journalists was wearing thin. Women were wailing audibly. There were over half-a-dozen fire fighters attempting to put out the flames. After a while, we were allowed to move closer to the shrine. The flames which had originated from the southern complex, a two-storey wooden structure painted green, were threatening to engulf the main white marbled mosque.

The lanes and bylanes were smothered in smoke. Practically everyone had fled. A few women were beating their breasts in despair.

Yusuf Jameel, the BBC man in Srinagar had questioned someone who had identified himself as Ghulam Rasool about the events leading to the fire. The man fumbled for words. 'We were herded out of our houses last night and lodged inside the REC (Regional Engineering College) complex. But there was no one in the area except the military' and that had prompted him to conclude that the 'military' had set ablaze the southern portion of the complex. While we were talking to residents, a soldier spotted us and asked us to 'clear out.' Later we received confirmation that, on the night of October 15, the BSF had cordoned off the shrine complex.

The decision to cordon off the shrine had been taken after a meeting of the Unified headquarters, held at the residence of Gen. Zaki. The decision was prompted by the reports that militants had broken open the locks of two doors leading to the safe housing the holy relic. The militants wanted to 'play havoc.' Even before the BSF columns were dispatched to cordon off Hazratbal, as Abdul Aziz, one of the inmates who had spent 32 days in the shrine, later recalled, many militants had already escaped by boat and very few were left within the shrine. Throughout, the inmates were exhorted not to lose courage. 'Allah is on our side.' Reporters were keen to see and talk to the militants inside. Yusuf and two photographers asked Rehman whether they could go inside, Rehman readily agreed but as three of them were about to enter the main complex, a strong voice asked them to step back. It was Brig. S. P .S. Kanwar who was in charge of the operation. Yusuf tried to argue that Rehman had given him permission to move. 'I order you to come back immediately, come back or I will bring you out.' Yusuf reluctantly obeyed. Rehman had no words to pacify the ruffled temper of the army officer. Media men in Kashmir, were in any case, used to the blunt words of men in uniform.

The BSF had been replaced by the army at seven that morning. There were about 110 militants (inside) all of them armed; some of them were foreigners. Brig. Kanwar said that the soldiers were under clear instructions not to enter the shrine complex but, if they believed that there was danger to any part of the possession of the shrine they might do so. But everything depended on how the situation developed and the orders received from their superiors. All this left many questions unanswered. How could the army foretell the dangers it was describing if they did not have intelligence about what was happening inside? We soon found out the answer to this; the shrine was being tapped.

The nightmare vision of the troops storming into the Hazratbal shrine haunted the minds of all Kashmiris. What would be its repercussions throughout the Valley? The prospect of the diplomatic loss of face for India in the Muslim world was inconceivably dreadful to the authorities. But on the other hand, what if the militants themselves tried to harm the shrine and the *Moi-Muqaddas* (holy relic). Everything was possible but every option was dangerous and fraught with catastrophic consequences.

Central Government's Reaction

The Internal Security Minister Rajesh Pilot was in the north-eastern state of Mizoram, when the shrine was cordonned off. He was furious with the Jammu and Kashmir Government for not informing him about it. But given his relationship with the Governor, he could hardly have expected anything else. Gen. Rao had issued clear instructions to his senior officers particularly those holding key positions to cease all communication with the Minister. Gen. Rao, who was very close to Prime Minister P.V. Narasimha Rao always acted independently of the central ministers, and without any consideration for the niceties of the State-Centre relationship. It turned out, later, that Gen. Rao himself had first ordered the BSF and later the army, to cordon off the shrine without informing Delhi. In fact, the Union Home Secretary N. N. Vohra had learned about it through foreign broadcasts, which one of his colleagues had accidentally heard.

The Home Minister S. B. Chavan had been informed by one of his journalist friends in Delhi. He immediately rang up the Home Secretary who confirmed the episode. The telephone lines between Srinagar and Delhi were kept very busy for a long time afterwards. When Chavan asked Gen. Rao why he had undertaken a course of action which was fraught with such far-reaching implications without first informing him, Gen. Rao curtly told the Home Minister that the matter was a local affair and he therefore saw no point in informing him. And to add salt to the wound the Governor said that if he required any assistance, he would speak to the Prime Minister.

The Central Intelligence Agencies began to issue regular bulletins while the news agencies were running one flash after another. The Home Minister was worried about the pace of events unfolding in Srinagar and the Governor's uncompromising stance added to his anger and frustration.

Finally, when the Prime Minister came to know about the episode which was making headlines in the international media he summoned both Chavan and Pilot to review the situation.

He had before him a brief sketch of the events faxed to him by the Governor. It was decided that Gen. Rao be allowed to handle the situation for the time being. He would be recalled, if he failed. To keep an eye on the situation in Srinagar, it was also decided that the Special Secretary (Home) V. K. Jain be sent to Srinagar. Jain's brief was to monitor the situation independently and report directly to the Home Ministry. This agreement was worked out to assuage the hurt feelings of Pilot, who besides being the Minister of State for Home (Internal Security) was also the Minister for Kashmir Affairs. The Prime Minister requested that he remain in Delhi and proceed to Srinagar in the event of need, to supervise the situation and resolve the matters, as he had done, when the police force in Kashmir had revolted following the custodial death of a Jammu and Kashmir police constable.

Preliminary Negotiations

Firemen were now battling the last of the flames. Suri soon decided on something on the spur of moment. Moving close to the shrine complex, he shouted at the holed up militants and other inmates: *Aap Bahar Ao Jayo, Aap Se Hamdardi, Se Salook Kiya Jayaga.* (If you come out you will be dealt with sympathy). He repeated this appeal urging the holed up people to 'come out' and promising them a 'sympathetic deal,' several times before an angry shout from inside the shrine replied, asking Suri 'not to waste time. We will die and not surrender come what may.' When Suri moved towards the complex, guns were pointed towards him. He was only 30 yards away from the main shrine, standing against the backdrop of smoke billowing out of the shrine complex. He went unaccompanied without even his personal security guard, Inder. Undeterred by the discouraging response from the other side, he tried persuasion, 'Look, I am a man from the Kashmir police and I do not have any weapons on my person, listen, why do you want to desecrate the holy shrine?' This time the response was a chorus asking the policeman to do whatever he wanted 'We will not come out.' They also retorted, in a fit of extreme anger, 'Who are you to tell us what to do about our shrine? You tried to burn the shrine and the evidence is before you.' Suri protested, 'You set ablaze the shrine complex, not us.'

The voices from the shrine said, 'We have the proof of who set it ablaze. You please go away. We do not want any sermons from you.'

Suri persisted and asked them to release the innocent pilgrims who had nothing to do with their violent activities. He knew this would further infuriate those with whom he was speaking. The response was shrill, 'You go away.' This was followed by the chanting of slogans; there was a sprinkling of women's voices saying, 'We will live and die with *Mujahadeen"* (holy warriors) 'rather than come out.'

By dusk, six women pilgrims had left the shrine. One of them was carrying as much as Rs. 15,000 in cash. They were too scared by the events of the past 24 hours to say anything. 'We don't know' was the stock reply that they gave to all our questions: how many pilgrims there were inside, how many women and children and so on. They would not even say how many militants there were inside and what weapons they possessed. Such was the litany of 'don't knows' that Brig. Kanwar in exasperation asked his people to 'let them go.'

It was clear that there was no option but to storm into the shrine and flush out the militants. Or to repeat operation Black Thunder which was first enacted in August 1988 to force the Punjab militants to surrender at the Golden Temple in Amritsar. Storming into the shrine implied damage to the main shrine which had remained intact despite the big blaze earlier in the day, which had gutted out the southern section of the shrine complex. The officials were also deeply concerned that, confronted by the sight of the troops storming into the shrine, the holed up militants, might in desperation blow up the entire shrine. That would be simply catastrophic.

If the government had had any doubts on that score these were removed the following morning. Two militant leaders, who came out of the main shrine in response to Suri's calls for talks told him categorically that no talks could be held with the government unless the 'siege' was lifted.' 'And if any attempt is made by troops to enter the shrine complex, it would be blown up. We have laid explosives all over the shrine,' Suri reminded the reporters of the words of militants. 'This can be a serious threat,' Suri concluded.

Enter Wajahat Habibullah

By afternoon, Wajahat Habibullah, a suave and highly polished IAS officer holding the post of Divisional Commissioner, Kashmir, had joined Suri in the negotiations. He appeared on the scene for two reasons. The Governor Gen. K. V. Krishna Rao, wanted these negotiations to be conducted by a Muslim rather than a Hindu officer. Secondly, the militants had specifically asked for Wajahat, by name for future negotiations.

The negotiations were fixed for 3 p.m. TV camera-crews, photographers and reporters had lined up to capture the event. The press was given access because the militants had declined to enter into any talks without the presence of the media. They were keener on having the international press there. It was clear that they wanted to draw maximum mileage, in terms of publicity. The government interpreted it as an act prompted by the Inter Services Intelligence (ISI). It was disclosed that the militants had been in direct communication with Pakistan through a wireless set.

At the end of the talks, what emerged was that the militants would not come out and vacate the shrine until the curfew was lifted from downtown in Srinagar. A group of religious clerics and scholars would be allowed inside the shrine to verify the safety of the relic.

This was a ploy to get away from the shrine without surrendering and handing over arms to authorities by mingling with the crowds. Gen. Rao understood the argument and to him it was becoming clear that it was not the minds of the militants which were at work; there were finer brains behind the planning. The implication was obvious: Pakistan was directing the show.

Gen. Rao conveyed this to the Home Minister S. B. Chavan. On this, he was asked by the North Block to work towards the storming of the shrine. The Home Minister promised all help. Special National Security Guards (NSG) commandos with all the requisite back-up would be made available to the State Government. The Army too favoured this approach. Even the Border Security Force (BSF) offered to finish the whole operation within 35 minutes. Faced with mounting pressure to storm the shrine, Gen. Rao said he would prefer to resign rather than allow the use of force.

That was the end of the matter. The Prime Minister knew that the resignation of Gen. Rao or his recall at that stage would be disastrous for him politically and also dent India's image in the Muslim world. The choices were limited and a wait and watch policy was adopted. Gen. Rao was asked to visit Delhi but he declined. Rao's instructions were that Wajahat should continue talking to the holed up militants and not get provoked even if the militants were to make absurd demands. Suri was asked to remove himself from the scene of negotiations and 'mind his duty of looking after law and order.' Politics was showing its face. The first thing Wajahat did upon getting a free hand was to request for the removal of the press-persons at the platform on the northern side of the shrine complex, just outside the main shrine. 'I don't know how talks can be held with TV cameras watching you all the time,' he pointed out. His argument was simple: whatever the press needed to know would be made available to them at regular press briefings, jointly held by Rehman, and Sabharwal. But with the change in the government strategy and non-acceptance of the demands of militants, the attitude of the holed up militants also hardened. They refused to talk unless the press persons were brought back to the shrine at the time of negotiations.

Promising that he would get a 'fair deal' for the people, Wajahat was able to persuade G. M. Bakshi and Kabir Sheikh, fathers of Shakeel Ahmed Bakshi, the arrested Islamic Students League (ISL) leader, who was later released in June 1994 and Abdul Hamid,[7] leader of JKLF who was later slain to join in the negotiations. However, the involvement of Bakshi and Kabir Sheikh did not yield any dramatic results. But Wajahat did not give up. He wanted to use the private channels of communications as long as it was possible. His persistence with this kind of approach was certainly annoying the government lobby which was pleading and did so strongly, for storming into the shrine. The Governor, however, listened to the Divisional Commissioner, Kashmir, whose soft approach he appreciated. Complications were developing, in other sectors even as the government was trying to grapple with the challenge posed by militants, who had occupied the shrine.

Further Complications

The People's Conference Chairman Abdul Ghani Lone announced on October 18, that he would lead a protest march to Hazratbal to 'liberate the shrine from the siege of Indian troops.' This announcement reflected more than the commitment to 'liberate' the shrine. People's Conference, one of the 24 constituents of the All Parties Hurriyat Conference (APHC) was expected to do what it wanted to do. But Lone's announcement underlined the fact that the battle for leadership supremacy was on in the Hurriyat Conference. On the afternoon of October 19, a procession of about 300 people led by Lone, distinguishable from the others by his tall structure and the Karakulli cap he was wearing, marched ahead from Batmaloo. Although the march involved only a small number of people, it revealed the feeling of many in Kashmir that it would not allow itself to be taken lightly at all. The high-pitched slogan shouting could be heard from a distance. BSF men attempted to stop the procession and were mercilessly beating the marchers with gun butts and *lathis* (*canes*). There was no provocation for such a brutal use of force. The women folk watching from half-opened windows concluded that Lone would be killed. Lone and Nayem Khan, leader of the People's League, were arrested. Tension was rising high on October 22, the first Friday after the 'siege' was laid. Large-scale violent protests were feared. The Government had only one means of restraining potential violence: the imposition of curfew in the Kashmir Valley besides the interior parts of Srinagar city, which had been under curfew since the morning of October 16.

The impression of calm on Friday, was dispelled when the Jamaiti-Islamic leader Syed Ali Shah Geelani, whose party, otherwise guided by Islamic teachings, does not believe much in shrines, announced that protest marches would be undertaken after the afternoon prayers on October 22, to liberate the shrine. 'We cannot tolerate any siege around our shrines. It is direct interference in our religious affairs,' he told pressmen at a hurriedly convened press conference at Hotel Adhoos on the evening of October 21.

Journalists' Dilemma

Even before I was fully awakened by the morning light, I was being repeatedly asked by my colleagues, how I intended to venture out as the city was under curfew. Surinder, whom we affectionately addressed by his nickname 'Lovely'[8] informed me that journalists and photographers at Ahdoos were not being allowed out. The local journalists, most of whom live at Partap Park, were facing a similar dilemma. Throughout all this I kept wondering what I ought to do. It was 9 a.m. when I rang up Yusuf Jameel to find out the latest news. There was no response. I tried Mukhtiar Ahmed, the ABC correspondent's number. No one picked up the receiver at the other end. Now I was dialling Lovely's number; it was constantly busy.

Something was wrong somewhere. And without waiting further, I stepped out. From M.A. Road, I made my way towards Partap Park. At the Poloview crossing, a couple of yards from Ahdoos, BSF men stopped me and asked me to 'go back.' I pleaded that I had to meet someone at Ahdoos. On hearing my destination, they were enraged and ordered me to *Bhagte Nazar Aayo* (disappear).

More than 150 journalists and photographers were on their way to seek curfew passes at Lal Chowk. The administration was adamant. 'It is for your safety that we are doing so,' Wajahat and Suri were telling the journalists, who saw no logic behind this statement. Arguments and counter arguments followed.

Suri asked one of his friends to 'cooperate.' But the journalist retorted: 'It is a matter of my profession. I must be allowed to go wherever I want to.' Others joined in. 'Give us curfew passes or arrest us.'

The situation was definitely getting out of hand. Wireless operators crackled one message after another on the spot of the newly arisen situation. The Governor who was in Raj Bhawan was informed of the journalists' protest. He would brook no argument and simply 'no' to curfew passes for them. 'What is to be done with the journalists?' After prolonged discussions, it was decided that the journalists would be transported in police vehicles. Senior Superintendent of Police (SSP) Srinagar Ram Lubiya was asked to accompany the 'obstinate' journalists.

I had no other option but to monitor the whole turn of events by telephone. At Safakadal, a pitched battle was going on. Stones were being hurled by protestors and the police responded with firing and tear gas. At Dalgate the scene was similar. Khanyar resounded with bullet shots. It was all concentrated on the city. Geelani was arrested when he emerged from the mosque following afternoon prayers. Those who followed him were spared. It was in sharp contrast to what had happened to Lone and others three days before. Come what may, I said to myself, I would go out.

Once again I found myself on Maulana Azad Road; a government vehicle stopped near me. Hamid, driver of Director Information K. L. Dhar[9] was there, asking me to get in. Dhar's was one of few cars permitted to move about on this day. Hamid was on his way to the Tourist Reception Centre; at the TRC we noted a police vehicle following the car. There, Tavleen Singh, a reputed columnist addressed a press conference of her own before the arrival of Rahman and Sabharwal. 'No. I don't think it was stage-managed. It was all spontaneous.' She referred to Safa Kadal where paramilitary policemen had resorted to firing; the incident was the centre of all discussions. No one had any idea as to how many had been killed or injured in this violent incident. For they had moved out of the scene of the action before things worsened.

Escalation of Violence

Scores of people came out on to the streets to demand the lifting of the siege by the army around the shrine. Some of the protestors also pelted stones on the police. The violence intensified when journalists stopped the police vehicles in which they were travelling, to witness the scene for themselves. As photographers rushed to capture the moments of the day, the chanting and shouting became more intense and more and more people—men, women, children came out to join the demonstrators who were already engaged in battle with the police in the narrow streets. The officials said one person had died and several others were wounded. But the reporters did not believe the official version. As I was to about to compile my story for the day, as though guided by instinct, I rang up one of the senior officers. He sounded disturbed. It soon became obvious why. There were extremely alarming reports from Bijbehra, the highway town on the Srinagar-Jammu national highway 46 kms from Srinagar. The day ended with 43 killed, 112 injured, 27 dead and 70 injured from Bijbehra. When I conveyed this to Chandan Mitra,[10] Associate Editor, *HT*, he was too shocked to comment. So the day was over and the Hazratbal crisis snowballed into a bigger issue. And I knew that all the journalists staying in Ahdoos,[11] Grand Hotel and locals in Partap Park were waiting for sunrise of October 23 to ascertain how things had happened in Bijbehra. There was yet another big story for all of us. But at what cost ... I refused to reflect on it for the thought itself was dreadful.

Reporters who had visited Bijbehra in the morning had had a providential escape. The army men would not allow them into town. They were particularly harsh towards Mekhla Deva, a reporter of the *Eyewitness* and her camera crew and foreign journalists. Mekhla was in tears at the kind of filthy and abusive language with which she was greeted by the army officers. Taxis carrying reporters returned with broken window panes and reporters with bruises inflicted by gun butts.

I started my journey to Bijbehra when other journalists were returning, knowing from my experience that by now the fury of the security forces might have subsided. On the outskirts of Bijbehra, army troops stopped my car and asked me to get down. My immediate fears that it was now my turn, were dispelled almost instantaneously as an officer of Major rank greeted me with 'Good afternoon' acknowledging my name and the newspaper I represented. An ambulance carrying two bodies was also there. He showed me the bodies of Javed and Khursheed, who had succumbed to their wounds at a hospital in Srinagar. Neither of them was a militant. One of the relatives of the deceased, a government employee told me how it happened and later on it was corroborated by other witnesses and policemen. On Friday morning October 22, a patrol party of BSF was fired on by militants, one of the *jawans* (troopers) was injured. The BSF men gave chase but the militants had vanished.

A demonstration had been decided on after the afternoon prayers in the main mosque. Militant leaders, though without arms, had demanded that everyone had to join the procession. themselves in the procession demanding the withdrawal of troops from the Hazratbal shrine. Once they were on the highway, the demonstrators marched towards Anantnag. Suddenly, they heard a shot from a distant place. But they ignored it as the chanting *Allah O Akbar* and *Hazratbal Ka Mohasara Tod Do Tod Do"* (Lift siege around Hazratbal) was reaching a crescendo. Then there was a shower of bullets. None knew why. And the final toll of 36 graves and the cremation of a 13-year-old Hindu boy cast a pall of gloom over the town for days to come.

Subsequent magisterial and BSF inquiry found[14] BSF troopers and officials including an Assistant Commandant guilty. All of them were dismissed from the service.

It was Sunday. At the Northern Command headquarters of the Army, the soldiers were partying. But Lt. Gen. Surinder Singh, General officer commanding the Northern Command and Maj. Gen. A. S. Sethi, were incensed by the messages which had been relayed to them from Badami Bagh Cantonment on October 24. Had Gen. Rao gone mad? Their inability to stop what was being done at Hazratbal in contravention to the agreed strategy further exasperated them. The army had cut power and water supply to the Hazratbal shrine to force the militants and other pilgrims out. Lt. Gen. Padmanabhan had earlier declared that he had no mercy to offer to terrorists. 'Our basic task is to save the shrine, maintain its purity and force the terrorists out.'

But Wajahat Habibullah had managed to secure a huge quantity of rice, chicken, mutton preparation, and several boxes of fruit for those holed up inside the shrine. He had overruled objections from the army saying that sending in food was necessary to bring about a solution to the crisis. He had somehow convinced Gen. Rao that sending in food would help resolve matters. The argument was that it would 'soften' the militants and they would come out. The Governor, who did not know anything about the ground realities in Kashmir, allowed Wajahat to do what he wanted. Gen. Rao and Wajahat were close to 10 Janpath. Wajahat did not allow the army to check what was being sent inside. Infuriated over this, the army soldiers directed their anger towards Brig. Kanwar, who in turn rushed to Gen. Padmanabhan. Even Gen. Zaki, Advisor (Home) had been kept in the dark. The media was barred from covering this. Wajahat had ordered the Doordarshan crew not to film the eatables being sent inside and the crew had to stop midway. Maj. Gen. Sethi failed in his attempt to reach Gen. Zaki. He called the Raj Bhawan and left a message questioning the decision of sending 'food to terrorists.' Gen. Rao summoned Wajahat and demanded to know why he had annoyed the army by not allowing them to check what was being sent inside the shrine. Wajahat was able to convince the Governor that he was employing the right tactics to induce the militants to leave the shrine.

Preparations to Storm the Shrine

Next day October 26, Gen. Surinder Singh flew into Srinagar from Udhampur and held an approximately hour-long meeting with Gen. Rao to iron out all thorny issues. The army was to be kept informed of all proceedings; however it again ruled out Wajahat's decision to send food replenishments into the shrine. The Director General of NSG himself came over. Special Secretary Home V.K. Jain, was already in Srinagar. Gen. Padmanabhan, NSG Chief, Brig. Kanwar and Jain were closeted for six hours late in the evening and the plan to storm the shrine was kept ready. Two planeloads of specially trained NSG men were also flown in.

All these preparations and plans were conveyed to the Governor, who took the Divisional Commissioner into his confidence. Wajahat said he should be allowed to pursue his course to its logical conclusion and requested for an additional day's grace. Although the plan was supposed to be kept secret, details kept leaking out. It became clear that the entire plan had been revealed to some of the ministers when the External Affairs

Ministry was told by the US State Department that the Government of India should not repeat the June 1984 mistake, when it had ordered troops to storm the holiest of Sikh shrine Golden Temple in Amritsar. That put an end to the plan to storm the shrine. The leakage of the whole plan to US officials was later traced to a senior official in the Jammu and Kashmir Government. The government was unable to take any disciplinary action against the officer in question as he had strong political connections.

It was beginning to dawn on Gen. Rao that Wajahat would probably not be able to achieve his objective. The Chief Secretary Sheikh Ghulam Rasool, who had not been informed throughout, was now brought into the picture. This was strongly resented by Gen. Zaki and Rehman. Their opposition stemmed from their belief that the Sheikh's appointment as Chief Secretary the previous year, superceding that of Jaitley, Tyabji and Ashok Kumar, would complicate matters. Some of these officers had even gone to the extent of suggesting that the Sheikh was sympathetic to the militants. Wajahat, however, was in favour of giving the Sheikh a role. Until then, he had been considered a man belonging to the Jaitley camp along with the other bureaucrats Tyabji, B.R.Singh and Rehman. This group also had the support of Sushma Chowdhary and Iqbal Khanday in the bureaucracy. The Sheikh experiment began on October 27. A strategy was worked out at Sheikh's Gupkar Road residence.

Hurriyat Leaders Join the Negotiations

Two Hurriyat Conference leaders Prof. Abdul Ghani Bhat and Moulvi Abbas Ansari were prepared to mediate on condition that the Muslim Aquaf Trust (MAT), be allowed to send food inside the shrine.

Accordingly, a court order was obtained and on the afternoon of October 29 the supply of food was resumed. That day, two more people, unable to withstand the hunger had left the shrine. A militant, Meraj-ud-Din, who belonged to the Hizb-ul-Mujahadeen, had fallen sick and was sent to the Police Hospital. Other evacuees included six women pilgrims and a deranged person.

By midnight all media persons were woken up by the report that a solution would soon be at hand. All the senior officials had rushed to Hazratbal, thus confirming that something was imminent. An arrangement had been worked out. The militants would come out. It appeared that a deal had been worked out with the help of the two Hurriyat leaders whose mediation had been authorized by the APHC executive council. Prof. Ghani and Maulna Abbas Ansari had accomplished the mission.

Hope Glimmers and Fades

Things suddenly started looking bright. Wajahat was the hero. His efforts were about to bear fruit. Someone tuned to Voice of America and we heard the statement of Ms. Robin Raphael, US Assistant Secretary of State, South Asia saying that the accession of State of Jammu and Kashmir to India was not legal. This gave rise to speculations that the US would intervene. Yet the crisis had been resolved without the militants landing in custody. They had also probably got an inkling as to how the US had prevented the storming in of the shrine. Prof. Ghani and Moulvi Abbas Ansari, who found her friendly, at their meeting with Ms. Raphael in June 1993, when she visited Kashmir as First Secretary of the US embassy in Delhi, felt that things were now going for them. The officers returned without any success. The drama of the day was over.

On October 30, Prof. Ghani disclosed, at a press conference, that no plan had been worked out for the militants to vacate the shrine. He said that the militants were 'determined not to surrender.' He reiterated that the militants would come out only after the siege was lifted. There were no foreign nationals inside the shrine, he claimed for he was the only leader of Kashmiris, who had been inside. In fact, he was repeating what the inmates inside had been telling the media men at regular intervals, 'We are starving, some of us are sick but we would not surrender to the Indian army. Whatever happens, as a result of our deteriorating condition, the responsibility would be that of the Government of India.' They also sent an appeal for the 'intervention of the international community.' The appeal was especially targetted at the United Nations, US President Bill Clinton, British Premier John Major and Pakistan Premier Benazir Bhutto. The media would report back and the publicity which it engendered, would further complicate matters.

November 2nd was a night full of excitement. I had finished my story for the day. Qaisar, the operator had just finished reading it. I glanced at my wrist- watch. It was 10.00 p.m. The telephone rang. A deal had been worked out and militants were coming out after midnight. I changed the story and waited for the outcome of the deal. The officials reached Hazratbal. Loud prayers were heard from inside the shrine giving rise to the hope that the militants would come out at any moment.

Suddenly, as had happened in the past, the militants appeared with the fresh demand that the army cordon be replaced by Jammu and Kashmir Armed Police personnel. The militants and pilgrims would be screened within the shrine complex and not outside as had been agreed upon. Wajahat pleaded with the militants to stick to their earlier agreement.

He was snubbed. They warned him to comply with their instructions failing which they would remain within the shrine. He informed the adviser Gen. Zaki and army officers of their new demand. They too snubbed him. Wajahat was like a lost man. He had burnt one bridge after another. The meeting he had with the Governor the following day in the presence of Gen. Zaki and Sheikh Ghulam Rasool was a disaster. New formulas were being discussed. The Governor asked Gen. Zaki and Wajahat to meet him at 10 a.m. on November 4.

It was decided that the solution would include partial acceptance of the demands of the militants. Rehman was also present at the meeting. On their return, Zaki offered Wajahat a lift. He made Rehman a similar offer but he said he would be slightly late.

Rehman Resumes Negotiations

At the UN crossing, a few yards away from the residence of Gen. Zaki, a military truck knocked down the car of Gen. Zaki, seriously injuring both him and Wajahat. And the Governor, after visiting the army hospital, called for Rehman and asked him to resume negotiations with the militants. Rehman was the ideal choice as chief negotiator for obvious reasons. First. Rehman, in his capacity as Additional Chief Secretary (Home) knew every detail about the whole affair and the progress that Wajahat had made during his talks with the militants. Moreover, since Rehman had been briefing the press daily about Hazratbal, he was aware of the public's response.

Secondly, as a civil servant who had been in the state service for more than a quarter of a century he was familiar with the psyche of the people of Kashmir. Furthermore, as ACS (Home) he had the means to exploit other factors including the stream of information which he continuously received. But, the Governor certainly had none of these things in mind. Had these factors counted for him, the responsibility would have been assigned to Rehman instead of Wajahat Habibullah from the outset.

Instantly, a section of the media, particularly the local section tried to disparage Rehman and his capacity to play the role that the Governor had assigned to him. The media was doing so at the behest of some of the officials in the state bureaucracy who were opposed to Rehman.

Both Gen. Zaki and Wajahat Habibullah were struggling for their lives. The doctors at the hospital were finding it extremely difficult to handle Wajahat's case.

His wife was grief-stricken. Even while doctors were making determined efforts PTI ran a story saying that Wajahat. Habibullah had been killed in the accident. Later, it had to withdraw the item as Wajahat was shifted to Soura for treatment. The chances of his survival were reported to be slim. By November 5 evening, Gen. M. A. Zaki submitted his resignation. Many thought that Gen. Zaki's resignation was linked to the accident of the previous day. But it was not. The resignation letter had been typed at least two days before the mishap and requested that he be relieved of his responsibilities by December 1. The resignation was the direct outcome of differences in the relationship between Gen. Zaki and the Governor on the Kashmir situation.

The day after the accident, he called his son Capt. Zaki and asked him to bring a particular file from his residence. He signed the already typed resignation letter from his hospital bed and sent it via a special army emissary to the Raj Bhawan. A copy was faxed to the then Union Home Secretary N. N.

Vohra. Days went by and in the meantime, the Supreme Court ordered that the inmates inside the shrine be given 1200 calories of food every day.

Besides this, the SC also allowed doctors to regularly examine the inmates. This reflected the strength of the Indian judiciary, which not only maintained its independence by overruling objections put forward by the State Government that allowing food inside the shrine would prolong the crisis and complicate matters. The SC would have none of it. The talks stalled. The militants stuck to their demands that there should be no TV crew around the shrine when they came out. They asked for some form of guarantee that they would not be handed over to Army custody. There was also dispute over how and when all of them would be released after their arrest. In fact, these were some of the issues that had prevented the resolution of crisis on the night of October 3.

No solution appeared in sight, hopes alternatively rose and fell. On November 10, the Hurriyat Conference suggested that the JKAP be given charge of the entire shrine area and the army be completely withdrawn, with safe passage for all. This was however not acceptable to the authorities. Life in the Kashmir Valley was completely paralysed by these events and the common man was feeling the strain of the situation. The Kashmiris were disillusioned with the Hurriyat Conference whom they felt was unable to play an effective role beyond calling for indefinite general strikes.

They were infuriated with the militants holed up in the shrine and appalled at the sacrifice of lives in Bijbehra and other parts of Kashmir Valley on their behalf. Exasperation was mounting within the government. They felt that while the militants were being given food, to eat, candles for light and medicines for the sick and life was being made generally comfortable for them, they had no reason for leaving the shrine. Earlier, the government had been under the impression that the militants would break down from the strain once they no longer received morale boosting instructions from the outside. That had not happened. For the first few days, their only link had been by telephone. No wireless set was recovered on the day of their evacuation.

Conflict Resolved

Militants mounted another pressure on the government when they refused to take food on November 13 and 14. Nor did they allow any doctors inside. The strategy was clear that a death due to starvation or sickness would force the government to comply with their demands.

The Prime Minister was coming under tremenduous pressure from the international community. He called a meeting of his Home Minister Chavan and his Deputy Rajesh Pilot. The operation was handed over to the intelligence bureau (I.B.) A.P. Bhatnagar, Joint Director and Upadhaya, Deputy Director were asked to do the background work to bring the stalemate that had been causing a dent in Indian's image to an end.

A compromise formula was worked out. The Governor and his administration were kept in the dark until it was finalized and acceptance secured from the militants and the army. Rahman was brought into the picture on November 15 afternoon, when it was stated that the talks had been resumed. According to the terms of the proposal, the militants would come out in the presence of some local leaders. Secondly, they would hand themselves over to the local police and not to the army nor to the BSF or the CRPF or any other central police force as they were apprehensive that they would be eliminated by these forces. All innocent pilgrims were to be released within 48 hours of their arrest. Others would be screened and released within a week's time. The militants on their part were to lay down arms and would not object to the presence of the TV crews though the rest of the media would not be allowed at this stage. Two well-known locals G. M. Daga and G. M. Bakshi were brought to Rehman's residence. They were informed about the agreement and asked to be witnesses. They were taken to Hazratbal shrine where both sides read the agreements and the two stood as witness.

A hiccup developed at the last minute. What of the two PoK nationals? They did not form part of the agreement. After deliberations and frantic calls to Delhi, it was decided that they would be returned to PoK.

The process for the vacation of the shrine had started. The first batch of 35 came out at 2.45 a.m., the second, of 25, an hour later and ten minutes after that, Idnis and Umar also vacated the shrine. The thirty-two-day-long drama was finally over.

Endnotes

1. Dr. Abdul Ahad Guru, a famous cardiologist in Kashmir, considered to be a think- tank of JKLF.He was kidnapped and executed by suspected militants of Hizb-ul-Mujahadeen.

2. These questions were asked by reporters at a press conference at which the author was present in May 1991 on the eve of the first death anniversary of his father.

3. Hazratbal is a revered Muslim shrine. This shrine houses a holy relic hair of Prophet Muhammad.

4. STD-Straight Trunk Dialling

5. Gen. K. V. Krishna Rao. Former Chief of Staff of the Indian Army who served twice as Governor of Jammu and Kashmir from July 1989 to January 1990 and March 1993 to May 1998.

6. Ahsan Dar, first chief of the Hizb-ul-Mujahadeen, who later parted ways and formed his own group Muslim Mujahadeen.

7. Abdul Hamid, a JKLF leader.

8. Lovely is the nickname of Surinder Singh Oberoi, who worked for AFP and later Star News and currently with ICRC.

9. K. L. Dhar, a senior officer who retired as Director Information, the head of the Government's press and publicity department.

10. Chandan Mitra, a senior journalist in India, who is now editor of the Delhi-based English daily *Pioneer* and also a member of Rajya Sabha, the Upper House of the Indian Parliament.

11. Ahdoos Hotel, a modest hotel famous for its delicacies in the heart of Srinagar city on Residency Road.

12

Rise and Fall of the Kashmir Separatists

JKLF 1994: Yasin's Release

Mohd.Yasin Malik's release on May 17 on bail orders of the Supreme Court of India and his subsequent arrival in Srinagar the next day marked yet another phase in the ongoing militancy in Kashmir.

His release had come at a time when his group the Jammu Kashmir Liberation Front (JKLF) was almost entirely decimated and had no strike power left. For fear of reprisal from pro-Pakistan groups, even its long-term supporters had either deserted the group or maintained a discreet distance. The JKLF was no longer seen as a protectorate of its supporters because its very own top militants were afraid of taking on its pro-Pakistan adversaries.

Yasin was back. A reception of sorts was organized. The security forces did not, rather surprisingly interfere with the several hundred JKLF supporters who had assembled, although there was a blanket ban on processions. This change in tactics on the part of security forces was attributed to the Government of India's directive not to create any unpleasant situation which would offset the gains that had brought down the level of support for militants especially after their surrender at the Hazratbal shrine.

These directives were implemented despite repeated attempts on the part of Governor Rao, to stall the entry of Yasin into Kashmir. He telephoned Vohra, at least twice on May 17 requesting that he retain the JKLF leader in Delhi for a few more days. These requests were turned down.

Governor Rao was always reluctant to talk to anyone apart from the Prime Minister. He had a rather offhand attitude towards important functionaries in the Government of India; he had once kept the Indian Home Minister S. B. Chavan waiting for over 20 minutes before receiving him.

Yasin arrived. It seemed, at first that there would not be much fanfare. These assumptions were soon proved wrong. A cavalcade of vehicles with Yasin Malik's car at the head made its way towards Idgah, a large terrain between the bridges of Navakadal and Safakadal, two downtown districts in the capital city of Srinagar, where *Id* (Muslim festival) prayers are offered by Kashmiris. The Parks of Idgah have been converted into *Maazar-e-Shauda* (Martyrs' graveyard) where leading separatists killed in encounters with the security forces are laid to rest. On reaching Idgah, Yasin paid homage to the 'martyrs.'

He broke down at the sight of the graves of two of his most cherished colleagues, Ashfaq Majid Wani and Hamid Sheikh, both of whom had been killed in encounters with the security forces. The crowd of some 4000 people who had turned up at Idgah to hear him were disappointed when he did not address them.

Testing the Ground for Revival of the Political Process

His release was, in itself, a matter of controversy. Ostensibly, a prominent human rights activist, Rajinder Sacchar had moved a petition in the Supreme Court citing Yasin's 'deteriorating health' as ground for his release. But things were not as simple as they were made to appear.

The man accused of the murder of five Indian Air Force (IAF) officers at Rawalpora on the outskirts of Srinagar could not have been set free so easily. The CBI had a very strong case against him and had things been allowed to move to their logical conclusion, Yasin would not have escaped the gallows.

But the Government of India had something else in mind. Its intention was to test the ground for the revival of the political process in Kashmir, for the second time round. Its first attempt to set free the five leaders: Syed Ali Shah Geelani of Jamait-i-Islami, Abdul Ghani Lone of People's Conference, Moulvi Abbas Ansari, former convenor of the Muslim United Front (MUF), Prof. Abdul Ghani of the Muslim Conference and Qazi Nissar Ahmed, also a leader of the erstwhile MUF in April 1992 had failed. Qazi Nissar was assassinated on June 20, 1994. His supporters believed that it was the Hizb that had killed him. Qazi had been summoned from his house and taken to a village where he was shot dead. Early next morning his body was found. His death sparked off massive anti-Pakistan and anti-Hizb demonstrations. This in itself was a signal of how times had changed. Throughout my childhood years and afterwards, only pro-Pakistan slogans were to be heard in the streets of Anantnag. People had always known the truth behind each and every assassination in Kashmir. The difference was that they were now voicing it publicly.

Yasin himself denied that he had been released to stir up political activity in Kashmir. He pointedly poured scorn on the Indian newspapers, some of which had described him as the 'Future Chief Minister of J&K.' But Kashmiris no longer accepted his disclaimers at face value in the way they had accepted the repudiations of the five erstwhile MUF leaders. They had learnt to be deeply suspicious of their leaders, a legacy of Sheikh Mohammad Abdullah. They knew that their actions rarely matched their words, especially when they were out of sight, beyond Kashmir.

Yasin Adopts Gandhi's Tactics

Yasin Malik would be entering the Hazratbal shrine. This was the clarion call which reached all journalists at about 8 p.m. on July 28, 1994. Since Hazratbal had become such an emotive issue, anything happening there was bound to make headlines in the newspapers, so we, the scribes could not resist the temptation to be there. The Jammu Kashmir Liberation Front (JKLF) the organization of which Yasin was the head, had even arranged a minibus for the journalists. Yasin himself was in a taxi accompanied by Shakeel Ahmed Bakshi, chief patron of Islamic Students League or the ISL.

The government, it would seem, had no inkling of the plan of the two separatist leaders. The journalists were anticipating a big story and were speculating about possible leads. Their thoughts were interrupted by a shower of bullets.[1] Two of the bullets hit their vehicle and all of them, 20 in all, jumped out and hugged the ground. There was a hushed silence pierced by the sound of bullets. One of the daredevil cameramen did not miss the opportunity of capturing the moment. But Yasin had moved way ahead of us. By the time we recovered and resumed our journey towards the shrine in pitch darkness, there was another rain of bullets. This time we decided to take shelter in the Jammu and Kashmir Armed Police (JKAP) manned bunker. Ironically, Yasin was on his way to undertake a hunger strike to pressurize the government into removing the bunkers from Hazratbal.

Separatists' Response to the Hazratbal Siege

The bunkers around the Hazratbal were manned by either the Border Security Force (BSF) or by the JKAP. When the bunkers were first erected on November 17, 1993, they had been entrusted to the BSF. But in January 1994, five bunkers were handed over to the JKAP, as part of a unilateral move to soften the attitude of the All Parties Hurriyat Conference (APHC) which had called for the removal of the bunkers. The APHC had requested the Muslim Aquaf Trust (MAT) not to take charge of the shrine nor identify the holy relic, a hair of Prophet Muhammad, until the bunkers had been completely pulled out. In response to the Hurriyat call, even the devout had not been visiting the shrine. No prayers had been offered at the shrine throughout these months.

On July 5, the Harkat-ul-Ansar,[2] a group of foreign militants threatened to disrupt the annual Hindu pilgrimage of Amarnath, if the government did not lift the bunkers from Hazratbal by August 4 noon. It claimed that it had been compelled to 'ban' the Amarnath Yatra, in retaliation for the maintenance of the bunkers around the Hazratbal shrine, as this was offensive to the Muslims. The threat was instantly supported by various pro-Pakistan groups, particularly 'Hizb-ul-Mujahadeen,' 'Jamait-ul-Mujahadeen,'[3] 'Al-Umar-Mujahadeen,' 'Al-Jehad,' 'Hizbullah,' 'Allah Tigers,' 'Jehad Force.'

The people in Kashmir were appalled by this turn of events. While there was profound objection to the presence of bunkers, around the shrine the call to ban the Amarnath yatra appeared utterly disproportionate. Kashmiris, who are known for their religious tolerance, silently condemned the proposed 'ban.' They were even more outraged when they learnt that even the APHC had come out in support of the ban. People understood then that extremists were calling the shots and that the voice of the moderates had been stifled.

It was in October-November 1993, that the Hurriyat had first called for indefinite Valley-wide strikes on the issue of the 'siege.' Then it had formed, what it called death squads to liberate the Hazratbal shrine on December 7, 1993. However, the government had arrested the top Hurriyat leaders when they came out of Mirwaiz Manzil, headquarters of the Awami Action Committee, one of the prominent constituents of the Hurriyat Conference.

Then, the wait began for the *Meraj-ul-Alam*, (the day when the Prophet joined Allah) which fell on January 11, 1994. The government was completely unnerved by reports that the shrine would be stormed and the bunkers torn down by the thousands of demonstrators who were expected on the streets. Negotiations were hurriedly resumed with the All Parties Hurriyat Conference and also with the Muslim Aquaf Trust (MAT);[4] the shrine was declared open for prayers. As a gesture the government offered to replace the BSF at four of the 11 bunkers. But the Hurriyat was uncompromising and called instead for a complete shutdown to protest against the Government's refusal to lift the bunkers. The strike was carried out throughout Kashmir. Both the government and the Hurriyat Conference kept the deadlock unresolved waiting for the occasion when both sides would be pushed to end the impasse. 'Jamait-ul-Mujahadeen,' a strong militant group that had been responsible for several killings, announced on March 20 that it would launch a violent campaign if the 'siege' around the Hazratbal shrine were not lifted. It was true to its word. Several government offices and vehicles were burnt. So great was the fear, that government officers abandoned the use of their official vehicles, hiring private taxis for official purposes.

Governor Rao had adamantly turned down any suggestion of removing the bunkers from the shrine. 'Unless they (MAT) give in writing that they would not allow the use of the shrine for other than religious purposes, the bunkers would stay in place,' he told his adviser D. D. Saklani who was considered to be a moderate and in favour of the lifting of the bunkers.

So it seemed that the bunkers would continue to be at Hazratbal as long as Rao was the Governor of Jammu and Kashmir. The Union Home Minister S. B. Chavan, took the same stand as Gen. Rao.

The announcement made on July 5 stated that a 'ban' would be imposed on the pilgrimage because the 'siege' was continuing at Hazratbal shrine.

The day arrived when the government finally lifted the bunkers and the Muslim Aquaf Trust took over the management of the shrine without giving any of the guarantees that the Governor had sought. What occurred on August 6, 1994, was preceded by a rapid succession of events which left the government with no option but to order the removal of the bunkers, almost unconditionally.

When Yasin Malik was arrested on the evening of July 28, and released and hospitalized on July 30, it was assumed that, that would be the end of the matter and every thing would remain unchanged at the Hazratbal shrine. The government was in no mood to 'surrender' to the threat of 'Harkart-ul-Ansar.' With Yasin Malik on hunger strike, and in hospital, the government thought that matters would not get out of hand and the All Parties Hurriyat Conference (APHC) or others would be able to persuade Yasin to end the hunger strike. But these calculations proved to be greviously wrong as was revealed in the coming days. Yasin moved out of the hospital, refusing all forms of medication including the life saving drugs which he needed following a bypass surgery that he had undergone during his four-year detention. He was a chronic heart patient. The logic behind his indefinite hunger strike was to use peaceful means to force the government to succumb. It sounded odd, absurd and ironic that the young man, who was among the first to have introduced gun culture into Kashmir in 1988 should now talk of adopting a Gandhian way to achieve his ends. The pro-Pakistan groups mocked at his transformation, some criticized him, others even came out with veiled threats, few were indifferent to it. One after another, pro-Pakistan groups like 'Harkat-ul-Ansar,' 'Hizbul-ul-Mujahadeen,' 'Jamait-ul-Mujahadeen,' and 'Al-Umar-Mujahadeen,'[5] questioned Yasin's unilateral decision to go on a hunger strike. These groups specifically stated that non-violent means would not help resolve matters. 'Force needs to be met with force.' That was the argument in favour of their own strategy. 'Gandhian' ways were prohibited in Kashmir. Such means were meant to 'undermine our armed struggle and innumerable sacrifices.'

The JKLF chief did not react to the charges and threats. He went ahead with his hunger strike. He moved back to his house from the SMHS hospital and continued with his hunger strike on July 30. In the evening, however, he made up his mind to re-enter the Hazratbal shrine. He agreed to the pleas of the authorities and others to move to the medical institute, Soura. He boarded the ambulance specially arranged for him. When the ambulance rolled on to Maulana Azad Road on its way to Soura institute, SSP Srinagar, Ram Lubiya, informed his superiors that Yasin had gone to Soura. Rajinder Tickoo I. G. P. Kashmir tapped his forehead despairingly when the message from Hazratbal came, only minutes after the SSP's flash, that Yasin Malik had re-entered the shrine. Panic gripped the entire administration. The decision to re-arrest Yasin was taken around midnight at the residence of Gen. Zaki. The telephone calls from Delhi were keeping Zaki, Rehman, Sabharwal and Aivelli awake. What is to be done and how it is to be done, were the questions being repeatedly asked.

The dawn of July 31 opened with the rumour that Yasin had died. Zaki summoned all senior officers, trying to ascertain the truth. The Governor was in Leh. The Army was put on the alert. The BSF and CRPF contingents began patrolling the streets. The North Block mandarins were informed of the unconfirmed report. Two hours later, the government was able to confirm that Yasin was alive, but critically ill. That was a solace. The JKAP men were asked to bodily lift the ailing JKLF President and have him moved to Soura. At Soura, again, Yasin would refuse to consume anything. His condition further deteriorated and the Soura Medical Institute superintendent Dr. Allaqaband became extremely worried. He suggested that the militant leader be shifted to the All India Institute of Medical Sciences (AIIMS) where he might obtain better treatment as the doctors there were well-acquainted with his case, having treated him throughout his detention.

This suggestion of the doctors at Soura, was something like a God-sent gift for the Union Home Ministry. Prime Minister P. V. Narasimha Rao had entrusted the case to Rajesh Pilot. Pilot and his men insisted on Yasin's transfer to Delhi. When the doctor's recommendation came, a special Border Security Force aircraft, was sent from Delhi and on July 31, evening, Yasin was in Delhi.

Pilot's brief was simple—make Yasin end the fast and announce the removal of the bunkers around the Hazratbal shrine. The two leading human rights activists of India, Kuldip Nayar, Chairman of Citizens for Democracy and Justice Rajinder Sachar, President of Peoples Union of Civil Liberties (PUCL) were asked to step in. The duo had helped the government out of a similar crisis, when Yasin and his colleagues had gone on an indefinite hunger strike in jail in January 1993 to demand that the people of Jammu and Kashmir be consulted on any dialogue on Kashmir.

The Nayar Sachar team obtained a statement from the government to approve the 'shift and relocation of bunkers.'

Yasin however, promptly insisted that there was 'no question of bunkers getting relocated. Those will be removed. That is the categorical assurance I have been conveyed.' And he accepted a glass of apple juice and broke his six-day-long fast on August 2 afternoon.

Discrediting the JKLF

The government's assurance which the JKLF interpreted as its victory, however, raised several doubts about the whole thing. It was purported that everything had been stage- managed by the government to create fissures among the various militant groups. JKLF was given credit for having worked for the removal of the bunkers. But if the government had wanted to give credit to the JKLF, it failed in its objective. The JKLF neither obtained any credit nor did it retain the credibility of the masses.

Instead, it came to be seen as an extension of the Government of India. Moreover, the JKLF had also lost its platform at Hazratbal as future events revealed. Amidst all this, the attitude of the pro-Pakistan groups, particularly that of 'Harkat-ul-Ansar,' had hardened. For it, the simple removal of bunkers cordoning off the Hazratbal shrine was not sufficient exchange for calling-off the threat to disrupt the Hindu pilgrimage of Amarnath. It wanted the government to remove troops from and around all mosques, Muslim shrines and educational institutions. The dilapidated mosques and Muslim shrines were to be renovated and opened for Muslims. The Indian Home Minister had to undertake that there would be no interference in the religious affairs of Muslims. The deadline for the fulfilment of these conditions was set at 12 noon on August 4. All the major pro-Pakistan groups reiterated their support for Harkat.

The All Parties Hurriyat Conference, while supporting the

pro-Pakistan groups had denounced the JKLF describing Yasin's hunger strike as 'un-Islamic.' But, when the government started negotiations with the Aquaf Trust on the removal of bunkers, the APHC guided the Trust from behind the scenes.

On August 5 evening everything was finalized. The MAT announced that it would take over the management of the shrine as the government had agreed to 'unconditional and complete' withdrawal of bunkers from around the shrine. The Governor duly issued a statement confirming the government's decision to remove the bunkers.

The statement read: 'It is a matter of great happiness that by the grace of Almighty and the support of the people and blessings of elders, the *deedar* of the holy relic will be organized at the Hazratbal shrine and prayers would be offered by the devotees as usual.'

Next morning at 6 a.m., Gen. M. A. Zaki who was again appointed advisor, was at the Hazratbal shrine. The bunkers had disappeared. Rehman and Sabharwal and Additional Director General of Police (CID), Mr. Veerena Aivelli, the trio that had brought about the resolution of the crisis by prolonged negotiations with the MAT, were also there. Even when everything was settled, the authorities were apprehensive as the MAT representatives had not appeared on the scene at the scheduled hour. And when they came, instead of heading straight to the shrine, they moved into a house and started deliberating with the authorities; it seemed as if the MAT and Hurriyat Conference leaders were trying to delay the takeover on instructions from Pakistan.

But all doubts evaporated as Prof. Abdul Ghani, a prominent leader and spokesman of the APHC along with Qazi Ahadullah, Yaquob Vakil, and MAT members emerged from the house and walked towards the shrine with the shouts of *Allah O Akbar* and "we want freedom.' 'This is the victory of people,' Prof. Ghani told the gathering. He said the 'resolution of the Hazratbal crisis after the government had renounced its intransigent stance goes to prove that it does not pay to be obdurate."It suggested that means should be devised to resolve the Kashmir crisis in a similar fashion by involving all the concerned parties—India, Pakistan and Kashmiris. His words were accompanied by an appeal to Harkat to 'lift the ban on the Amarnath pilgrimage to demonstrate the rich Kashmiri traditions of religious tolerance.' But the advice was not heeded.

However the Amarnath pilgrimage was over as the State government, with the active cooperation of the Army, para-military police force and the police had managed a successful *yatra*—the turnout of 45,000 pilgrims was a respectable figure. But this was not the end of the matter. A single brick does not make up an entire building.

Shabir Shah: People's League

The same year on September 14, Shabir Shah of the People's League was released after five years in jail. He was given a rousing reception. He was set free from Jammu's central jail and his supporters greeted him with the chant: 'We want freedom.' He made his way to Doda and travelled on to Srinagar. Crowds waited for him at Lal Chowk, Srinagar, well past midnight. The man who had promised to knit everyone with his 'needle and thread' was the idol of the moment. He was persuaded to join the Hurriyat Conference which he did, only to part from it two years later. 'Shah Shah Badshah' had lost his shine. He was simultaneously a subject of envy and ridicule. He is the only separatist who has well-wishers in all the three regions of the State and that may be what would make something of him in future, though at the moment he is on the road to nowhere.

Charar-E-Sharief: Fuelling Hostility towards the Separatists

It was March 1995. The Indian intelligence agencies had discovered the presence of more than a 100 militants in Charar-e-Sharief town in Budgam district. The town is famous for the shrine of Sheikh-Noor-ud-Din Noorani who preached Hindu-Muslim brotherhood. His message of peace and brotherhood has been expressed in folklores in the Kashmir Valley by people of all religions. The intelligence agencies suspected that a Pakistani militant Mast Gul,[6] a tall man with a flowing beard, was trying to replicate the Hazratbal incident there. The town was cordoned off by the BSF; it was suggested that the army would be able to do a better job. This left a sour taste in the mouth of BSF officers who started leaking each and every strategy of the army to a newspaper. The militants on being informed of the plans of the army, adopted a counter strategy.

Mast Gul and his men had such a grip over the town that the army had to beseech him on their wireless sets to allow their men to pass with the promise that it would not target the militants. The army kept its word. It showed exemplary inaction even when the militants razed the entire town on May 9, 1995. Two days later they burnt the shrine and fled the scene. The Corps Commander 15 Corps said that the army was there neither to protect the shrine nor to arrest the militants. What was it doing there then for two months, in siege mode? It had no answers.

The burning of the shrine brought an open outcry against the Hurriyat leaders. Hurriyat leaders who attempted to visit the blazing town, were rough-handled by its residents. Shah and Lone were greeted with go-back slogans. It was much in the same way that the Hurriyat leaders had been hounded out of Anantnag when they went to offer their condolences on the death of Qazi Nissar, a year earlier.

The burning of the Charar-e-Sharief shrine, when there were hundreds of soldiers guarding the township on all sides, was a shame for the Indian army. When the shrine was burnt and Mast Gul, the man whom India blamed for the heinous act, escaped, the army generals said: 'We were not there to save the shrine or to prevent the escape of militants.' They had no reply to the question: What was the army there for?

Kukka Parray: Militant Recreant

Pankaj Pachuri, who is now with NDTV India, had come from London to do a series of stories on Kashmir in the aftermath of the burning down of Charar-e-Sharief in Budgam district in May 1995. He stayed with me. We were on our way to Hajjan to meet Kukka Parray[7] who was called father of counter-insurgency for he had stood rock-like against the onslaught of pro-Pakistan militant outfits. He had initially joined the militancy but soon turned his back on it. Eventually, he made so much money that he was able to maintain a cadre of personal supporters. His writ ran firm. Kukka Parray, who was then operating under the code name of Jamshed Shrizai, had turned against the militancy after the Hizb-ul-Mujahadeen militants had gunned down seven of his villagers. He was aghast and unable to face his villagers who wondered why he remained in the militancy when his own people were being killed.

I overheard his supporters talking among themselves which showed how things had started changing in this part of Kashmir. 'The Hizb men say that the army burnt Charar-e-Sharief shrine, we don't believe that. We know Hizb doesn't believe in shrines. They burnt it and blamed it on the Indian army. I knew for certain that this group of armed young men did not know that I understood Kashmiri, the language in which they were conversing.

We returned disappointed because we could not see Kukka Parray. A month later, I met Kukka Parray at the height of the crisis involving the captivity of five foreigners by Al-Faran.[8] Two of the journalists had been kidnapped by Kukka's men for not publishing articles about his group Ikwan-ul-Musilomoon. Kukka Parray arrogantly took the entire press corps in Kashmir to account. 'You people don't write even a word about us, while you fill column after column with the utterances of those killers because you fear their guns. I will show you that I can also use my guns.'

Kukka Parray knew how to get things done. Manzoor Anjum, who edited *Uqab*, had requested (and we were with him in this) Kukka Parray for the release of two of our colleagues held hostage by him. 'You leave it to me, whether I kill or spare them,' his words were ruthless. When one of us tried to argue, Javed Shah ordered him to keep quiet. The colleagues were released two days later. But in the same year there was an attack on Yusuf Jameel of BBC now with *Asian Age*. The parcel bomb was delivered for him, but Mushtaq Ali who opened it, was killed instead. Towards the end of December, Zafar Meraj was waylaid and injured critically. He survived. All these attacks were attributed to Kukka Parray's men, though he himself denied his role in these incidents.

Kukka Parray had actively started working for the army. The army was using him not only to neutralize the militant outfits with pro-Pakistan leanings but also settling its own scores with the media. Kukka Parray had his own men and women in the media who projected him as the saviour of the people of Kashmir and built a larger than life image of him.

Second Hazratbal Crisis

It was on March 24, 1996 at about 11.30 a.m. An armed group of

JKLF militants (Amanullah faction) led by their self-styled Commander in Chief, Basharat Raza, had tried to force entry into the Hazratbal Shrine. This was resisted by the Jammu and Kashmir Armed Police guards. There was an exchange of fire in which nine militants including Basharat Raza and self-styled Military Advisor Code name Nik Boi were killed. A Sub-Inspector, an ASI (Assistant Sub-Inspector) and three Constables of the JKAP Guard also received bullet injuries; the Sub-Inspector did not survive his wounds. In the melée that followed, a number of armed JKLF militants managed to rush inside the premises of the Shrine premises. Officers from the Hazratbal area later apprehended five JKLF militants from whom a number of AK rifles, one UMG, seven grenades and a telephone were recovered. Immediately after the exchange of fire, Senior Police and (Security force) officers including the Additional Director General of Law and Order, Inspector General of Police Kashmir, Inspector General of Border Security Force reached the spot and started attempts to persuade the militants to vacate the shrine. This was effected on March 25, 1996. Soon after their arrival in Srinagar, the Advisor (Home) and DG visited the shrine. The JKLF militants had timed the attack to create problems for the Government of India and the State as Jammu and Kashmir was approaching its first parliamentary elections, after the November 1989 elections. It was generally believed that Pakistan had played a role in planning this crisis. The JKLF leader Shabir Siddiqui is reported to have drawn Rs three crores from a bank in New Delhi. The amount was purportedly transferred into the bank by some conduits working for Pakistan's interservice intelligence. It was immediately after his return to Srinagar that the second operation to capture the shrine was made. The first such attempt was made in October 1993 and it had lasted for over a month ending with the surrender of the militants. For Pakistan, creating a fresh crisis could have served two purposes.

It could have disrupted elections and simultaneously create a crisis of a wider magnitude.

The authorities first made the attempt to resolve the crisis through negotiations. The help of a number of eminent residents of Hazratbal was enlisted. Others also volunteered their help. They tried to persuade the militants to vacate the shrine. On the evening of March 25, the latter announced through the public address system that the holy relic was in their possession. Accordingly plans were made to smoke them out. The National Security Guard (NSG) was requisitioned for the purpose. The NSG contingent arrived at Srinagar during the night of March 25/26 and operations were to be launched on March 26/27.

On March 26, efforts to persuade the JKLF activists to vacate the shrine continued. Eight dead bodies including that of Nissar Ahmad Bhat @ Basharat Raza, Commander-in-Chief were removed from the shrine premises. The Police secured the shrine with the help of the Muslim Auqaf Trust (MAT) and on joint inspection of the Shrine premises by the police and MAT the locks for the outer gate of the vault containing the Holy Relic were found to have been tampered with. An attempt had also been made to force open the safe whose handle had been broken by the militants indicating possibly their intention to destroy the relic. The safe was, however, locked and on joint inspection together with the special committee of residents of Hazratbal, at the premises of MAT, the Holy Relic was found to be safe and secure. The safe was re-sealed by the MAT. The shrine was cleaned after its vacation on March 27 and prayers were resumed the day after that. However, JKLF activists led by Masood Alam, who had succeeded Basharat Raza as Commander-in-Chief continued attempts to draw sympathy for their outfit. At the same time, they sought to threaten the Muslim Auqaf Trust and the men who had assisted in the negotiations to vacate the Shrine.

As a result, Auqaf advised devotees not to visit the shrine. On March 29/30 the police cordoned off the building occupied by the JKLF militants. The militants were directed to come out and lay down their weapons. Three militants surrendered in response to the call. In addition, three women and two children also came out of the building. At that point, the militants started firing from the house. Twenty-four people were killed in the exchange which followed including Shabir Sidiqi (President JKLF). And so ended the second Hazratbal crisis even as Kashmir took the first tentative steps towards democracy.

Endnotes

1. The Hizb men were suspected of attacking the reporters for they suspected that JKLF loyalists of Yasin Malik were in the mini-bus.

2. In July 1994, the HUA (Harkat-ul-Ansar) threatened to disrupt the Himalayan Hindu pilgrimage to Amarnath, the cave shrine of Lord Shiva if the bunkers manned by BSF around the shrine complex were not lifted.

3. JuM is Jamait-ul-Mujahadeen, a strong fundamentalist group. It also joined HUA in threatening to disrupt the Amarnath pilgrimage on the same issue.

4. MAT-Muslim Aquaf Trust, the body managing the affairs of Muslim shrines in the Valley. MAT refused to take responsibility for the shrine even when the army had lifted its siege on November 15, 1993 and the militants had left the shrine. The Hurriyat Conference together with other militant groups told MAT not to act until the BSF bunkers were also removed.

5. Al-Umar Mujahadeen, a Srinagar-based terrorist group known for its ruthless killings. Its chief Mushtaq Ahmad Zargar was set free from Srinagar jail and transported to Kandahar in Afghanistan along with Maulna Masood Azhar, now the founder of the Jaish-e-Mohammad, a formidable terrorist group, in exchange for the passengers of an Indian airliner IC 814 in December 1999.

6. Mast Gul, a Pakistani militant who had camped in Charar-e-Sharief and is blamed by India for the burning down of Charar-e-Sharief town and the shrine of Sufi saint Sheikh Noor-ud-Din Noorani.

7. Kukka Parray-A militant turned counter-insurgent. He was assassinated in September 2003 by Jaish-e-Mohammad men.

8. Al-Faran-A front of HUA-Harkat-ul-Ansar that appeared in the limelight for abducting five foreigners all of whom were executed in captivity.

Part V

13

Kashmir's Second Dalliance with Democracy

The flames of secessionism were leaping high. Violence was taking its toll. India was losing its grip over Kashmir day by day even though hundreds of troops were being poured in almost daily. After the Hazratbal episode people's attention was once more directed to their day-to-day problems.

They found the regime of the advisors under President's rule (Jammu and Kashmir is the only state in India that is brought under Governor's rule for the first six months of Central rule, thereafter, it becomes the President's rule with the approval of the Indian parliament) in the state corrupt and indifferent. The advisors had denied all access to the people. The common man did not have any recourse to address his daily grievanaces.

The militants were still *mujahadeen* for many, despite their having committed unspeakable atrocities on the people of Kashmir for whom they were supposed to be fighting. There were countless untold stories of the rape of young girls, looting and coercion. They were thieves in the real sense. The halo of their being freedom fighters was fading but the fear which they inspired was palpable.

I remember a night at Watlab, an enchantingly beautiful place close to Wullar lake, the largest fresh water lake in Asia. Its beauty is mesmerizing. I had been on a visit to the shrine of Baba Shukur-ud-Din, a shrine built in the memory of a Kashmiri saint whose love for humanity was immense and the magical effect of his message for peace, harmony and communal brotherhood had made a vast impact on the people of the area.

I was taken there by a journalist friend. Our host was a businessman. He sounded a disappointed man. What he told us was astonishing. 'Let things turn in favour of the security forces, I will not give even four days to these thieves (militants).' It was a revelation, I had heard stories of how the militants were forcing their entry into the homes of the people, demanding food, shelter and even girls. Hundreds of stories of intimidation and harassment were floating around. This was something which gave me an insight into the minds of the people who were being harassed by militants day in and day out. They wanted to get rid of this cult of violence that had enchained their thoughts and their freedom of expression.

Kashmir was in the grip of terror. The security forces were no friends of the people either. They were burning them alive. The stories of their torture only fuelled the anger and frustration of the masses and made them irreparably hostile to India. The situation was worsening.

The two sides of the conflict rejoiced over their successes and shocked at their losses, which were relayed with great exaggeration to the media. The number of militants killed was a thing of joy for the security forces and each of their press notes would begin with: 'a major success was achieved when security forces killed this number of militants....' That meant a time of mourning for the militants. But the armed rebels also had their moments of success. They would kill people and claim responsibility. For them anyone whose killing could make news was good, no matter even if that happened to be the aged and infirm like Moulana Masoodi, a close associate of Sheikh Abdullah. He was shot dead in his bed in Ganderbal on December 13, 1990.

Politicians were getting restless. It was the fear of the gun that was keeping them out of business but that was no dampener to their aspirations. They were watching with acute helplessness the way the Governor and his advisors were revelling in power. A high degree of frustration and desperation was also creeping in. All sorts of politicians believe that power prevents guns and bullets from reaching them because of the security that comes with power. Vulnerability was equated with the lack of power.

In Kashmir where political workers were dying by the dozen every month, political leaders who were enjoying power and those aspiring to be in power were devising their own ways to stay on course. A number of proposals were being floated to restore power to the politicians. One of these was to revive the dissolved Legislative Assembly, allowing it to fulfil the remainder of its term, which would end in March 1993 so that it could live out its full term. Another proposal was to discount the period when the Assembly had been dissolved and to count the three years from the day when it would be revived. Congress leaders, in particular, were getting restive.

PCC chief Ghulam Rasool Kar, who had enjoyed ministerial privileges as Power Minister in the National Conference-Congress coalition government, regretted the day when Farooq Abdullah had submitted his resignation. 'It was a big mistake,' he told me emphatically several times. But these expressions of discontent were only made after the death of Rajiv Gandhi for it was Rajiv who had suggested or rather pressed Farooq to resign in January 1990 to protest the re-appointment of Jagmohan as Governor of Jammu and Kashmir.

Farooq was far away in London: shielded from the violence which gripped the Valley. 'I didn't want to become a martyr like Moulvi Mirwaiz Farooq,' he told me and Rahul Bedi of *The Telegraph*, London and a British journalist. Sitting on his lawns where flowers were in full bloom and offered a full view of Gupkar, the spring of 1995, I could see anger filling his eyes.

Somehow, he tried to control himself. There were moments of silence. I thought of filling those moments by asking yet another question. But Farooq interrupted me and pointed towards the mosque across the road.

'It was from there that they would pour all the filth in our ears. They would hurl obscenities from the mosque against me, my family, my daughters. There was no escape. I would bolt all the doors and try to screen my daughters from the profanities streaming from the loudspeakers; where could I keep my family?' he asked, his eyes clouding over with the bitter memories of those days. His father had often been absent during the formative years of his life: he had been jailed by the Maharajah when Farooq was a child. 'I have known the pain of not being with my father.'

He had seen the writing on the wall and that the guns would reign for a long time in the Valley and that the pro-India politicians would be the targets. Though he called his temporary migration an act of wisdom, he would never be forgiven, in the history of Kashmir, for having deserted his people when they needed him most. They were seeking guidance from the leader of the party which claimed that it would live and die for them. Farooq had left them to swim or sink in the whirlpools of blood in Kashmir rather than rise to the occasion to be with his people and tell them what was good or bad. He baulked from paying the price of leadership. There were innumerable examples of leaders who had fled from the place of their origin only to return when conditions permitted. History has proved that Farooq's act was dictated by self-preservation for his brother Sheikh Mustafa Kamall had stayed on and survived the years of violence and bloodshed. He had carried on with his work as a medical practitioner, examining patients at his cottage in Tangmarg, a place which was extremely vulnerable to the action of militancy and all the threats which it posed. Kashmiris were being sorely tried by the harshness of life in Kashmir. Pro-India politicians were also feeling the heat. But those camping on in Jammu and Delhi were casting about for ways to gain power or be part of it.

They were taking advantage of Delhi's recognition of the advantages of having an elected government in Jammu and Kashmir where all acts of omission and commission were currently being attributed to the federal government as it was exercising direct rule over the state, giving credence moreover to the assertion that India was holding on to Kashmir by force. Prime Minister P. V. Narasimha Rao was having a difficult time explaining the absence of a democratic government in Jammu and Kashmir. At the same time he had to answer the question: why was the number of the Indian army soldiers constantly on the rise in the Valley? He tried his best to explain that the soldiers were there because of the developments on the ground. He told the Pakistani ambassador in Singapore in 1995 that the presence of Indian troops was the outcome of Pakistan's terrorist campaign which made it necessary to send more troops to the Valley.

The envoy had asked Rao how he could justify India's claim on Kashmir; to which Rao had retorted with another question: Why had there not been as many soldiers in the Valley prior to 1989, the calendar year of the beginning of turmoil in the state of Jammu and Kashmir? But these questions and answers did not convince world opinion. The international community had come to recognize Kashmir as a genuine indigenous struggle rather than what India would have the world believe 'Pakistan sponsored cross-border terrorism' or 'proxy war.' The international community did believe the Indian version, but underlined the need for a political solution based on the wishes of the Kashmiri people.

The only way to counter international perceptions was to have some kind of democratic set-up in place: to show the world that Kashmir was being governed by the politically expressed will of the people. That was a difficult task. The Prime Minister first chose Rajesh Pilot, his Minister for Communications to break the ice. Pilot sought to rebuild his bridges with the leaders whom he had known since the 1980s when he had negotiated an accord between Rajiv Gandhi and Farooq Abdullah. He was also courting Moulvi Iftikhar Hussain Ansari, a Shia leader and Mian Bashir Ahmad, a popular Gujjar leader. He also asked Ghulam Rasool Kar, Taj Mohi-ud-Din and several other Congress leaders to remain in the Valley. He maintained his lines of communications with Farooq Abdullah in London.

Pilot also sought to build his image among the militants by promising that the government would ensure that relatives of arrested persons be informed within 24 hours. He promised that there would be no more extrajudicial killings. The local government in Kashmir took umbrage at his manoeuvrings. Governor Girish Chandra Saxena[2] was quite miffed. He even barred officers from meeting Pilot. He thought that Pilot was interfering in the governing process in Kashmir and trying to build his image nationally by foisting impractical ideas on Kashmir. Saxena finally left on March 10, 1993; he could not put up with the dual control.

These sentiments were gradually shared by his successor, Gen. Rao, who at one stage became a bitter critic of Pilot. He made it known to Narasimha Rao that Pilot should be taken off Kashmir affairs. In 1994, Narasimha Rao assumed direct control of Kashmir affairs, breaking the long practice of the Home Ministry's looking after the affairs of the sensitive state. This announcement came within days of the National Conference's executive committee meeting in Jammu in November 1994 which called for the restoration of the pre-1953 autonomous status of the state. But this demand was not an overnight development. In London, Farooq had been hearing from time to time, stories of the horror and torture afflicting the State. These were reported in the British press in London where he had taken his family; and whenever he was in Delhi he would come across them in the Indian national dailies and occasionally he would come back to the Valley and return as ever a disappointed man. He spent hours with his colleagues and friends, discussing the ways and means of getting out of this impasse. There appeared to be blind walls of hatred which India could not demolish. The Indian leadership was at an utter loss. He was struck by the idea of autonomy. The meaning of autonomy had changed by then. It was not what the Maharaja Hari Singh had sought for his subjects in the instrument of accession that he had signed with Government of India. It was not merely restoring to Kashmir what it had lost over the years. It was not the question of restoring the titles of *Sadar-e-Riyasat* for head of the state or *Wazire-Azam* for head of the government. Its dimensions had changed tremendously. What was at issue was the restoration of the dignity and honour of the people of Kashmir and also saving Kashmir for India. In 1994, when the NC revived the demand for autonomy, Prime Minister Rao took over charge of Kashmir affairs. It could have been a mere coincidence that, at this juncture, Farooq was reviving the issue of the restoration of autonomy and wanted direct handling of Kashmir affairs to be the responsibility of the PM. Rao obliged him. Farooq termed it a Diwali 'gift' for the people of the State. Narasimha Rao whose mind was preoccupied with the Kashmir elections, called both Ansari and Mian Bashir Ahmad, a respected Gujar leader. He offered as much as Rs 50 lakh to both of them for preparing ground for the elections in Kashmir Valley. 'No way,' replied Mian Bashir Ahmad who knew the consequences of talking of elections in Kashmir. He was not worried about himself. His fear was that the moment it was revealed that a Gujar leader was working for the elections, the community would be targeted. He did not want that to happen. He told the Prime Minister that it would be more prudent to select a Kashmiri leader. The only credible candidate was Farooq Abdullah, whose charisma was unparalleled. Gen. Rao was desperate to hold elections but was haunted by fears: what if the militants were to target Farooq Abdullah? Who would or could step forward? India would lose both a great opportunity and face before the international community. He was genuinely worried.

Farooq who had defended the Indian stand on Kashmir at international forums was, an unwilling player, though he was being nudged forward by politicians in Delhi. He needed some face-saving stratagem to stage a comeback: unless autonomy was granted or assured, he would not participate in the polls. Narasimha Rao told the Parliament that if the granting of autonomy was an issue, the 'sky is the limit;' the air was electrified with anticipation at that announcement. Farooq was adamant.

He even declared in early 1995 that if and when he came back to power, he would return as 'Prime Minister and not Chief Minister.' He was heightening the hype and putting pressure on the Centre. Narasimha Rao hoped that the air was clearing for the polls. Election fever was gradually building up in the media and in official circles. The elections to the Ladakh Autonomous Hill Development Council indicated that the people in the Buddhist dominated part, as well as Shia Kargil and the Jammu region were for the polls. Similar feelings were permeating the Valley but fear prevented the people from voicing their innermost desires.

T. N. Seshan, Chief Election Commissioner in June 1995

who had been overwhelmed by the destruction of Charar-e-Sharief shrine and the violence that ensued, cautioned that it might not be the opportune moment for elections. Towards the end of 1995, enthusiasm for elections again re-surfaced and Narasimha Rao hinted that something big was imminent. He merely announced that the titles of *Sadar-e-Riyasat* (instead of Governor) and *Wazir-e-Azam* or Prime Minister instead of Chief Minister could be revived as part of the political package. Farooq pooh-poohed the idea. For him, the change of titles would not mean anything unless accompanied by the restoration of real powers. He held a meeting of the executive committee of the National Conference in Srinagar and informed the Governor that the NC could take part in elections. That was the end of the chapter on elections in that year.

In 1996, sensing that India might conduct polling in the state, Pakistan tried, by exploiting the JKLF, to recapture the Hazratbal shrine, in order to create a stand- off. Responding in true military fashion, Gen. Rao ordered the police to enter and flush out militants. This occurred in March 1996 and thereafter the message was clear: the polls would be held in May for the Indian parliament. Voting was enforced in many instances. It was plain to the people in Kashmir that the Government of India had emerged as winner and that the militants would not be allowed to disrupt the polling process.

Farooq Consents to Participate

There was a change in government at the national level and the United Front Government conceded that Jammu and Kashmir required something more than what it had had. Farooq finally consented to participate in the polls. It was only then that H. D. Deve Gowda, Narasimha Rao's successor announced that Jammu and Kashmir was a special state and deserved special attention and powers. The general secretary of CPI-M,

Harkrishen Singh Surjeet, a prominent communist leader in India, had played a crucial role in it. Speaking at an all parties function organized by the Left Front in the Banquet Hall, a dilapidated architectural marvel at M. A. Road in Srinagar, in the presence of Harkrishen Singh Surjeet and Mufti, Rao's successor had urged Farooq to contest in the elections.... 'It is in the interest of the nation and the state and you should not shirk this responsibility.'

It was generally believed, then, that unless Farooq and the National Conference participated, the elections would lack credibility. Farooq was under pressure from all sides to contest. Mufti was one of the many mounting pressure on him. That the elections should not look a one-sided affair, the Government of India asked the militants who had surrendered to take part as well.

As far back as May 1990, Jagmohan had been preparing his own election plan after dissolving the Assembly on February 19. He was eager for fresh polling and wanted the JKLF to take part in it. And the Government of India was even keener than he was on the issue.

If it was the idea of Prime Minister Vishwanath Pratap Singh,[3] then, it was equally the brainchild of Mufti Mohammad Sayeed to restore the pre-1953 status to Kashmir and have the JKLF participate in the polls. The Intelligence Bureau undertook an extensive study in 1990 to find out what would satisfy the people of the State short of *azadi*. They had only one reservation: if it was proposed that the 'pre-1953 autonomous status of Jammu and Kashmir (be) restored.' The people had little or no objection but they wanted this issue to be discussed and decided by JKLF.

As intent as they were on *azadi*, the JKLF leadership would not entertain anything short of freedom.

The issue was revived on the eve of the 1991 parliamentary elections, which Jammu and Kashmir had missed. The IB discussed this with Yasin Malik in Tihar jail, but he refused to budge. The moot point was that the JKLF was not sure of the intentions of the Government of India and moreover, it was aware of the fluid political situation at the national level where the BJP had pulled the rug from under the government of V. P. Singh and Chandra Shekhar was surviving on the life support system offered by Rajiv Gandhi and Congress. The JKLF, which had very intelligent brains in its think tank both in Kashmir and other parts of the world, particularly the US and the UK, did not want to land itself in any trouble. It wanted the Indian political system to stabilize so that it might be in a position to offer some concrete guarantees. The JKLF did not want to repeat any of the mistakes it had made in the past. Having come so far on the road, it was unwilling to retrace its steps. Dr. Ghulam Qadir Wani, a Jamait-i-Islami activist who had joined forces with the JKLF, told me in December 1990 that 'the Government of India was not to be trusted.' He was more liberal in his outlook and possessed a more profound knowledge of Islam and Kashmiri society than his contemporaries in the fundamentalist party.

He was the spokesman of the JKLF at that time. It was my first interaction with any of the militant leaders in Kashmir. It all started like this. One of my friends, who was working in the Central Government service, asked me if I would be interested in interviewing a JKLF leader. Without any hesitation, I agreed. A couple of days later, I received a call from a local Urdu weekly editor asking me where I might be picked up from. I indicated Partap Park, which I have always regarded as the Fleet Street of Kashmir. I was taking a risk. I knew it. But I also knew that the JKLF would not harm any journalist at this point in time, when it was locked in battle with the Hizb-ul-Mujahadeen. At the back of my mind was the knowledge that I had the blessings of my Kashmiri friends. So I was taken in an autorickshaw or three-wheeler, a popular commuter cab in India, to Sarai Bala, located across the River Jhelum. There followed a long walk through an endless maze of lanes and bylanes and finally my guide and I found ourselves at the doorway of a modest house. I spotted Dr. Wani sitting in the company of eight young men. 'Please sit down Mr. Joshi,' Dr. Wani invited me after receiving me in the traditional Kashmiri: getting up, drawing his hand out from the *pheran*, warmed by the heat of *kangri*. Thereafter the conversation began. I started asking all sorts of questions, most of which were rather difficult and I was afraid that I might antagonize him. Dr. Wani kept his cool, however. To the question what if you get the 1953 status, he replied: 'Where is the guarantee, how can we trust Delhi? It betrayed Sheikh Abdullah. It broke its word with the people of Kashmir. Didn't Jawaharlal Nehru promise plebiscite to the people of Kashmir?' He was sure that now 'when the guns have brought the Kashmir issue out of cold storage, we cannot accept this proposition.' He was making a premium case for guns. Dr.Wani was killed at his Bandipore residence after his return from Pakistan in November 1998.

But in the 1996 polls, Farooq had specific targets: The Centre's rule, the alienation of the people with autonomy as the solution offered by the National Conference. He played with finesse on the hopes of the people and projected their worries and spoke of their identity and self-respect. He had nothing to explain. The accountability of the bureaucrats was not there. He lambasted the terrorists as much for the trouble they caused as the security forces for perpetuating the turmoil. People had forgotten many of his failures and how he had deserted them. What they remembered most was that he had picked up the theme of the honour and dignity of the people under the autonomy slogan. He promised that he would get them autonomy and also peace gradually. 'I don't have a magic wand to transform things overnight. But I will certainly strive for it.' His campaign was extremely promising. He lifted the hand of Sheikh Ghulam Rasool, a former Chief Secretary and one of his voters in the Ganderbal constituency and announced: 'I am going to give him a very big responsibility,' which he never did and in revenge, the ex-CS, was to work assiduously against Abdullah. Farooq who had developed cold feet in campaigning for the elections was being persuaded to contest. He had a premonition that the task that he had chosen for himself in the 1996 campaign was beyond him, his will or capacity. That realization had dawned on him because he had the MLAs as ministers against whom he hardly dared raise his voice. He could not take them to task. There were leaders like Ghulam Mohi-ud-Din Shah, Bashir Ahmad Kitchloo, Mohammad Shafi Uri who would want power but were not willing to take any risk.

Then there was Moulvi Iftikhar Hussain Ansari who wanted to have a finger in every pie. He was elected on the Congress ticket but had no qualms in joining the National Conference ministry. For their part, the ministers and the MLAs were self-servers. With such an unpromising team, Farooq could not have hoped to undo the damage inflicted by the militancy over the past seven to eight years, nor could he have inspired confidence among the people. So he knew that the road blocks were bigger and more impenetrable than he had anticipated.

Farooq promised a ministerial posting to every NC contestant in 1996 as a lure for them to strive to obtain more votes in the elections. He was haunted by the prospect of a dismal debacle as the people were shying away from his rallies. The counter-insurgents, whose guns he blamed for the series of extortion and rapes in Kashmir was another source of disquiet.

At every stage he tried to seek justice from the Election Commission. 'I am hopeful that the Election Commission will see how the *ikhwanis* (renegades) were misusing their guns to harass the voters.' Kukka Parrey, the father of counter-insurgency was the only counter-insurgent to have won a seat in 1996, contesting from the Sonawari constituency in Baramullah.

The low turn out of people at his rallies and the fear that had paralyzed his party men was reflected in Farooq's words and election speeches. He himself was not confident of making a landslide victory and such a prospect among his party men, was even less likely. For this reason, he chose to address the first election rally at Pattan, the constituency of Moulvi Iftikhar Hussain Ansari, who was fighting the election on the Congress ticket. But it was because of the bonhomie between Farooq and the All India Congress Committee General Secretary Ghulam Nabi Azad whose protégé Ansari was, that Farooq too befriended the Moulvi, forgetting that it was the same man who had played a key role in toppling his government in July 1984 and abused his mother in the legislative Assembly. But Ansari could draw crowds and had loyal followers behind him. None of Farooq's own party men had a similar capacity to attract the crowds or command such loyalty among their followers. And Farooq badly needed crowds to live up to his image of a popular Kashmiri leader who could even make his arch-rival Mufti Mohammad Sayeed envious. Mufti had re-joined the Congress after leaving the Janta Dal for he had not been accommodated in the ministry of the United Front Government following his defeat in the parliamentary elections which he had contested from Bihar and subsequently lost despite the confidence and assurance of Laloo Yadav,[4] the maverick leader of the eastern state. He bitterly regretted his decision to contest in the elections. 'I should not have contested like Inder Gujral.' Gujral was chosen as Foreign Minister by H. D. Deve Gowda, a shabby figure who was propelled to the Prime Minister's post in June 1996 after the ignominious 13-day rule of the BJP. What was still more painful to Mufti was that his own protégé Mohammad Maqbool had won from Anantnag, a parliamentary constituency of south Kashmir that Mufti had always regarded as his own, and had, eventually, become a Union minister. In frustration, he abandoned his Rajya Sabha seat and waited in the sidelines, biding his time until the day when he was suddenly to return to the Congress.

Victory for Farooq

Farooq won the elections and set about to form the government. The results had been well beyond his expectations. He would frequently recall in his speeches, how on his return from London, he was teased by his son and daughters about the number of seats the National Conference had won. 'They asked me to guess how many seats we had won, I said: 25. They said guess again and they kept on teasing me before revealing that the NC had won a two-third majority in the House of 87.' Farooq was flabbergasted because he had not expected the NC to win more than forty seats.

Barely after five months into the government, Farooq offered to dissolve the Assembly and asked the APHC to come forward and contest the elections in February 1997. He told an audience in the auditorium of Jammu University that 'if that brings peace, I will dissolve the Assembly today but let the Hurriyat Conference leaders say that they will participate in the polls.' Among those listening to him were the US ambassador to India, Frank Wisner, who was harping on the familiar American theme that the Kashmir issue should be addressed in accordance with the wishes of the people of Kashmir. He had no answers if the elections were not a test of the wishes of the people. Wisner obviously had some reservations. He was more convinced by the American media reports that the people had been hustled into the army trucks to vote than that they had voted out of their free will. Agreed that, had that been the case, for the sake of argument, one might well ask, why then had the voters chosen the National Conference and Farooq Abdullah? If they had not found a credible alternative to him and his party, why had not the voters simply invalidated their votes? I might add, as a reminder, that in the May 1996 parliamentary polls, which the National Conference had not contested, the voters, at many places, had invalidated their vote by drawing the plough symbol on the ballot paper and stamped on it. That was a measure of the popularity of the party.

Another fact that Americans in particular and the Western world at large, have conveniently chosen to ignore is that the Separatists and their armed guerrillas had harassed and intimidated voters and threatened them with dire consequences if they were to defy their call to boycott polling. If the free will of the people were to be determined, this could only be done by people voting at the risk of their very lives. Why then could the National Conference not be the sole beneficiary of the 'manipulated victory,' as they termed it? What about the 29 non-National Conference men who had won the polls in 1996? How could they have won if the NC had rigged the elections and that too under the direct supervision of Delhi? How then had the one-third strength of the House got elected in the first place? Again for the sake of argument supposing that the National Conference had its men in place in the Kashmir Valley, how could it have won four seats from the predominantly Hindu district of Jammu and three from Buddhist-dominated Ladakh division? The Western view is clouded by such misgivings that it is difficult to correct them overnight. The West has its own prejudices. The British are always harping on the theme that

Jammu and Kashmir is a core issue between India and Pakistan and a constant source of tension in South Asia.

I have personally interacted with the people from the Western media who come to Jammu and Kashmir with deep prejudices imprinted on their minds against India. They don't listen to any reason. For them India is guilty on all counts in Kashmir. Sure it is on many counts and the Indian media has raked the army and the government on coals in a fashion that it would be very difficult for many in the Western world ever to imagine.

Endnotes

1. Sheikh Mustafa Kamal, the youngest son of Sheikh Abdullah who was twice minister in his eldest brother Farooq Abdullah's cabinet.

2. Girish Chandra Saxena was the former RAW chief who became twice Governor of Jammu and Kashmir (May 1990 to March 1993) and (May 1998 to May 2003)

3. Vishwanath Pratap Singh was Prime Minister of India from November 1989 to November 1991.

4. Laloo Yadav was the former Chief Minister of the Indian eastern state of Bihar and now Railway Minister in the federal government.

14

Pre-Kargil Political Scenario

The February 1998 parliamentary polls in which Omar Abdullah made his debut in politics, were a complement to the 1996 Assembly elections. The people's participation this time was more voluntary and emphatic. Mufti Mohammad Sayeed had won a seat for Congress, from Anantnag. The National Conference won three seats and the BJP two. Mufti's victory at Anantnag may be attributed to the weakness of the National Conference candidate Mohammad Yusuf Taing, who had authored Sheikh Abdullah's biography *Aatish-e-Chinar*.[1] Taing was the choice of Begum Akbar Jehan – the widow of Sheikh Abdullah, whom her loyalist camp in the National Conference called "*Mader-e-Meharban*" (kind mother).

Farooq's party supported Atal Bihari Vajpayee's[2] government after the February 1998 elections. Right from the start of his appointment as Prime Minister in March 1998, Vajpayee had attempted to find a solution to the Kashmir crisis. First he tried to browbeat Pakistan by ordering the detonation of nuclear explosions in May 1998 only to find Pakistan responding with even greater ferocity, by triggering off its own set of nuclear explosions. The US was furious that India had exploded five bombs in a row at Pokhran in the Thar desert of Rajasthan and managed to conceal them from the spy satellites. India was wild with joy, which the soldiers in Kashmir expressed in bouts of bulletfiring. The Kashmiris were aghast. Had India then superseded Pakistan, in the arms race? It was a development that might impair the Kashmir cause.

From within, pressure mounted on Pakistan to retaliate with a tit for tat series of explosions. The Pakistan Government gave in and the Chagai hills in Baluchistan reverberated with nuclear explosions within a fortnight of India's explosions. Pakistan had levelled the score of explosions. This bolstered Pakistan's spirits. India's superiority in conventional warfare was neutralized and the next step was a clash to be seen in Kargil.

Farooq who had been castigated on all sides for casting his lot with the National Democratic Alliance (NDA)[3] government led by the Hindu fundamentalist party Bhartiya Janta Party (BJP), was greeted by more finger-pointing in the state. He explained himself in these terms. 'We are a backward state and we cannot afford to have any confrontation with the Centre. My father (Sheikh Mohammad Abdullah) had told me that even if the Rashtriya Sawayam Sewak Sangh (RSS), (whose overt aim is to make India a Hindu nation) were to come to power in Delhi, we should be supporting them for the sake of the people and their welfare in a state like Jammu and Kashmir.'

Few accepted the logic of the argument. Many within his own party were opposed to this decision. It was inconceivable that the National Conference which had been keeping afloat the flag of secularism and Hindu-Muslim-Sikh unity should side with a party that was fundamentalist to the core. Such an alliance could only have been prompted by political opportunism. It had its roots in the dismissal of the National Conference government as a result of the machinations of the Centre and of which Farooq himself had been the victim first of the Congress in July 1984 and then that of the National Front Government[4] of Vishwanath Pratap Singh in which his *bête noire* Mufti Mohammad Sayed was the Home Minister.

Farooq was concerned for the survival of his government. Had Farooq not been a partner in the NDA, it is very likely that his government would not have survived the series of brutal killings which rocked Jammu and Kashmir. Unsuspecting villagers were slaughtered in their sleep, and young children hacked to death in unspeakable acts of brutality. Such massacres occurred repeatedlly in a city where neither funeral processions nor wedding parties were spared. All this was a poor reflection on the rule of law in the state and also a question mark over the performance of Farooq's government. But since his party held four crucial votes in the Lok Sabha on which the survival of the Vajpayee government depended, the National Conference government was left unperturbed.

Leaving the NDA would signify Omar Abdullah's exit from the union ministry while remaining implied putting up with the humiliation of being a partner of the very government that had summarily rejected the autonomy resolution passed by the state legislature. The National Conference working committee was in session, deliberating on the issue; 'hawks' like Ghulam Mohi-ud-Din Shah, Mohammad Shafi and Abdul Rahim Rather were clamouring for the NC to leave the NDA to redeem the honour and prestige of the Party which was now jeopardized by the autonomy resolution. 'If we cannot take a stand today on the issue, tomorrow, we would not even be in the pages of history,' Mohammad Shafi Uri, a senior minister in the Farooq Abdullah cabinet said, underlining the mood of the people who were opposed to Omar's presence in the Union Cabinet and the votaries of perpetual confrontation between Srinagar and Delhi. A new chapter of bitter confrontation between the state and the Centre was opening. The death of Farooq's mother momentarily relegated discussion of the central issue to the background. The Chief Minister had become, in effect, a pawn in the hands of his senior colleagues. There was no exit route for Farooq after he had passed the resolution and challenged the Centre. Nor was there any longer room for him to manoeuvre either politically both within his party or vis-a-vis Delhi.

The death of Begum Akbar Jehan in July 2000 changed the political landscape. As patron of the National Conference, her role was essentially a ceremonial one. Nonetheless, she exerted a powerful personal influence over the party and some of its leaders and had in particular a moderating effect on Farooq Abdullah. Her death deferred the moment of confrontation with Delhi which did not take place until July 2003.

A lull in terrorist violence brought Bollywood back to the Valley; the shooting of Boney Kapoor's film *Mere Apne* was followed by others. The apparent calm was soon disrupted by a series of massacres in Udhampur and Doda. Even the neighbouring state of Himachal Pradesh was not spared.

This was the militants' response to the process of normalization that was taking place and also a rebuff to the pro-active policy that Home Minister L K. Advani had come to announce.

But the people of Kashmir, wearied by the trauma of violence and bloodshed, desired peace. Hope sprung up in them when Prime Minister Atal Bihari Vajpayee announced his journey, by bus, to Lahore to open a new chapter in Indo-Pak friendship. The gesture was welcomed by the international community and to some extent even Pakistan Prime Minister Mian Moahmmad Nawaz Sharief[5] was a willing partner to the script of peace that Vajpayee was seeking to write. Vajpayee's poem *Jang na hone denge* (We will not allow war to take place between the two nations) at Minar-e-Pakistan was hailed not only as a masterpiece in poetry but a genuine expression of friendship between the two nations that had turned hostile to each other. India had consistently accused Pakistan of sponsoring cross-border terrorism, a charge that Islamabad kept denying.

However, even as the Lahore declaration was being penned, Pakistani soldiers under the command of Pervez Musharraf were climbing the Himalayan heights in Kargil and had intruded into the Indian bunkers and posts, which, as part of an unspoken agreement between the armies of the two countries were to be occupied only during summer and could, in good faith, be abandoned, during the freezing winter. This was a breach of trust.

But it was also a demonstration of the failure of the Indian Army itself. The abandoning of posts during winter did not mean giving up the monitoring of the situation along the Line of Control (LOC) which divides Jammu and Kashmir. Although the posts were to be abandoned during winter the troops had to move down to posts at lower heights and regular aerial surveys of the posts were to be undertaken. The complacency of ignoring the posts altogether had assumed a pattern that the Pakistani army had not missed and had taken advantage of. The Pakistani army had been eyeing the opportunity for this kind of intrusion for a long time. This was the startling disclosure by former Pakistani Prime Minister Benazir Bhutto[6] who had told Vir Sanghvi in a Star Talk interview that Gen. Pervez Musharraf had mooted this idea when she was the premier. She claimed that she had shot it down. There were no denials by Musharraf and the Pakistani army, which gives credence to what Ms. Bhutto was saying. The Indian army, it became apparent after the interview, was just taking things too lightly. It had no clue whatsoever of the intentions and preparations of Pakistan to take over the Kargil[7] heights. It was so complacent that it ignored all the signals in the form of the banging of mortar and the shelling of artillery. The first signals of how things had deteriorated in Kargil came when in March 1997 Pakistani troops shelled Kargil—a single market town on the banks of the Suru, a glacial river, killing more than a dozen people and destroying several homes. Kargilis were asking: why us? It had never happened before. They thought that the simple answer was that they had not cooperated with the Pakistani army in facilitating infiltration, hence this punishment.

It was repeated again in October that year and the phenomenon continued. The Indian army sought solace in the fact that the shelling was a temporary phenomenon, refusing to read the writing on the mountains. Pakistan was gaining a foothold amongst people who were unhappy with the way they were being treated by the Indian army. So the circumstances were set for a major war on the Himalayan heights.

Yet some of the Kargil Muslims reported suspicious movement of the tall men in bunkers in the Batalik hills to the army only to have their reports dismissed as the fabrication of mere shepherds. The army also did not take cognizance of the reports that Pakistani helicopters were conducting aerial surveys of the snow-clad mountains.

Pakistan troops intruded and captured the main heights holding Srinagar-Leh[8] highway under shelling range. They were in a position to cut off this highway which meant not only the isolation of Kargil and Leh but also denial of the Siachen[9] glacier to Indian access. This was to be the highest battlefield in the world at an elevation of about 18,000 feet or so.

Pakistan's other military strategic purpose was to get the Indian troops to fight in Kargil where the position of Pak troops gave them an advantage for they needed only to roll stones down from the heights and the Indian troops would be incapacitated. Pakistan, then could have opened another frontier into the plains and taken Indian territory.Indian superiority in conventional war would no longer be a threat for this time Islamabad too had nuclear weapons in its possession.

It was in mid-May that the Indian army woke to the full horrors of the intrusion. Pakistan claimed that it was the intrusion by the *mujahadeen* fighting Indian rule in Kashmir. It never acknowledged the presence of its troops. It was only after US President Bill Clinton had called for the inviolability of the LoC putting pressure on Pakistan to toe the line, that Pakistan responded with the withdrawal of its troops in July. For President Clinton feared, as the rest of the world did, that the two South Asian nations might be driven into a nuclear encounter, and trigger a holocaust that the world was keen to avoid.

Nawaz Sharief, worried over the potential number of casualties of the intense air campaign under Operation Vijay of the Indian army and Air Force, rang up President Clinton on the night of July 3, on the eve of America's Independence Day for an appointment with President Clinton. Clinton responded and asked him to come over to Washington. Even as Nawaz was on his way, Clinton invited Vajpayee to join in the deliberations. Vajpayee refused saying that he had nothing to discuss with the Pakistani Prime Minister.

Vajpayee told Clinton that he had already done enough by not allowing the troops to cross the LoC and he promised that he would abide by whatever the US President would decide. Pakistan was asked to withdraw its troops immediately to its side of the LoC and India asked to keep its military might in check until Pakistani troops had been withdrawn. As the Pakistani troops withdrew, India recorded victories on Tiger Hills, one of the major heights in the Drass region of Kargil among other places.

Kargil to me was a land which belonged to another world. I had passed through Kargil in 1993 and had not much idea about the place and the people. When Operation Vijay[10] began, and with it the call of duty, I visited Kargil first by aircraft with Chief Minister Farooq Abdullah. We spoke to the soldiers and realised how they had been taken for a ride by the commanders and had no clue that men from Turtuk, a rocky belt in Nubra on the edges of the LoC, had been to Pakistan for training and brought in arms and ammunition. Nor did they realize that the Pakistanis had entered five to ten kms deep into Indian territory. This then was the situation. I was filled with an overwhelming sense of outrage that the top brass of the Army had taken things so casually and left such a sensitive border so unguarded and unprotected.

When I visited Kargil, the shells were exploding everywhere. It was an ongoing war. Since all journalists were staying in Siachen Hotel, I also checked in there. The hotel owner is Mohammad Sadiq, the perfect host who personally saw to it that his guests were made comfortable. He forcefully denounced Pakistan because its shelling had ruined the lives and business of the people in the town. Transporters were afraid to go out in their vehicles as the Leh-Srinagar road was dotted with burned-out trucks which had been carrying supplies, rather like irregular milestones zigzagging along the highway. For those plying the road, each moment was one of prayer. The taxi drivers would pray for a long time, before putting cars into gear particularly in the Drass zone where the Pakistani shells would destroy everything in their range.

They were pounding the Brigade headquarters every now and then. These have since been moved into the slopes, well out of Pakistani view.

But on the streets of Kargil, I sensed deep divisions. The Kargil Muslims were not blaming Pakistan alone for the trouble. The Indian army too was being held guilty. At that moment itself I had the feeling that even if India were to win this war, it may never perhaps win the hearts and minds of the people- and which is indeed happening.

Parliamentary Elections 1999

The National Conference also played a role in the September 1999 elections which were effectively thrust on the people. One of its MPs, Saif-ud-Din Soz who was promised a ministerial berth by Congress in its prospective government, voted against the Vajpayee Government in the crucial confidence vote on March 30. He justified his decision to vote against the BJP-led Government on the ground of 'conscience.' Partly in order to appease the BJP which many regarded, at that time, as the potential winner and partly to underline the fact that Farooq would brook no challenge to his leadership, the NC had no qualms in removing Soz for his audacious move. Farooq was resorting to survival politics with a party which considered him to be a security risk and whose lack of ideological underpinning was compatible with that of the National Conference. For the people in the Valley, Farooq Abdullah's party represented a distinctive Kashmiri identity for the people in the Valley, while the BJP wanted an Indian veneer over it. There had been a tussle between the two parties ever since the birth of India. The BJP which is the reincarnation of the Bhartiya Jan Sangh[11] of Dr. Shyama Prasad Mukerjee who had launched a crusade against Sheikh Abdullah in Jammu. Jammu had its own version of the episode which had taken place under the banner of Praja Parishad who, so the belief goes had been blessed by Dr. Karan Singh, who was then *Sadar-e-Riyasat* or Head of the State which was once ruled by his father. That the Maharaja Hari Singh's family and that of Sheikh Abdullah would tie the political knot on the eve of the 1996 polls had been unthinkable. Dr. Karan Singh had become a Rajya Sabha member with the support of the National Conference and before that he had agreed to head the State Autonomy panel, much to the surprise and shock of his supporters in Jammu. Though he was to resign nine months later, the dent which he himself had inflicted on his image was irreparable. Karan Singh knowing that what he had done was reprehensible, avoided further discussion about it. But he did admit to me in October 1999 that the decision to be Chairman of the autonomy panel, had been erroneous. He was loudly reflecting on his decision of November 1996 in the sprawling grounds of Karan Mahal at the extreme end of the Gupkar Road which overlooks the vast expanse of the shimmering waters of Dal Lake, that was as enchantingly beautiful as ever. This was after his loss in the Lok Sabha election against Atal Behari Vajpayee in Lucknow as Congress candidate. He had quit his Rajya Sabha seat before contesting again in the parliamentary elections, for the first time after a lapse of fifteen years. He had lost to Janak Raj Gupta, Congress candidate, in the parliamentary elections in December 1984 and had not been able to reconcile himself to the defeat. He had broken his private vow not to contest ever again in elections.

Even after his resignation from the Rajya Sabha and almost two years after he had renounced the chairmanship of the State Autonomy Panel in July 1997, he had kept his youngest son Ajat Shatru Singh in the Farooq Abdullah Government. There was a joke in the National Conference circles that Farooq had gone a step ahead of his father and made the Maharaja's family the bearers of the flag inscribed with the plough which had been the symbol of resistance to the Maharaja Hari Singh.

Although Dr. Karan Singh was rather dejected, he adopted a high moral stance speaking contemptuously of the people of Jammu, whom he described as 'ungrateful.' Dr. Karan Singh was disappointed over the fact that Jammu had never supported him. But on this count there is deliberate if unconscious amnesia on his part, for it was the Udhampur parliamentary constituency that had returned him four times to the Lok Sabha and saw him becoming the minister in the Union cabinet. But he recalls that after the 1977 Congress debacle he had turned hostile towards Indira Gandhi and even deposed against her and her son Sanjay Gandhi before the Shah Commission.

At the meeting of the state cabinet in August 1997 which had been convened to deliberate on Dr. Singh's resignation his son Ajat Shatru Singh,[12] had not only verbally condemned his father's action but intended to issue a statement to that effect. It was Farooq Abdullah who restrained him from carrying out his threat. Ajat himself rejoined Congress. Farooq could not accept the betrayal. However, he felt that it was for Dr. Singh to explain why he had resigned from the autonomy panel adding that he did not bear him any ill will. However, this did not prevent him from arresting all the Hurriyat leaders engaged in the anti-election campaign, during the September 1999 elections, to ensure that their violent activities did not derail the prospects of victory for himself and his party. Syed Ali Shah Geelani, Abdul Ghani Bhat, Moulvi Abbas Ansari and Yasin Malik were the key figures arrested. Farooq was aware that things were not going his way. He calculated correctly that their arrest would help him win the elections. But the truth was that he could no longer tolerate the idea of defeat having tasted victory over Mufti Mohammad Sayeed in the February 1998 parliamentary elections.[13]

But Farooq was deeply worried by the low turnout of the voters. The percentage of voters in the Srinagar-Budgam constituency from where Omar Abdullah was contesting against Mufti's daughter Mehbooba Mufti was so low that he publicly reprimanded two police officers, the Director General of Police, Gurbachan Jagat and Inspector General of Police, Kashmir division, P.S. Gill for not exerting control over the militants in the parliamentary constituency and so create the conditions to draw people out to vote. The less than five per cent voter turnout in his own constituency in Ganderbal (one of the segments of the Srinagar-Budgam parliamentary constituency) which he represented in the Assembly, was particularly troubling.

I remember the sight of those empty booths where not a single voter would show up for hours on end. This was a damning indictment of the Farooq Abdullah government that was later confirmed with the defeat of Omar in the 2002 assembly elections.

Worse still, Governor Girish Chandra Saxena and Farooq himself had gone to see the new golf course during polling hours. At the same time, the Valley was observing yet another strike on the call of the All Parties Hurriyat Conference. Farooq knew that the violent campaign of militants would have some impact, but he had not forseen that it would result in the drastically low turnout of voters. He had taken things for granted, believing that there would be pockets of good turnout here and there comparable perhaps to the February- March 1998 parliamentary elections when the participation of voters was voluntary and high.

Mohammad Shafi Uri,[14] took a more objective view of the situation. He was convinced that the Kargil conflict had affected the security grid and that the militants had gained access to areas in the interior. This had resulted in widespread voter intimidation. The sight of the *fidayeen* or suicide terrorists attacking the army establishments and killing and maiming the security personnel with impunity caused widespread fear. If the armed forces could not be safe in their cantonments, what were the chances of security for ordinary people? Fears ran high, particularly in the countryside where the troops which had been originally detailed for counter insurgency operations were now transferred to the borders in Kargil where Pakistan's intrusion into the Indian side had provoked a mini war that lasted for almost two months. That war had disrupted everything and the people were afraid of defying the militants who had come to kill and die. This was the most deadly brand of militants that had yet stepped onto the soil of Kashmir. That voters had been harassed and would not venture to cast their vote at the cost of their lives was to be expected. Farooq was not fully responsible for this situation. But he was the Chief Minister and had to bear some of the blame. The arrest of the separatist conglomerate All Parties Hurriyat Conference's leaders were powerless to stem the tide of violence.

New Cult

It was Lashkar-e-Toiba or LeT[15] who introduced the new cult of violence into Kashmir: instilling fear through suicide attacks and setting new standards for the local militants. They gained a new confidence. The deadly combination of the local militants becoming guides and the Lashkar militants mounting attacks on the army, the presence of BSF and the police camps made the Valley hostage to these marauders. The security forces were becoming helpless. They had not imagined that the militants would have the audacity to attack them in their cantonments. One of the explanations for this was that no degree of security could deter a man on a mission to die. The examples of the suicide bombings in Israel were cited. Lashkar activists had mastered the art of suicide attacks. They often attacked at dusk or dawn when the soldiers were bleary eyed and less alert than usual. Disguise was also used. Militants would appear in combat uniform and on almost every occasion they were mistaken for fellow soldiers till the moment when they would set off grenades or open fire. By then it was too late for the soldiers to retaliate. The damage was done both in terms of the loss of men and also prestige. This was a new element in the reign of violence, terror and brutality in Kashmir since 1990.

The most spectacular attack was mounted by two of the Lashkar men on the PRO's office in Badami Bagh cantonment complex in Srinagar on November 3, 1999. Major P. Purshotam was the PRO of the army who had already been transferred out, but had come to say goodbye to his journalist friends, little knowing that he would be bidding farewell forever to this world.

Fayaz Ahmad Latha, who was working as a freelance cameraman and contributing his footage to the NDTV that was running the Star News show on satellite television, was accompanying Tariq and Habib Ullah Naqash. Tariq worked for ANI, or Asian News International and Naqash was a photographer with *The Asian Age*. Tariq had some work with Major Purshotam. Journalists in Kashmir would often visit the army PRO's office for some subsidized items available at the CSD canteen. Naqash was driving the car. Tariq went inside. Naqash became impatient and demanded that we leave immediately.

Purshotam welcomed them and offered tea. Suddenly, they heard the sound of explosions. He dismissed it as the firing of crackers by some soldiers ahead of Diwali, the festival of lights which Hindus celebrate mostly by bursting crackers. Tariq sensed something ominous. 'No sir, I believe this is something else.' It was getting dark. Purshotam sent a member of his staff to see what was happening. The latter was shot and came in bleeding profusely to report to his officer: 'Sir, terrorists have come.' Purshotam asked the journalists and one of his men to get inside the toilet. He bolted them from outside ignoring all the protests of the journalists, who did not want Purshotam to run into any danger. Fayaz was to recall this almost daily.

Purshotam started working on the telephone wanting to know why there was no response to check the terrorists. Then suddenly, the gunman came inside and opened fire. The journalists and others saw it happening through the chinks of the toilet door. 'We held our breaths and I offered even my last prayers,' recalled Tariq. The gunman was inside for a few minutes and, after satisfying himself that he had no one else left whom he could shoot, moved out. There was a nightlong gun battle that followed and the journalists had their own story to tell. Fayaz who had survived a landmine explosion in November 1998 thought that his end had come. No one believed that they had been directed to the toilet by Major Purshotam. The army men were angry. Had the fourth man, a soldier, not confirmed what the journalists were saying, the three would have been shot dead. In such situations army men rarely ask questions or listen to logic. The three were interrogated and as the version of each tallied with that of the others, they were handed over to fellow journalists the next morning. I was in Jammu on that day. There is often fierce competition among journalists and some can barely stand the sight of others. Still there are occasions when they show rare unity of thought and action. The whole journalistic community in Kashmir did not sleep that night. My phone never stopped ringing. Next day, the journalists, as a mark of gratitude, offered floral tributes to Major Purshotam. They were aware of the possible cost and consequences of expressing their gratitude to someone who had saved them and now lay dead. But this time they were not afraid.

Journalists in Kashmir are great in more than one way. My own survival in Kashmir and the way I visited places is a story of great human compassion and love. 'He is one of us,' Ataf Hussain then the *Times of India* correspondent in Srinagar told Wajahat Habibullah, the Divisional Commissioner Kashmir when the government was surreptitiously attempting to sow discord between journalists. I remember the way all of us would sometimes join forces against any voice levelled against one of us.

This is just a glimpse of the things that had started happening after the Kargil conflict when security forces were reduced following the transfer of troops from the counter-insurgency grid to the borders.

IC-814

Farooq knew what was coming. The afternoon of December 30, was mild with the sun shining on the grass of the Chief Minister's bungalow at Wazarat Road, Jammu. He was sitting on a chair. One might have thought that he was enjoying the warmth of the winter sun. 'Ask him to come here,' I overheard him saying loudly to Rashid Baba, his personal guard and trusted man of all seasons.

'Tell me,' he demanded. By now I knew that whenever Farooq used crisp sentences or one liners, there was some problem on his mind. Farooq is voluble and talks endlessly, giving no chance for interruption whenever he is extremely angry or delighted. He is a man of extremes. So is his love for Kashmir. He was clearly tense and obviously greatly disturbed. I was right: he was under pressure from Azhar Masood's men at Kandahar in Afghanistan, the capital of Taliban.

Farooq had a fundamental and unshaken principle-no compromise with terrorists. He had tendered his resignation over the release of five hardcore Jammu and Kashmir Liberation Front (JKLF) men in December 1989 in exchange for the release of the Home Minister's daughter. Now, it was the same situation ten years later. Five men had hijacked the Indian Airlines flight IC 814 which had taken off from Kathmandu, the Nepalese capital, on its journey to Delhi, the Indian capital. The hijackers had given a list of 37 men to be released from Indian jails. All of them were Pakistanis. That left no one in doubt about the Pakistani connections over the hijacking episode that had turned bloody from the very beginning with the murder of Rupian

Katyal, who had been married for only a month and who, by one account had attempted to offer some resistance to the hijackers who had coined strange names for themselves like Burger, etc. The plane was hijacked on Christmas Eve and four tense days had passed with the Government of India and its mandarins behaving in the most incompetent fashion. They sang clueless about the events and the designs. It was the usual song that Pakistan was behind it but there was no attempt at any stage to see what was transpiring behind the scenes. There were endless discussions on TV panels and one statement after another followed by politicians—some amusing, some derisory that the government was doing everything to get the passengers released. In fact nothing was happening. The Kashmir angle was clear in this sordid saga of hijacking and the focus of the Indian leadership was on some form of short-term solution.

Delhi's interest was in getting the passengers released. It had no valid argument before the hysterically protesting relatives and family friends of the hostages that there was no reason why their friends and relatives should not be exchanged for jailed militants, if five JKLF men had been exchanged for the daughter of the Home Minister. The Vajpayee and Advani duo who had criticized the V. P. Singh Government for giving in to terrorists' demands, were now about to repeat the same mistake with as dangerous consequences as those of a decade earlier. Indian diplomacy had failed miserably. Pakistan could not be pressurized by the United States into playing its part to get the hostages freed. It was clearly because the Indian diplomats had no idea what was being cooked up. India was in a mess, so was its political leadership and diplomacy.

India's Foreign Minister Jaswant Singh whose only qualification for the job was that he was verbose could not gather up the guts to condemn those who were harassing his colleague Foreign Ministry spokesperson, Nirupama Rao during the Agra summit (July 2001). Vajpayee was leaning on him and Defence Minister George Fernandes who visited Siachen more than a dozen times (now it is more than 30 times) but had no idea of the intrusion in Kargil hills. He was the one who gave the Pakistan government a clean chit when Pakistani intrusion was first detected in May 1999.It was Vajpayee's politics for he did not want his number two Advani to outscore him in any game. It was perhaps rightly remarked about Vajpayee that he wears a mask and his real self is different. The Prime Minister did not know that his politics of settling scores with his own colleague was putting the interests of the nation at risk, interests which he was supposed to have safeguarded at all costs—even at the cost of his life. He failed and instead dispatched his trusted man A. S. Dullat, RAW chief, now OSD in the Prime Minister's office, to Jammu.

Farooq was aware of what was happening. It was the source of his tension. As I sat silently without answering his query, he did not take a minute to understand that I had seen through the tensions at the back of his mind. 'What have you heard?' he asked me without completing the sentence as if to find out how close I was to discovering the tensions brewing in his mind. 'I am told that they were asking for Maulana Masood Azhar, Mushtaq Zargar and Sheikh Omar Sayeed and Mushtaq-ul-Islam.' He could not conceal his surprise. 'Who told you so?' he asked. It was a rhetorical question, for he did not expect me to reveal my source.

Then without waiting for my answer, he continued, 'this is going to be terrible. I am not going to say yes. We have suffered once and we cannot afford to repeat the same mistake again. It will be a disaster.'

'They should learn some lessons from what happened ten years ago,' he said while making unmistakable reference to the

Rubiya Sayeed episode of 1989. 'So I say that you are opposed to the release of any terrorists in exchange of the hostages?' I asked and heard him saying rather loudly, 'Yes... I left the place, knowing that the next few hours were going to be crucial.

Farooq's worries were centred on the fate that was to befall Kashmir. He was flamboyant, he could not care in the least about the things happening around him; Farooq was the image of a happy-go-lucky man. There was no danger to his chair as he had a comfortable majority.

'Kashmir will burn and we will have to pay a heavy price,' his words spoken on January 18, 1990, instantly came to my mind, when he drove to Raj Bhavan in Jammu to submit his resignation to Governor Gen. K. V. Krishna Rao whom he had kept waiting till midnight before submitting the resignation of his government. 'There can be no compromise with terrorists,' he was saying to himself and was unwilling to reveal more.

The same worries had come to haunt him again. What will happen if Maulana is released? Why are they asking for Maulana? Why is he so important? R. V. Raju, an IPS officer of the Kashmir cadre, one of the greatest investigators of the times I have ever seen, knew the answers. He had headed the CBI team which was investigating the assassination of Rajiv Gandhi. The ISI is not worried about the militants whom it arms with guns and grenades. They are deputed on the mission to fight and die and they are expendable. There is no need to hijack planes and take Westerners hostage. Their mission is *jihad* and let them die but ISI needed people who can motivate these men for *jihad*.

Raju's argument was valid. He had already briefed his boss about it, so I presumed. The Chief Minister's anxieties were not the outcome of some superstitions. He had known from experience that compromises with the terrorists only bred more terrorism. He had seen it happening all these years and was resolute that he would not become a partner to any deal that would help terrorists to expand their base and kill more people.

Harinder Baweja, a journalist while profiling Azhar, whom she first met in February 1994 in Srinagar's army cantonment writes: 'His behaviour in custody then, in February 1994, was no different from the kind of treatment meted out to me in Kabul by the Taliban in October 1996. Azhar refused to look me in the eye for his religion forbade eye contact with women. It didn't matter at all that he was surrounded by the Indian army or that he was in captivity. He had no problems, rather no reservations narrating what he had done in the two days that he had spent in the Valley. He was fortunate, I remember him telling me, that Allah had chosen him for what he called an Islamic duty and his only regret was that he had been captured and not killed. Had he been tortured, I asked him. Driven by rage—he broke his own rule—and looking me straight in the eye said saracstically. 'No, the army has been showering me with petals.'

He spent months after that in the hands of various interrogating officials drawn from different agencies like the Intelligence Bureau and the Research and Analysis Wing. The interrogating officer for Kashmir's counter intelligence wing, after several days trying to break Azhar, interestingly noted in his report that 'he (Azhar) was not himself involved in any subversive activity in Kashmir.'

Unknown to his interrogators, the Pakistan establishment was devising desperate strategies to secure the Maulana's release. The first plan of action was put into place within a few months after his arrest. In June, the same year 1994-the Harkat-ul-Ansar kidnapped two British nationals while they were trekking near Pahalgam in Kashmir's Anantnag district. One of them, Kim Housego, was the son of David Housego, a reputed Delhi-based journalist. High on the list of demands put forth by the HUA was Azhar's release. But when that didn't work, another plot was hatched four months later in the month of October.

This time, Omar Sheikh (later implicated in the kidnapping and death of Daniel Pearl, *Wall Street Journal's* South Asia correspondent) was sent to India with the express purpose of kidnapping foreigners to secure Maulana's release. He managed to befriend an American and three British tourists and keep them chained at a safe house on the outskirts of Delhi but was soon apprehended by the police. Like Azhar, he found himself in jail and both languished there for years without much progress on their legal cases. Pakistan did not give up despite Sheikh's arrest and in the following year, in 1995, five more foreigners were kidnapped by the Al Faran, a front name for the HUA. Again, the name that topped the list of the militants the Al Faran wanted released in exchange for the hostages was Azhar's. Kashmiri authorities continued negotiations with the captors for many months before the link snapped and the hostages were given up for dead. The Maulana's importance for the Pakistani establishment can be judged from the fact that their High Commission in India approached the Ministry for External Affairs for his release on the plea that he was a journalist.

Technically, that is how the Maulana began—as the editor of *Sada- I-Mujahid.* But he was much more than that. As a master motivator, his mind was more lethal than that of an AK-47, his words more dangerous than bullets. His speeches hit home and indoctrinated many minds. Even when in jail, Azhar continued with his writing, smuggling letters out with help from sympathetic jail sources.

'Ultimately the whole thing is going to happen in Kashmir.

I know it for certain. These people will intensify the violence in Kashmir and there would be more people dead. All this will happen to the people in Jammu and Kashmir. My heart bleeds for them and how can I allow this to happen? These are my people. I can understand Pakistan doing it for its sinister designs. Pakistan has no love lost for the people of Kashmir, why is the country's leadership not understanding our woes?', Farooq spoke half in anger and half in disgust at the growing violence in Kashmir for he was becoming tired of visiting the grieving families of the massacred victims and he could not bear the sight of more deaths. 'Who is dying? It is a Kashmiri,' he said continuing with his monologue.

He did not want more bloodshed in Kashmir. Releasing Masood Azhar would mean doing exactly the opposite. The Government of India, naïve as it proved to be, thought that he was a mere cleric and could pose no danger once set free and Jaswant Singh saw no harm in accompanying him in the official aircraft on the shameful flight from Delhi to Kandahar.

Maulana was released. So were Umar Sheikh from Tihar jail in Delhi and Mushtaq Zargar better known as Mushtaq Latram from Central jail, Srinagar. Dullat[16] had been able to get a nod from Farooq after an overnight debate and discussions. He heard Farooq's angry words and shared his distress. Like a typical intelligence man he listened with extreme patience. 'But what if they blow up the plane and all the passengers go with it?' he asked Farooq and, without waiting for a reaction, he went on to tell him, 'you will be blamed and can you forgive your conscience with the thought that these innocents died because you did not cooperate?' Dullat had played his trump card. He knew that his words had had an impact. He told Farooq that he was talking about something that had not happened as yet, while there was immediate and imminent danger to the lives of the passengers, innocent children and women.

Dullat was trying his argument for his feedback from his organization was that the hijackers were bent upon blowing up the plane and they would not settle anything short of the release of Azhar, and Umar. Mushtaq Latram seemed to be an appendage just to give a Kashimri flavour or perhaps a last minute change in lieu of the body of Sajjad Afghani which is buried in a graveyard which one can view easily from the rear of the Chief Minister's house in Jammu on the banks of Tawi river that moves sluggishly to Pakistan. Farooq gave in. But nevertheless his premonitions started coming true. The first gory glimpse was the massacre of 35 Sikhs in Chittisinghpora in Anantnag in south Kashmir about 60 kms from Srinagar. There was global outrage. But the militants were at work. Farooq could not contain his anger and frustration. He was unhappy that the government had not listened to him and the price was being paid. They did save those passengers but what about the hundreds of people who were dying every day?

Maulana Masood Azhar on his freedom in Kandahar found his way to Pakistan where he announced the formation of Jaish-e-Mohammad and a new saga of terrorism began. Kashmir was the prime target.

Endnotes

1. *Aatish-e-Chinar*—Flames of Chinar – This is the title of a biography on Sheikh Abdullah. The Chinar is a tree associated with Kashmir.

2. Atal Bihari Vajpayee : India's Prime Minister from 1998 to 2004.

3. NDA: National Democratic Alliance : An alliance of more than 24 parties that formed the federal government in Delhi in 1998.

4. National Front-It was the name of the parties that formed the federal coalition government in November 1989 under the premiership of Vishwanath Pratap Singh.

5. Mohammad Nawaz Sharief : Pakistan's Prime Minister whose government was involved in the tit for tat exchange of nuclear tests with India. He was deposed on October 12, 1999, jailed and exiled by Pakistan's army chief Gen. Pervez Musharraf, who is now also President of his country.

6. Benazir Bhutto: First woman Prime Minister of Pakistan in 1988; now living in exile.

7. Kargil, a Himalayan district in the north of Kashmir. Kargil lies in the Ladakh region of Jammu and Kashmir. The state has three regions: Hindu-dominated Jammu region, Muslim majority Kashmir Valley and Buddhist majority Ladakh region.

8. Leh : The town which serves as headquarters of the Leh district of Ladakh region.

9. Siachen glacier: The 40 sq. km glacier in the Himalayas contested by both India and Pakistan. In military terms, it is regarded as the highest battle-ground (18,000 feet) in the world.

10. Operation Vijay is the code name of the military operation under which the Indian army launched the attack to push back the intruders from Kargil in the summer of 1999. The Kargil war which officially started with 'Operation Vijay' on May 19, 1999 lasted till July 26, 1999. More than 500 Indian soldiers were killed in this operation.

11. Bhartiya Jan Sangh was a party of Hindu nationalists before its merger with the Janta Party in 1977 and later in 1979, it was renamed Bhartiya Janta Party or BJP.

12. Ajat Shatru Singh : Son of Dr. Karan Singh, who was elected on an NC ticket from the Nagrota assembly constituency on the periphery of Jammu. He was a minister in the Farooq Abdullah government from 1996 to 2002. He joined Congress in 2002, after his defeat in the Assembly elections.

13. The 1998 parliamentary elections were held following the dissolution of the United Front Government headed by Inder Kumar Gujral,

upon the withdrawal of support by Congress. Jammu and Kashmir contributed six seats to the Lok Sabha (having the strength of 543 seats).

14. Mohammad Shafi Uri : A senior NC leader who is considered a popular leader of the border town of Uri. He is considered a strong political man. He was a minister in the Sheikh Abdullah Government (1977–1982) and also minister in the Farooq Abdullah Government. But he was defeated in the 2002 elections by merely 67 votes.

15. Lashakr-e-Toiba or LeT, the terrorist group that launched suicide attacks in Kashmir. It also been listed as a terrorist organization by the United States.

16. A. S. Dullat, former RAW chief, who on his retirement in 2000 became officer on special duty in the Prime Minister's office during the Vajpayee Government.

15

Millennium Kashmir

'Why did you write that?' Farooq asked me. He was referring to my published story that the All Parties Hurriyat Conference leaders were about to be released. He seemed to suggest that I had written something against him. I heard Farooq telling me: 'They suspected us of having leaked the story.' It was a quite a bit of a shock to me because I had never spoken to Farooq about the stories nor did I intend to, as a journalist. I could understand the repercussions because the Centre had always suspected Farooq of sabotaging its efforts directed at securing peace with the separatists. This time was no exception. Farooq is discreet enough never to ask any questions about the sources, though his media bashing at times is notorious.

I myself have been subjected to this. When Farooq is angry, he fires right, left and middle. He goes to extremes. Though the very next day his anger may subside and he might even be seen apologizing. That is his style and many media people in Jammu and Kashmir have come to live with it. His words, which he repeats quite often, 'you will remember me once I am no more,' sometimes touch the hearts of even the bitterest of his critics.

Farooq in this case was obviously worried over the fact that he might be suspected of having leaked the story to the press. That morning, several of his friends had called him from Delhi saying that the Home Minister L.K. Advani suspected him of having whispered the story.

The complexity of Kashmir politics could not have been more bizarre. In this particular case, Abdul Ghani Lone, the senior Hurriyat leader, who was in the United States when his colleagues in the Hurriyat Conference were arrested in

September 1999 for opposing the parliamentary elections and justifying the violence that had been launched by the militants hell bent upon derailing the election process, was pressurizing the Government of India through the men who visited him, that jailed leaders should be freed. The arrested leaders, particularly Syed Ali Shah Geelani, who then headed the secessionist conglomerate of APHC, were gaining points with Pakistan because it pleased Islamabad that some people were fiercely furthering its agenda in Kashmir. Hizb-ul-Mujahadeen and Lashkare-Toiba had upset Delhi when it massacred 35 Sikhs in Chittisinghpora in Anantnag on March 20, 2000, the day US President Bill Clinton had arrived in India on his five-day tour of South Asia in the last year of his presidency.

Secondly, the arrested leaders were also getting international attention. The international community repeated pleas to Delhi to release the separatists. US President Bill Clinton had personally taken up this issue with Prime Minister Atal Behari Vajpayee.

Vajpayee began experimenting once again, by ordering the release of the APHC leaders in April 2000. This time Delhi also needed some alibi to work for the release of the Hurriyat Conference leaders. It was guided by two objectives. One, it wanted to start a dialogue with the separatists so that the simmering issue of Kashmir could be resolved. It was also looking for alternatives to Farooq Abdullah whose aggressive tone often worried Delhi. The Central leadership was becoming sceptical of the National Conference.

At the same time leaders like Mufti Mohammad Sayeed were keen on the dismissal of the National Conference Government. Mufti's campaign theme was that the NC regime had been thrust on the people of the State rather than having come to rule as a result of the popular will of the people of

Kashmir. Disparaging the Abdullah family has been a permanent feature of Mufti's agenda since the beginning of his political career in the 1970s when he attempted to challenge the unassailable Sheikh Mohammad Abdullah. Having failed to do so, he battled against Farooq Abdullah who had replaced his father as Chief Minister. Farooq's son, Omar Abdullah was now the target of Mufti and his daughter Mehbooba Mufti. She was particularly bitter after she had lost the 1999 parliamentary elections to Omar in the Srinagar-Budgam constituency. Omar won that election for a second time. His maiden victory was in February 1998 from the same parliamentary constituency. That was a prestigious victory for Omar and a humiliating defeat for Mehbooba. She could not forget the agony of that defeat and launched a scathing attack and virulent campaign against Farooq Abdullah and his son. Her strategy was to talk about human rights violations. She spoke of the wrongs suffered by the people. The Abdullahs were complacent to the point of being indifferent. While Mehbooba moved, the Abdullahs remained stagnant. Against this background and with the separatists refusing to accept Farooq Abdullah as genuine leader of the people of Kashmir, the Centre was looking for other credible options.

Negotiations with the Hurriyat Conference

Delhi was fully aware that the Hurriyat Conference had no *locus standi* among the people. It had never tested its electoral popularity. It had shied away from participating in elections under the pretext that the elections under the Indian Constitution would deliver no solution. Its slogan was and continues to be 'no election, no selection, only solution.' This solution, it seeks through the grant of the right of self-determination for the people of the State and tirelessly reminds the Indian leadership of the promises that the first Indian Prime Minister Jawaharlal Nehru had made on the floor of the Indian

Parliament, that the people of Kashmir would decide their destiny through plebiscite, something that the United Nations endorsed through its resolutions. There were various forms of elections suggested by the Hurriyat Conference. 'Let all the Indian forces go back to the barracks and let there be international observers and let the elections be held at district-level (in each of Jammu Kashmir's fourteen districts), then let the people vote in a free and fair manner. Then, the people would show who the real representatives were,' Geelani has said so many times.

But who would silence the guns of the militants? How would they disappear? Geelani and the likes of him had no answers to these questions. In fact, there were no answers. And that was the only reply that the separatists could come up with to justify their non-participation and opposition to the elections.

They were probably afraid of facing the people in the elections: first it would have exposed them in the eyes of the people as opportunists who could shift sides with the changing times. The people who had responded to the call of *jihad* and the liberation of Kashmir from Indian rule made by these leaders and paid heavily in the process could not be expected to contemplate their leaders' participation in the polls. If elections were to pave the way for a solution, how were the leaders to justify the sacrifice of the tens of thousands of lives that had been made? The objectives of freedom for Kashmir or merger with Pakistan had died long ago. The masses knew that the Hurriyat Conference lacked the will and was also incapable of leading them in any particular direction. If it was freedom, then where was the 'azadi' that these leaders had promised and the image of which had lured tens of thousands of people to their graves? If their death was martyrdom, for a cause, where was that cause and its status? If elections could offer a solution then why were there so many graveyards of 'martyrs?'

The separatists had created a make-believe world for the people and they had sustained the hopes of Kashmiris by telling them that the international community was coming to their rescue and the day was not far when they would be part of the free nation called Kashmir. America was watching. The gullible people were taken in by the statements that came from the United States and also from other countries. Each anti-India statement on Kashmir of Robin Raphael, the Assistant Secretary of State for South Asia, was seen as a step towards the realization of their hopes. Their dreams were conjectured by leaders who themselves lacked conviction. And that was where they knew that their escape route was in opposing the elections. Accepting anything Indian would have provoked the people's ire.

And that would have been the end of their game.

It was this which led them to oppose the elections. Apart from that, Kashmir is gripped by the belief that democracy is being trampled underfoot by India in the name of national interest. And this interest drowns all voices of dissent, however powerful or genuine these might be.

Nevertheless, Vajpayee's order to release the APHC leaders in April 2000 was executed. APHC chairman Syed Ali Shah Geelani was sought out by the Prime Minister's emissaries R. K. Mishra and Wajahat Habibullah, and there were several rounds of talks but these could not progress because in the meantime, Farooq Abdullah had thrown a spanner in the works.

Farooq's Autonomy Report

The autonomy report was tabled in the State Legislative Assembly by his government in the full glare of the cameras in April 2000, almost at the same time when the Hurriyat leaders were set free. A link was seen in the tabling of the report at the end of the budget session of the state legislature and the release of Hurriyat leaders. It was interpreted by critics of the National Conference as the ruling party's counter to the moves of the Centre to open negotiations with the separatists. The NC feared this because it believed that if separatists were to participate in the polls, Abdullah's party would face a tough times. Ironically, now that the NC had lost its power in the 2002 polls, it is the strongest advocate of talks with separatists. Even today the participation of the separatists in the polls could turn tables on any mainstream political party. This is the paradox of Kashmir. Even the hated people can win. The Hurriyat, had it consented to contest in the elections,would have been in a somewhat similar position as was Sheikh Abdullah in 1975 after having buried the plebiscite slogan. Sheikh Abdullah had won the 1977 elections. Hurriyat too could have tasted victory. That prospect haunted the NC in 2000. Critics were quick to point out that the National Conference had chosen the timing of the tabling of the autonomy report when it was known that the NDA Government in which the BJP was a dominant party was opposed to the granting of autonomy to Jammu and Kashmir. 'National Conference is insincere in handling the autonomy issue. It could have passed a bill on autonomy to show its sincerity and seriousness,' Mufti had commented.

But the legal position is that the State Legislative Assembly cannot table any bill involving Centre-State relations without the prior permission of the President of India. Hence, the tabling of the bill was a remote possibility. Mufti was only playing a political point scoring game and deliberately obscuring the constitutional obligation.

Mufti had his own reasons for denouncing Farooq and the National Conference but the fact was that as a leader of Kashmiri origin he could not oppose the autonomy. His party MLAs supported the autonomy resolution when it came up for discussion and voting at the special session of the state legislature in Srinagar in June 2000. But another equally important fact was that the National Conference had wasted precious time in the preparation of the report. It was submitted after a full gap of 41 months after the constitution of the autonomy panel in November 1996. The report was prepared in a slapdash manner. There was nothing to suggest that extraordinary homework had been done or any in-depth studies had been undertaken by those who prepared the report. The panel was headed by Ghulam Mohi-ud-Din Shah who had replaced Dr. Karan Singh as the Chairman of the autonomy panel. It was at best a cut and paste job, of different agreements between Delhi and Srinagar. Nevertheless it was a report and it had the sanctity of the excerpts from the constitution and also agreements signed by various leaders of Kashmir and India.

Although Farooq had said that the autonomy report had nothing to do with the Centre's moves to start the dialogue with the separatists, the timing did not leave anyone in doubt that Farooq was trying to seek his pound of flesh when he was threatened by the prospect of the Centre- separatists making a breakthrough. The critics were unsparing.

Vajpayee was angry with Farooq for playing spoil sport and responded by rejecting the National Conference's autonomy resolution passed by both Houses of the state legislature without even going through it. That was too much of an insult to be borne by Abdullah. But he neither opted for fresh Assembly elections nor did he withdraw his son from the Union Ministry once again proving that what mattered most to him was power, though the general impression at that time was that, had Farooq opted for dissolution of the Assembly on the issue, he could have won the Assembly elections without difficulty.

Although he was exasperated by the rejection of the autonomy report, Farooq never took issue with the Centre about it. The point that he wished to drive home to the Kashmiri separatists was that they could hardly expect better treatment from Delhi when it was not even prepared to restore autonomy to the State of Jammu and Kashmir within the parameters of the Indian Constitution. How could they, the separatists, hope to obtain the freedom they were asking for, still less merger with Pakistan? Syed Ali Shah Geelani and Abdul Ghani Lone reacted the way Farooq had expected.

Geelani felt that though autonomy might not have been on their agenda, they had not after all, sacrificed the lives of tens of thousands of their people to that end, he concluded that they could hardly expect justice or fair treatment from the government since it had baulked at a simple report.

Farooq had carried the day though he had lost face before the people of Kashmir to whom he had promised autonomy at all costs. He could only lamely reiterate that the government should have opened discussion on the autonomy report. Quite apart from the personal threat to his leadership and that of the party, Farooq had made a request which he could not possibly expect to be granted. 'What are you going to talk to these Hurriyat leaders (about), their agenda is clear? They are the mouthpiece of Pakistan. They are asking for secession of Kashmir. Are you going to give them independence of Kashmir or hand over the Valley on a platter to Pakistan?' These were valid posers. If the National Conference was ruling the state and its representatives were sitting in the Assembly elected by the people under President's rule, why should its position have been undermined? This was the question to which Delhi had failed to respond. Worse still, the National Conference had lost its activists to the bullets of militants; ministers and functionaries had been killed and their lives shattered by militants merely because the National Conference had upheld the finality of

Jammu and Kashmir's accession to India. This was the sticking point.

But Farooq and the NC had not pursued the issue of autonomy to its logical conclusion. Farooq flinched. When the autonomy resolution was rejected, the NC lacked the guts to force the issue. It contributed to its own let- down before the eyes of the people of Kashmir. It was Farooq's ambition for his son to hold ministerial office in Delhi and to complete his six-year term and to ensure Omar's success by buying peace with the Centre which back-fired. The future was to demonstrate the people's rejection of the NC's continuance in power, the touchstone was the failure of the party leadership's failure to stand up to Delhi. Kashmiris hate nothing more in their leaders than their subjugation to Delhi.

Dialogue with the Separatists

Delhi's strategies have often baffled the people and political analysts alike. Vajpayee was only repeating what his predecessors had done in the past.

Where was the policy of fighting terrorism? 'No negotiations with terrorists,' BJP leaders and Vajpayee in particular had reiterated that there was no question of holding negotiations with terrorists. He had accused Congress of fostering terrorism by its flip-flop policies. 'Our stand is clear? We will not talk to Pakistan nor will we talk to terrorists unless Pakistan rolls back terrorism.' The words rang loud and clear and it was Vajpayee speaking to the people in Hira Nagar, not far from the international border in December 1998. Vajpayee had embarked on a bus journey to Lahore, Pakistan in 1999 only to be greeted by Pakistan's intrusion onto Indian soil, on the Kargil heights and he vowed that he would not talk to Pakistan come what may unless Islamabad rolled back cross- border terrorism. His posturing gladdened the hearts of the Indian nation, relieved that here was someone who could take Pakistan to task for the audacity of challenging Indian might. There were many who were mourning the loss of their dear and near as a consequence of Pakistan-sponsored terrorism; there were the families of soldiers who had sacrificed their lives in Kargil. And on June 13, 1999, when Vajpayee visited Kargil, the Pakistanis had greeted him with guns. Shells missed his helicopter by inches. Back in Srinagar, he told newsmen that there would be a war. We believed him. After all, this was a Prime Minister speaking. He was chagrined that what he had intended as a pilgrimage for peace should metamorphose into a war march towards the inexorable heights of Kargil. We witness here the restiveness of a poet and a politician aspiring to become a statesman. Vajpayee strongly believed that his claim to the Nobel peace prize or a niche in history, parallel to Jawaharlal Nehru's, lay in the philosophy of reaching out to the enemy. He might have drawn his lessons from Yithzak Rabin, the Israeli Prime Minister who was assassinated by a fellow Jew for broaching peace with the Palestinians and for his recognition of Yasir Arafat as their leader, whom other Israelis took for a terrorist and the master-mind behind all acts of terrorism. The 'Commander-in-Chief' of Hizb-ul-Mujahadeen, Majid Dar moved out of Pakistan lured by the Indian intelligence agencies. In Srinagar, he announced to the people of Kashmir a three-month long unilateral cease-fire and a bilateral dialogue with the Government of India to restore peace to the Valley. 'There has been enough of bloodshed and even if we continue to fight and bleed for the next ten years, the results would not be different. Let's begin a dialogue and search peace ... across the table.'

Abdul Majid Dar with whom the government had held negotiations in Dubai, got him transported to Srinagar. The

Government of India was resorting to the old practice of buying loyalties in Kashmir. It was using Majid Dar this time.

This was the usual ploy at the disposal of the RAW and the ISI. As Lone correctly assessed at his party convention in November 2000: 'Kashmir has become a pawn in the hands of the agencies of India and Pakistan."

India was fast losing ground because Pakistan was effectively stonewalling talks.

The Government of India moved according to script. A dialogue table was set up at Nehru Guest- House in Chashma Shahi and talks began. I wondered how the thousands who had been killed at the hands of militants might view the spectacle of the killers being accorded the honour of being seated at par with the Indian Home Secretary and his team.

All Parties Hurriyat Conference leader Abdul Ghani Lone was also surprised at the way the Vajpayee Government had been on its knees once Abdul Majid Dar of Hizb-ul-Mujahadeen announced unilateral cease fire in July 2000. 'They are buffoons. They don't even know the basic art of politics,' Lone remarked.

'If you declared that there would be no talks with terrorists, why did you hold talks? You compromised a situation and legitimized terrorism and rewarded those who picked up guns.' Lone was right. The Government of India was spineless. It had dashed with all pomp and ceremony to Srinagar to hold talks, which never went beyond the first round. August 3 was the beginning and the end of it all. Farooq had attempted to forestall Delhi. He was angry over the way the Government of India had conducted itself and bitten the dust. That had made his position as a pro-India politician quite vulnerable. India cannot be trusted, so why should Farooq be trusted? All anger was now directed at him. He was persuaded that it was all an attempt directed at marginalizing him. He was angry with Delhi not only for undermining his position by holding talks with terrorists or encouraging his political opponents. He resented the Government of India for not taking him into their confidence. 'I am willing to give up the chair of Chief Minister if that will help to bring peace in Kashmir,' he said. 'I have done it in the past,' he used to say, referring to his resignation in 1990. Before the public eye, Farooq welcomed the talks, but he had genuine fears and reservations. Besides, he held adamantly to the logic of not entertaining negotiations with terrorists. He knew that unless Pakistan stopped pulling the strings, nothing would be achieved. Contrary to sound political counsel, the present script was really the dictate of intelligence agencies. Political matters should not be left to the terrorists and the intelligence sleuths. His apprehensions proved correct.

Within a couple of days of Majid Dar's announcement of the unilateral cease-fire, his boss Syed Salahauddin made it conditional on Pakistan's participation. This was not in the original version of the cease-fire announced in Srinagar. Pakistan, feared that the commencement of talks between the Hizb, the formidable group of Kashmiri separatists and the Government of India, would lead, inevitably to the neutralization of foreign militant outfits. It could pave the way for peace in the Valley. Once that happened the whole operation in which Islamabad had invested so heavily in terms of men and money would turn to nought. Pakistan did not want that to happen. Pakistan again undertook to thwart the peace process.

Pakistan sponsored a series of massacres on the intervening night of July 31 and August 1, 2000 in which nearly 100 Hindus were killed all across south Kashmir and parts of the Jammu region. It was the first time that the Hindu pilgrims of Amarnath1a Himalayan pilgrimage in south Kashmir were targeted. There was a universal condemnation of what had happened. The Hizb too had condemned these massacres washing its hands off the carnage that shocked the whole Indian nation. The Government of India, as gullible as it proved to be, believed that the Hizb had actually not played any role in it. How perceptions had changed or how much Delhi was living in its own make-believe world was obvious from this.

When 35 Sikhs had been massacred in Chitisinghpora in Anantnag, Delhi had rushed there saying that the Hizb-ul-Mujahadeen and Lashkar-e-Toiba were involved in the massacre. Three months later, the same Hizb-ul-Mujahadeen had become an angel in the eyes of the Government of India which had been short-changed. Not only had the talks collapsed but the level of violence had also picked up. The Hizb struck with greater terror as a car bomb exploded in the middle of the Residency Road on August 10, two days after it withdrew the cease-fire in Islamabad and Advani and Vajpayee wrung their hands and blamed Pakistan for the failure of talks the outcome of which had been pre-destined. Pakistan was once again in a win-win situation. It had achieved its objective by withdrawing the Hizb from the talks and Majid Dar was left helpless fretting and fuming while his aide Fazal-ul-Haq Qureshi[2] who had served as a mediator, rued the day he had taken up this assignment.

Vajpayee was not a man to give up his dreams and ambitions. He announced a unilateral cease-fire in November 2000 coinciding with the beginning of the Muslim holy month of Ramzan. It was extended twice and in all lasted for six months[3]. However, it failed in its objective and had the opposite effect in raising the level of violence. The year 2000 also saw the first suicide bombing by a local youth Afaq Ahmad who blew himself up in front of the cantonment gate in Batwara. Jaish had struck. It struck again in December 2000 when Prime Minister Atal Behari Vajpayee's ill-conceived Non-Initiation of

Combat Operation (NICO), better known as unilateral cease fire, was on. Vajpayee like his predecessors was fond of experimenting upon their favourite playground—Kashmir.

What happened in Agra, the city famous for the Taj Mahal, epitome of immortalized love, constructed by Mughal emperor Shahjahan, is another sordid story. The cease-fire was called off in the last week of May 2001. The Deputy Chairman Planning Commission, K. C. Pant[4] was appointed as interlocutor to hold talks with everyone in all parts of the state in an attempt to find a solution. Simultaneously an invitation was sent to the Pakistan Chief Executive Officer Gen. Pervez Musharraf to visit India and hold talks on all contentious issues, including Jammu and Kashmir.

Musharraf who, since his taking over the reins of Pakistan on October 12, 1999, had indicated that he was willing to dialogue with India at any time and at any place, welcomed the opportunity. By the ensuing month he had made himself President, just a week before he arrived in Delhi for the Agra summit. The General was in a sherwani not the army uniform. Moreover, it was a white sherwani, a symbol of peace. He was given a hero's welcome in India and greeted as a potential peace maker. Hopes in Kashmir skyrocketed. There was an air of optimism. Prayers for the success of the summit grabbed the newspaper headlines. There was widespread hope for a breakthrough. It was generally felt that only talks could yield results now and since Vajpayee was from a fundamentalist Hindu party, he was thought to be better placed than anyone else, whom the hard-line Hindus did not trust, to negotiate and obtain the desired objective. However, even Vajpayee was being labelled by Hindu fundamentalist groups as 'secular'—which, in their vocabulary, is a derogatory term. Ashok Singhal,[5] President of the Vishwa Hindu Parishad,[6] had even called him a 'coward.'

On the other side was an army General who was in total command of the situation in Pakistan, which had not been the case with civilian Prime Minister Mian Mohammad Nawaz Sharief at the time of the Lahore declaration. Since Pakistan is a country known to attribute its survival to the three As: Allah, America and Army, it was thought that Gen. Musharraf on behalf of the Pakistan army might be able to take effective measures to write a new chapter of peace between the two hostile nations. America has always hoped that both countries might sort out matters between them for Washington is deeply apprehensive of a nuclear conflict developing over Kashmir. However, Allah appears not to have blessed the Pakistan Army or America for the inevitable happened: the talks failed.

But then President Musharraf had made his intentions clear when he defied protocol and had high tea with the APHC leaders at the Pakistan High Commission against the wishes of his host nation, on the very first day of his arrival in Delhi, on July 13, 2001. The following day he was in Agra and the talks started.

Each and every one of his movements was being recorded. The satellite channels were falling over each other, in attempting to get close to him. He held talks with Vajpayee and also with Advani. Philosophically and poetically, Vajpayee gave the reason for his choice of Agra: 'I thought that, against the backdrop of Taj, a monument dedicated to love, the General would talk peace.' Vajpayee was living out a vision of his imagination. However, a breakthrough did appear imminent as Pakistan Foreign Minister Sartaj Aziz hinted at the signing of a joint declaration. But before that Musharraf had told editors of the leading dailies of India that he could not sign anything that compromised Pakistan's original stand on Kashmir. 'Kashmir is the core issue.'

'I am prepared to sign all other documents in a matter of seconds but let's first resolve Kashmir, the most contentious issue, thereafter whatever you may say: trade, business, tourism, I will do that.'

'If I am to give up my stand on Kashmir, then I would have to buy Nehar wali Haveli and live here,' he said showing how important the sorting out of the Kashmir issue was for him. Nehar wali Haveli was his childhood home in Delhi which he had left after the partition. He visited that home during his visit.

The Indian leadership was aghast at the audacity of their Pakistani guest. He had violated protocol. He had taken all the editorial cream of India for a ride. His breakfast meeting with editors was being telecast live by Pakistan TV and no one was aware of it, not the best Indian brains nor the intelligence agencies had had any hint of it.

That was the start of the undoing of the Agra summit. Pervez Musharraf returned home empty-handed and his ministers blamed Advani for his rigid stand which had prevented an agreement between the two countries.

India and Pakistan began blaming each other. Pervez Musharraf said that someone more powerful than Vajpayee had sabotaged the talks.[7] The reference was to Advani. 'The draft of the declaration was all ready for the penning of signatures. Something occurred and all the cards caved in. India was angry that Pakistan had spoken only of Kashmir and Kashmir alone. There was no willingness on the part of Pakistan to accept its role in the cross-border terrorism in Kashmir. That is where the talks failed, went the Indian argument. And so the balance game continues.

Endnotes

1. Amarnath: A Hindu shrine in the south of Kashmir nestled in Himalayas at the height of 13,500 feet.

2. Fazal-ul-Haq Qureshi of the People's Front who was the Hizb-ul-Mujahadeen's key man in the July-August 2000 talks with the Government of India. He was also a member of the five-member team of the Moulvi Abbas Ansari faction of the All Parties Hurriyat Conference which held talks with the Government of India in January 2004. However, he withdrew from talks to protest against the human rights abuses by the security forces before the second round on March 22.

3. The cease-fire was extended twice. It was announced on November 19, 2000 and came into effect on November 28-the beginning of the holy Muslim month of Ramzan. It was again extended for a month in December at the end of the fasting period. In January it was extended for four months. In all the cease-fire lasted for six months.

4. K. C. Pant. A senior leader of Congress who later joined the BJP and became Deputy Chairman of the Planning Commission. He was appointed as interlocutor to hold talks with all the Kashmiri groups in May 2001.

5. Ashok Singhal. International President of Vishwa Hindu Parishad, a group of Hindu fundamentalists committed to the objective of a pure nation of Hindus.

6. (VHP) Vishwa Hindu Parishad, a group of Hindu fundamentalists in India.

7. Pervez Musharraf's statement on Kashmir: 'On course despite hiccups,' *Hindustan Times*, July 17, 2001

16

Turning Point in Kashmir Terrorism: 9/11

America saw terrorism strike at its heart on 9/11. The twin towers of the World Trade Centre in New York came crumbling down. Pentagon was bleeding. Terrorists had hijacked commercial flights and turned them into missiles to strike at the symbols of military and economic power of the United States of America, the sole superpower in the world. Terrorists the world over were laughing over the fall of American might within America. This was beyond the worst nightmares of the American nation: to be forced to contemplate the twisted metals, searing human flesh, smoke and dust of ground zero which has choked the whole of America. The American nation was shocked. The dangers of growing terrorism which Indian leaders had tried to warn them of and which they had dismissed with derisive laughter, had come true.

Kashmiris who witnessed their own set of terrorist acts were aghast at the scale of the mayhem unleashed by terrorists in New York and Washington saddened over the loss of hundreds of lives in the United States.

But Farooq Abdullah felt that, at last, the 'giant has woken and expected America to fight terrorism in right earnest.' His feelings were mixed. Like most of his people he was sad over the momentous tragedy. But he was glad that his stand against terrorism had been vindicated. As America now realises.

The United States was on its knees. It sought to resurrect itself from the debris against the perpetuators of the acts of terror. President George W. Bush declared war against terror. 'The search is underway for those who are behind these evil acts...we will make no distinction between the terrorists who committed these acts and those who harbour them. We fight the terrorists and we fight all of those who give them aid. America has a message for the nations of the world: if you harbour terrorists, you are terrorist. If you train or arm a terrorist, you are a terrorist. If you feed a terrorist or fund a terrorist you are a terrorist. And you will be held accountable by the United States and our friends.' These words seemed to be 'imaging' Pakistan.

Pakistan Sides with the US for its Kashmiri Cause

Farooq indeed was happy. He felt that the noose around Pakistan would be tightened and that would ease the pressure of terrorism on Kashmir. For Pakistan was a haven for terrorists and the capital of terrorism where terrorist groups recruit terrorists, train and arm them. It was in Pakistan that terrorists plan their operations. Though 9/11 was thought to be planned in the lawless mountains of Afghanistan by Mullah Umar[1] and Osama bin Laden—the leaders of the Taliban and Al-Qaeda—the terrorist networks, Pakistan was within that frame. The terror networks owed their existence to the ISI of Pakistan and America knew this.

The immediate target was Afghanistan where the mastermind of terrorism, Osama bin Laden was hiding. To strike there, America needed Pakistan's help. Musharraf became a willing ally against the Taliban, the very force that Pakistan had, itself, created. Musharraf had no qualms of turning back on his own creation when it came to his own survival in power. He claimed to have done it in the national interest to prevent Pakistan from being labelled a terrorist nation.

Musharraf attempted to reason with the people of his nation on September 19, 2001. In a televised address to the nation, he said that America was asking for 'our support in three main specific areas. Information exchange, the use of air space and the third area (where) they need our support is logistic support. I also want to clarify that until this moment, their plans are not ready and so we don't have any details of what they plan. But I can tell you whatever America is planning, the United Nations General Assembly and Security Council have passed a resolution supporting them, and this resolution is to fight against terrorism. And I also wish to tell you that all Islamic nations supported this resolution.'

In the same speech he sought to make his people aware of the domestic situation in Pakistan. 'Pakistan is facing a very critical time. And I would say, after 1971, this is the most critical period in the nation's life. And at this point, our decisions will have far-reaching and decisive results. On the one hand, if we make any mistake, they can culminate in very bad ends. And on the other hand, if we make the right decisions, they would be very fruitful for us. The bad results can put into danger our very existence.'

President Musharraf knew better. He knew the intended target of the message. That Afghanistan would be targetted was a foregone conclusion drawn by everyone in the world. Pakistan too could not escape was the logical conclusion. The United States working out its road-map of war on terror. Musharraf knew that the time had come to throw the baby out with the bath water. It was a question of his personal survival and that of his nation. Pakistan was campaigning against extremism out of its national interest and not under pressure from anyone. Pakistan became an ally of America in the war against terror but its attitude towards India and particularly to Jammu and Kashmir remained unchanged.

On September 19 itself, Pervez Musharraf had declared

that he was helping America in its war against terrorism because that would help in 'our cause on Kashmir.' Pakistan which had failed to obtain effective American intervention in Kashmir, was setting its sights on the role of the US in Kashmir in lieu of Islamabad's turning its back on the Taliban and helping the Americans in their war against Osama bin Laden in Afghanistan. Pakistan was killing two birds with one stone. It was becoming a crucial ally of the United States in the war against terror and at the same time it was eyeing Americans working in its favour vis-à-vis its claim on Kashmir.

Hurriyat Presses for Negotiated Settlement

The All Parties Hurriyat Conference and the rest of the separatist leadership were closely watching the post-9/11 scenario. They observed how the Pakistan President was shifting sides. It could happen in Kashmir too. There was consternation: since Pakistan had given up on the Taliban today, tomorrow it could 'in its national interest' give up Kashmir. The Hurriyat Conference, however, was unable to break itself completely from the shackles of Islamabad. So it changed its tune. It started voicing concerns against extremism. This was an echo of the innermost voice of the Kashmiris. Pakistan had, after all, failed to live up to its reputation as saviour of the Kashmiris. It had not taken on India in 1990 when Kashmiris were being killed by security forces along the borders and within the Valley. The post-Kargil conflict had only brought more death and destruction through the *fidayeen,* a cult which had scant respect for Kashmiri sensitivities. Having understood this, the Hurriyat had started pressing for a negotiated settlement and distancing itself from the cult of guns, preferably through American intervention.

The Hurriyat leaders were eager to suggest that the post-9/11 world had no place for guns in Kashmir. 'Guns cannot provide a solution and we should not fall into the trap of the extremist forces,' Lone used to say. His argument was that Kashmiris would harm their own cause if they persisted in their recourse to arms. 'We cannot seek the support of the Americans and at the same time support those wielding weapons of terror.' The argument was indeed a valid one.

Renewal of Violence

But the change in mindset did not mean that Pakistan had changed. Farooq's happiness too was short-lived. Six days before America launched its air assault in Afghanistan, the events of October first occurred in Kashmir. Terrorists struck at the Legislative Assembly in Srinagar and left 38 people dead and many more wounded. Pakistan's move was a clear manifestation that it was pursuing its original agenda in Kashmir. The Indian response was awaited. There were several noises and finally Vajpayee wrote a letter to President Bush seeking his help in taming Pakistan and in checking its terror tactics. That made no impact. Instead, December 13 occurred. Five terrorists struck at the Indian Parliament and before they got killed what had become obvious was that India lacked the spine to launch its own war against terrorism though it had flexed its muscles and raised the expectations of the people. It mobilized troops to the borders only to withdraw them a year later, to the ridicule of the nation and its soldiers, who stood watching helplessly waiting, for orders for action, which never came.

Assassination of Abdul Gani Lone

Abdul Gani Lone's differences with theologians and the religious agenda of *jihad* was at the root of his assassination in May 2002 within a month after his meeting with the leaders of Pakistan-occupied Kashmir (PoK) in Dubai in the United Arab Emirates (UAE). Mirwaiz Umar Farooq was also with him during the talks they held with former PoK Prime Minister Sardar Abdul

Qayoom Khan. The common ground which the three shared was that foreign militants had no role to play in Kashmir. Lone became the loudest critic of the foreign militants outfits: Lashkar-e-Toiba and Jaish-e-Mohammad. 'Kashmir cannot be allowed to be used as a battle ground by those seeking to unfurl the Islamic flag on the Red Fort or the White House.' This was the favourite theme in his speeches months before his assassination. He told me that he hated the idea of militants with guns sitting across the discussion table. It was beyond his comprehension, 'How could militants with guns hold dialogue, that means their gun cult has been recognized as legal and logical.'

His assassins appointed May 21, 2002 as the day and Idgah as the place of his assassination. There was no room for mistakes. It was not by coincidence. It was by design. The aim was to silence the emerging anti-Jihadi voice: first that of Mirwaiz Molvi Farooq, and now of Abdul Ghani Lone. Mirwaiz Umar Farooq, son of the assassinated Mirwaiz Molvi Farooq was now left alone. But the frightening message was clear: you are next, if you continue to oppose *jihadis*.

India felt a jolt on learning of the assassination of Lone. Its hopes of seeing a rise in the voice of the moderates in the separatist camp were dashed. So an attempt was made to turn the moderates to the election process. A new balloon was floated: the Kashmir Committee set up by one of its maverick politicians, Ram Jethmalani,[2] through whom, in the late 1980s, anti-Congress forces attempted to pin down Prime Minister Rajiv by relentless daily interrogation. This time Prime Minister Vajpayee was using him to counter his all powerful deputy Advani, who had nominated his own crony Arun Jaitly to hold talks with the National Conference and other groups on the subject of the restoration of autonomy.

Jethmalani first played a political game with the

secessionist conglomerate All Parties Hurriyat Conference and advocated international mediation in the Kashmir dispute. The Hurriyat was delighted. At last, they felt, here was someone from the Indian establishment who had come alongside to endorse their viewpoint: when two sides cannot resolve their dispute on their own, room should be made for a third party. Pakistan, too, has consistently maintained this stance whatever changes there may have been in its leadership. Jethmalini's words were therefore music to the ears of the Pakistanis. And he further made Pakistan happy during his visit there, by observing that 'Kashmir is not an integral part of India.'

Since the start of the secessionist militancy in Kashmir in 1989, Pakistani leaders ranging from Benazir Bhutto to Nawaz Sharief and now the military ruler, General Pervez Musharraf had been advocating the same line. Naturally, the Americans were happy. They saw in it an opportunity to arm-twist India and Delhi was happily allowing itself to be exploited by the American-Pakistan nexus. The fractious leadership in Delhi lacked the courage to resist American pressures and one of the pressures was to have a committee that could open dialogue with the separatist camp. So Vajpayee obliged Washington. He has always done that, his denials notwithstanding.

Jethmalani's puzzle was falling into place. He set up a committee and filled it with the Prime Minister's men on Kashmir. Vajpayee was unhappy with the way Advani had bulldozed his missions via K. C. Pant and former RAW chief A. S. Dullat. So he struck by what appeared to him as a master stroke, little knowing that it would be an irrevocable disaster from the very beginning.

Kashmir Committee

The outcome of the mission fulfilled the prophecies of keen Kashmir observers. The KC, as it came to be known, started its high profile, widely publicized three-day visit of Kashmir from one end to another. It met the Jammu and Kashmir Democratic Freedom Party President, Shabir Ahmad Shah and expressed confidence that it would succeed in its mission to persuade the separatists to take part in the September-October 2002 polls. It met the Hurriyat leaders and drew a blank. In the end Farooq approached the KC, and asked if it was possible for them to persuade the Hurriyat to participate in the polls adding that he would step down and make way for the imposition of Governor's rule. Jethmalani's joy knew no bounds. He felt on top of the world. But his joy was short- lived as the Hurriyat delivered a stern reminder to Jethmalani and company that elections were no solution to the Kashmir crisis. 'How many times, (do) we have to repeat,' asked APHC chief Abdul Ghani Bhat and added unperturbed that 'elections were not a solution.'

He further reminded India's former Law Minister that elections held under the shadow of guns and without any solution in sight could not yield any lasting solution. Kashmir was not a dispute concerning the change of the government. It was a much wider issue that had assumed global significance.

In his lucid style, the professor in Bhat was at his best. 'We are looking for a solution, you are looking at elections. Tell me in what manner these elections can resolve a crisis which has claimed nearly 80,000 lives and when many more are dying every day? It is an issue of the people's wishes and the determination of their future status not who would form the next government.'

'You have come with an offer from Farooq Abdullah that he would step down, if we take part in the polls, what is the great deal in it? Farooq was not there in 1996 when the Government of India first wanted to re-introduce what it called democratic process in the state.'

'What you are saying is, let me say with as much politeness as I can command, meaningless.'

Those present at the meeting disclosed that Jethmalani was left speechless. He could not utter even a word. His arguments of free and fair elections were dismissed as inconsequential. 'We are looking for self-determination and you are talking about elections. There is no comparison between the two.'

There were more stinging remarks from Bilal Lone, eldest son of the assassinated separatist leader Abdul Ghani Lone. 'Mr. Jethmalani, why have you come? Prime Minister Vajpayee would talk to the elected representatives which means for earning a seat at the negotiation table, we must contest in the elections. We reject these elections. We are an aggrieved party. If you have to talk to us, talk, otherwise why are you wasting time on the things over which you have no control?'

These were home truths. The fact of the matter was that the Hurriyat could not jump into elections without having obtained something substantial to face the people. The talk of autonomy or of the devolution of powers was of no interest to it. It knew that on the issue of autonomy it was on a sticky wicket vis-à-vis the National Conference and the Centre. The National Conference had a very strong argument, or rather a fact, on its side that it had been asking for autonomy from the very beginning and at no stage did this justify the violence that had wreaked havoc in the Valley. The Hurriyat had no argument to counter that and moreover, it had become a pawn in the hands of Pakistan.

Farooq: Elections 2002

Farooq Abdullah was perspiring. Sitting in the Conference room of District Police Lines, Jammu, Farooq was sweating more because of the announcement of the elections that Chief Election

Commissioner J. M. Lyngdoh was expected to make rather than because of the humidity of the Jammu summer. It was August 2, 2002. He had come to the police lines to pay tribute to the policemen who were killed fighting terrorists responsible for the July 13 massacre at Rajiv Nagar, a suburb of the locality of Jammu in which 29 people had been killed.

It was disconcerting to hear talk of the holding of elections, which is a peacetime exercise, in a place where people were being killed by the dozens. The toll for the day, even as the CEC announced four-phase polling for Jammu and Kashmir, was more than two dozens and 15 of whom were army personnel. Militants had overrun the Dana post in the Machail sector in the north-west of Kashmir and killed one Captain and 15 soldiers and the militants had hurled a grenade at the PCC headquarters at busy Maulana Azad Road conveying their message of an anti-poll terror with a loud bang—something that the people in the Valley have become used to. The announcement of the polls had its own surprises.

Farooq feigned ignorance that the CEC (Chief Election Commissioner), J. M. Lyngdoh was going to announce the election schedule but he was very much aware of what was coming. It was not simply a matter of winning these elections. The credibility of all his previous victories was also at stake. His victory in these elections would vindicate his previous electoral successes. Ironically, such a victory would also incur a repetition of the charge levelled in 1987–that polling had been rigged.

He was happy that the elections had been announced without the Centre's having acceded to any of the demands of the opposition that the state be placed under the Governor's rule or that polling be postponed. The whole spectrum of the opposition, as anyone could see, was unanimous in asking for

Governor's rule in the State both as a matter of strategy and out of genuine fear. Mufti Syed and his daughter Mehbooba Mufti were the most vociferous. Congress was not far behind. The AICC General Secretary Ambika Soni even demanded that Governor G. C. Saxena be replaced. 'We have no faith in Governor Saxena. He is a friend of Farooq Abdullah and we fear that under such dispensation no free and fair elections can be held.' If the opposition had something to fear from its past experience it was also discrediting the National Conference ahead of polling. It was seeking an advantage before the elections, something which the National Conference did not see through. It had lulled itself into too much complacency. The thought of defeat was very remote from their thoughts. But this was a bigger challenge; he did not realize that the onus of ensuring free and fair polls rested squarely on his shoulders. He promised free and fair polls day in and day out and decried his political opponents for demanding the Governor's rule only to cover their failure to face the people. Farooq and his son Omar Abdullah challenged the opposition to show the clauses which made it obligatory for polling to be conducted under the Governor's rule. They were also quick to point out that their victory in the 1996 election had been under Delhi's direct rule. 'I was not in power at that time,' Farooq had argued endlessly. There was truth in his response because the polls were held under President's rule in September 1996 and the National Conference had won by a two-third majority in the House of 87.

But this election was different. The National Conference was standing for election, for the second time completing its term in the post-independence history of Jammu and Kashmir. It was also the first time, that Farooq Abdullah had completed the full tenure of government. Farooq's father Sheikh Abdullah had died in September 1982, before completing the full term of his election which began in 1977; it was Farooq who held the fort until June 1983, i.e. until fresh elections were held. Farooq himself had resigned in 1990 after winning the Assembly Elections in 1987.

The odds were weighed heavily against him this time. Since the polls had assumed an international dimension, the Government of India was wary of keeping Farooq to supervise the polls. There was greater distrust of Farooq than of the PDP, Congress or even the Hurriyat Conference.

The manner in which the Prime Minister and his Home Minister were making all sorts of promises to hold free and fair polls within the state appeared to imply that Farooq's past victory had been the result of rigging. They were preparing the ground for his exit. The Prime Minister in his April 18 speech in Srinagar claimed that all pre-2002 polls were bogus.

Rationale for Governor's Rule

As the tempo for the Assembly elections started building up, clamorous voices were raised over the question of Governor's rule in Jammu and Kashmir. There were many reasons for this. Farooq had his own objections to direct rule of Delhi in the state.

Those clamouring for Governor's rule were guided by their personal interests. The first ground for Governor's rule was that Farooq Abdullah was a big hurdle in the process of initiating dialogue with the separatists, so he had to go and the ground should be prepared for the dialogue. The first demand (for Governor's rule) came in 1998 when the Assembly elections were not even under consideration. The campaign also found an echo following each massacre of Hindus in the Jammu region. There was something mischievous in the campaign for Governor's rule at this juncture. It could not have been by chance that the clamour for Governor's rule should coincide with the demand for the removal of Farooq Abdullah in order to facilitate the opening of dialogue with the separatists on the one hand or that the call for the dismissal of Farooq's Government should follow upon the massacres of Hindus in Jammu. There was a single hand behind these two demands with a single purpose: The Government of India had set up the stage for Farooq's exit.

The clamour for Governor's rule grew louder at the end of the Kargil conflict. The suicide attacks started and Farooq was blamed for all the failures.

They came to the fore again in 1999 with the poor showing of voters during the Parliamentary Elections in September 1999 and the Farooq Abdullah Government was accused of having lost touch with the people and, had therefore, to be dismissed. This campaign overlooked the level of violence that had been unleashed by the Pakistan-sponsored militants in the run up to the parliamentary polls and also during the polling. The militants were incited to mount the violent attacks on the voters and politicians participating in the polls.

The second argument for Governor's rule was that the Assembly elections would be free and fair and there would be a level playing field for all the parties and participants. It was felt that the National Conference being the ruling party had arrogated to itself all powers and security. There were wild allegations that the political opponents did not get the same degree of security or protection. So the logic of the argument was that during Governor's rule there would be equality in terms of security and other matters. There was a ring of truth in this. The National Conference had the advantage of greater security and its workers did benefit from privileges accruing automatically to those belonging to the governing party which had more than 4,000 of its activists, Chief Minister, ministers, legislators and other functionaries listed as protected persons.

The National Conference saw things the other way. 'Yes we have as many people listed as protected persons, but look at the rate our men are getting killed every day,' National Conference President Omar Abdullah would say. He was also speaking the truth. The party had lost more than 450 of its activists. There was an obligation on the part of the government to protect the families of such people. Moreover, the National Conference had a wide network across the state. After all, the party had won with a two-third majority in the 1996 Assembly polls and had gone on to win the parliamentary polls. Furthermore, in February 2002 it had even won a parliamentary by-election from Jammu-Poonch which until then had been a bastion of the BJP and the Congress. The seat had fallen vacant with the death of Vaid Vishnu Dutt, the ailing BJP leader, and BJP thought that it could win hands down as it had done in 1998 and 1999. But that did not happen. The National Conference had won by fielding a Gujjar Muslim candidate Talib Hussain, thus consolidating its Muslim votes. In this constituency alone, the NC represented 10 out of 20 segments, while Congress represented four, the BJP four and the BSP two. There were charges of rigging and all the parties had joined hands against the National Conference, but the Election Commission overruled the objections and declared the result that Talib Hussain had won the seat by a margin of more than 45,000 votes.

This unprecedented election victory of the National Conference in the Hindu-dominated constituency set off alarm bells in the minds of the political parties in Jammu and Kashmir. They were not reconciled to this victory and deeply regretted the division of Hindu votes and the division within their own parties that facilitated the NC victory. Worse for these parties, the victory of a Muslim candidate was a big blow. Even for the National Conference's Hindu activists this was a negative situation because they did not want a Muslim to succeed in the polls. This indicated that the Muslim voters, if consolidated could, defeat the divided Hindus. It was an ominous signal which gave fresh ground for the demand for Governor's rule to hit at the NC.

Though it appears far-fetched, there was a sense that the demand for the trifurcation of the state had gained momentum with the humiliating defeat of the Congress and BJP at the hands of the National Conference in the parliamentary by-election. It would be wrong to say that the BJP or the RSS alone were promoting the cause of a separate state for Jammu, even Congress and many among the Hindu activists of the National Conference had offered their support behind the scene. These are typical of the double standards that are displayed in Indian politics in Jammu and Kashmir.

Congress had its own agenda in asking for Governor's rule. The party that had contested in the elections in alliance with the National Conference in 1987 when Rajiv Gandhi, husband of Sonia Gandhi, who now headed the party, was Prime Minister, suddenly saw the wider implications of the charges of rigging in the polls under the National Conference rule.

Congress was making a hue and cry over Governor's rule as one of its election issues rather than a condition for participation in the polls. This campaign had the elements of 'political blackmail' and fears of the possible outcome of the polls.

At the moment, the party was vigorously and rather aggressively asking for Governor's rule in the state as part of the campaign against National Conference for the sake of free and fair polls. The 1987 elections that it now alleged were rigged, were contested by the National Conference in alliance with Congress. The Centre was ruled by Congress.

The National Conference leaders demanded to know why, 'If things had not been right in the elections, Congress had not spoken out earlier. 'I hope Ambika Soni's memory has not failed her that much,' Omar Abdullah commented of Ms. Soni who was going hammer and tongs to the town for Governor's rule in the state.

There was a fear in the back of the mind of Congress that internal dissension might cause it to lose badly in the elections. It had won only seven seats in the 1996 Assembly elections against four out of six seats in the May 1996 Parliamentary elections under the same set up in which the Assembly polls were held. That decline was due to the fact that, in the parliamentary elections, the National Conference was out of the fray and it had almost no strong opposition to face and once the Assembly elections exposed its real position, the party had come to see what it was up against and where it needed to prepare the ground.

Again, the National Conference leader asked Ambika Soni how many times she or any other Congress leaders had visited when the state was under the direct rule of Delhi for six and a half years, when people were getting massacred. Most of the time Congress was ruling at the Centre.

Ambika was vitriolic in her attacks on the National Conference and Chief Minister Farooq Abdullah and declared that Congress would go it alone in the polls under the leadership of Ghulam Nabi Azad, forgetting or conveniently omitting the fact that the Jammu and Kashmir PCC chief was sitting in the Rajya Sabha with the support extended to him by the National Conference.

Similar political considerations were being weighed among the other opposition parties and they were mobilizing everyone in the state to ask for Governor's rule. The many demands which the Government of India and the major national political parties Congress and BJP were making in relation to the Jammu and Kashmir elections one day asking for the participation of the Hurriyat Conference in the polls and yet another demanding Governor's rule for the free and fair elections drew the attention of international observers who were beginning to find the whole situation rather suspect. The international community had no love lost for India. Ironically, these parties had brought international scrutiny to bear upon the elections in Jammu and Kashmir.

First, the Government of India by seeking the help of the international community in asking Pakistan to stop cross-border terrorism into Jammu and Kashmir, and then by amassing troops along the border after the December 13 terror assault on the Indian Parliament, it had raised the hype so that the international community was forced to take cognizance. The world could not afford to look the other way when two nuclear powered nations were close to war. It was a dangerous situation in South Asia was the common refrain of the global community that saw merit in intervening.

Jammu and Kashir is at the root of the problem between India and Pakistan. American Secretary of State Colin Powell whose own foreign policy was running in conflict with that of his own colleagues in the Bush administration had declared that 'Kashmir is on the international agenda.' This had infuriated the Indian political parties. But when he made this statement, he was also referring to the elections. British Foreign Secretary Jack Straw went a step further and said that the 'international community would be keenly watching the Kashmir polls.'

The Government of India was also asking, the international community, although not publicly for obvious reasons, to persuade the Hurriyat Conference to participate in the polls. By doing so, the Government had itself invited the international attention and intervention. The US ambassador to India, Robert Blackwill, was told by the Indian Home Minister L. K. Advani that Hurriyat was not participating and hinted that 'you could ask them to participate in the polls.' The American embassy sent a delegation to the Valley to talk to the Hurriyat and thereafter a European Union delegation followed with the same mission. The whole matter had been internationalized. What was the point in maintaining that the issue was not an international one and that the elections were purely a private affair of the people of the state. It was not. Embassies in Delhi have sent diplomats to oversee the polling. It is concern for the impact which might be made upon the international community that has prompted the Vajpayee Government and the Election Commission of India to start working towards 'free and fair elections.'

Endnotes

1. Mullah Umar, Chief of the Taliban in Afghanistan who went into hiding after the American assault on the Taliban and Al-Qaeda in Afghanistan in October 2001 in retaliation to 9/11.

2. Ram Jethmalani, a leading lawyer and law minister in the Vajpayee Government, used to ask Prime Minister, Rajiv Gandhi ten questions, daily, in 1989 on the purchase of Bofors guns. These ten questions were published by *The Indian Express.*

17

Fall of the Abdullah Dynasty

Defeat in the Legislative Assembly Elections

October 10, 2002 was like any other day—with the bright sun shine reflected on the shimmering waters of Dal Lake. But in the counting hall at the Centaur Hotel a massive political flame was flickering wildly; it spluttered and went out leaving behind darkness for the Abdullahs. The young scion of the Abdullah dynasty Omar Abdullah had lost his maiden election to the Legislative Assembly. Thousands of hammers had struck simultaneously. The dynasty was finished. The Abdullahs were out of power. The day had begun ominously for Omar despite the best wishes of his father and wife and their vast array of friends. Omar Abdullah would lose the election from Ganderbal. This nightmare for the Abdullah family could not have been dreamt up by even the most optimistic of his enemies in the opposition camp. Or so they would say though in their heart of hearts, they would not believe in their own rhetoric. He lost to Qazi Mohammad Afzal who until that day had only a dismal record of defeats against the Abdullahs. The victory goddess had come to smile on him. As the counting trends showed that Afzal was heading for a clear victory, Omar left the counting hall in a huff and started sipping tea from a flask under the vigilant eye of the cameras of satellite channels. It took him a lot to gather the courage to say: 'It happens. This is politics.'

He had never known defeat. He had only tasted victories. The debacle was inconceivable even in his worst nightmares. But the defeat was not his alone. With it, the Abdullah dynasty had lost control of the reins of power. It had been decisively defeated in the elections that the world would later came to hail as free and fair. The man who had hoped to be the youngest Chief Minister of the State, was nowhere. He had made the blunder of saying, too confidently that, come what may he would resign from his post as Union Minister. He was India's Junior Minister for External Affairs, a job that he performed so well that even Prime Minister Atal Bihari Vajpayee was unwilling to accept his resignation for well over three months. 'If nothing else (meaning if the National Conference, the party he headed did not win a majority) I would be at least an MLA.' But even that was not to be. He was simply a member of the Lok Sabha, the Lower House of the Indian parliament. The National Conference had even fixed October 14, 2002 as the day of swearing-in of the new government. Omar Abdullah had ordered a new suit for the occasion. It was taken as a foregone conclusion that he would be sworn in as Chief Minister succeeding his father. The team of ministers and key positions of bureaucrats had already been picked.

Failed Promises

The Abdullahs had taken the electoral fight lightly, out of a sense of complacency. They had not put their hearts into the campaign nor did they take note of the undercurrents that were welling up within the party and among the people.'We have faced tougher battles. We shall overcome,' Farooq would say. According to him the electoral battle in 1977 when his father Sheikh Abdullah was alive and the whole Government of India had started working against the National Conference, was far tougher. 'We won that. He hated the idea of being reminded that Sheikh Abdullah was still alive then and that, the National Conference was a vibrant political group and there were no regional political rivals to challenge the might and the popularity of the National Conference. It is not easy to bring home a point to Farooq Abdullah. That continues to be his biggest weakness.

Such was the level of complacency that even when the prevalent view was that the National Conference was on a sticky wicket, the Abdullahs had blamed it on the vicious campaign which had been launched against them by their adversaries. That something was wrong with them, their party and their rule—they would not accept.

The truth was that the promises of peace and autonomy made by the National Conference in 1996 were nowhere in sight after six years. The National Conference had lost on both counts. It could neither get autonomy for its people nor could it bring peace. These two issues had come as posers as it prepared to face the 2002 Assembly Elections. It had not been able to bring down the level of killings nor lift the people out of the quagmire of fear that gripped them. Neither could the government ensure the return of the Kashmiri Pandits to the Valley, the place that is their real home, nor did the life for the ordinary Kashmiri change. In fact, the militancy had crossed over to the south of Pir Panjal into the Jammu region. The people's faith had been badly shaken.

Corruption

Farooq Abdullah had also failed to check corruption. It was out of the necessity for crowds and voters in the 1996 assembly elections that Farooq Abdullah had condoned the acts of omission and commission of Moulvi Iftikhar Hussain Ansari and even got him acquitted in a stage-managed inquiry probing his role in a land scandal known as *sidhra scam* and re-inducted him into the cabinet after having kept him out of the ministry for almost two years. The police investigation that had zeroed in on Ansari and found him guilty of having committed fraud was never brought before the cabinet. Political necessities outweighed moral considerations. It was such acts of unnecessary magnanimity towards corruption that had tarnished Farooq's own image. Farooq was perceived to be shielding the guilty. National Conference ministers and legislators were making money. There was no denying the fact. They were guided by their fears that this was their last term either in the Assembly or the Government and should therefore make best use of the time they had at their disposal. They began selling jobs and tenders. They also started spending constituency development funds to further their own fortunes. 'Everything is on sale, had become the byword for the National Conference rule.

Visitors would meet the NC legislators, their pockets laden with currency notes and when they left their pockets were empty. There was a price tag on everything. This perception gained credence among those who could not get jobs. They spread the word with great ferocity against the National Conference Government. It was even reported that people had to pay money to obtain the cheque for ex-gratia relief given to the next of kin of those killed by militants.

Within the National Conference, the youth were becoming disgruntled. Under government order SRO 43, jobs were to be given to family members of the men killed by militants. However, the sons and daughters of the original National Conference leaders were preferred over genuine workers. These youths lost interest in party affairs and work when their claims were overruled in favour of those of sons and daughters of the NC leaders. They sided with the opposition. Not that the Abdullahs were unaware of the groundswell of anger which was gaining momentum among the party men, but they were unable to check it. As it happened, the party lost much of their ground support. The Abdullahs never thought even in the worst of their nightmares that they would ever be humbled at the hustings. For them victory had been a foregone conclusion.

Farooq Sets His Sight on the Vice-Presidency

It was against this backdrop that Farooq Abdullah first announced his intention to quit active politics and exhorted his party legislators to select a new leader for themselves after the expiry of the term of the Assembly. His sudden announcement in the first budget session of the Ninth Assembly took his party legislators by surprise. But there were others like Ali Mohammad Sagar who had been aspiring to become Chief Minister one day. They could not conceal their glee.

There were two motives behind it. Farooq was hoping for a slot of the Vice-Presidential post and he had made it a point to air his views in the Assembly in February 1997 while replying to a motion of thanks on the Governor's address aware of the fact that TV and radio were airing his views across the country. It was no secret that he was angling for the post. His hopes were there because he had very good ties with the United Front Government and he had obliged Congress leaders to achieve this end. He had inducted Ghulam Nabi Azad, that maverick of a politician into the Rajya Sabha with the support of the National Conference legislators in the hope that he would prevail over the Congress leadership to support him for the Vice-President's post. What Farooq thought was a clever move on the political chessboard of Indian politics, was in fact a sign of naivety. How could Azad whose party was not willing to give him a Rajya Sabha seat from any of the states, it ruled, help him slot for the contest or election of Vice-President? But then that is the way Farooq Abdullah is. The signs of his disappointment in failing to make it to the office of Vice- President in 1997 were obvious when he 'congratulated' Prime Minister Inder Kumar Gujral at Qazigund in south Kashmir on July 26 for having chosen Krishan Kant as the candidate for Vice-President.

Internecine Conflicts

It was with an eye to the Vice-Presidency for himself that he had placed Omar at the head of the National Conference organization in much the same fashion that his father Sheikh Mohammad Abdullah had done for Farooq Abdullah in 1980. Farooq Abdullah was at his emotional best while handing over the cap of his responsibility as President of the party on Omar's head. The cap did fit well. But it did not go well with many in the party. There was a trio consisting of Ghulam Mohi-ud-Din Shah, Mohammad Shafi Uri and Abdul Rahim Rather who felt belittled that this young man from nowhere had come to preside over them and squash their ambitions for ever. Each one of them wanted to be Chief Minister. Once they had conceded their position to Omar they knew that they would be nowhere.

Omar's uncles Sheikh Nazir Ahmad and Sheikh Mustafa Kamal too had their reservations. How could they be expected to supplicate before their own nephew—a child in politics, and worse still an alien to the land and the language? They did not raise the voice of protest but their whispers were audible to the people outside.

Omar was keen from day one that there would be no parallel power centres. He wanted to be both President of the party and Chief Minister. He could not fathom the resistance that was there. He had heard tales of internal sabotage but dismissed them with unconcealed contempt for he believed that there were going to be no challengers to his leadership. His word would be final, or so he thought. The clash of personalities and the generation gap was also to tell upon Omar and Farooq's relationship. Farooq was vexed by his son's popularity outstripping his own. Whenever he asked his operator whether there were any important phone calls, he would fume with anger when told that he had just two and he was piqued when he learnt that Omar had perhaps ten times more. 'I am still the Chief Minister and the people have already started deserting me,' he would quip; to which his son would respond: 'Dad times are changing.' And there were discussions at the dining table which underlined the differences between father and son. Omar is fond of *puri, bhaji* for breakfast. But he is also conscious that he should not have oil dripping from the fried stuff. He orders his orderly to soak it on a napkin something that amuses Farooq; 'You want to eat fried stuff and then you are scared of the oil dripping from the food. Get me all this. I am not worried. I have lived enough.' The voters were not indifferent to what they read in the newspapers nor what they heard in the streets.

That there was an inkling that these rounds of gossip might affect the prospects of Omar in Ganderbal had reached Gupkar Road. First, Farooq, now graduated to senior Abdullah, would pour scorn on any one who remotely suggested that Omar would be defeated from Ganderbal. 'It is all rubbish. You know who is doing it. My own people. They don't want Omar to come and succeed. They are afraid of accountability.'

As the disconcerting news unravelled that the ground was slipping, the Abdullahs sought to work miracles through their own men.

Sheikh Ghulam Rasool, an influential retired bureaucrat, was sulking. He had not been given any position in the government despite a firm promise by Farooq himself at the time of the 1996 elections. Farooq had raised his hand and told the audience that if elected to power, 'I would give him a major responsibility.' That was never to be. When father and son met him to seek his support, he asked them: 'Why have you come to me now, go to BR and Tony Jaitly whom you have been listening to all along these six years of your rule.' The request to let bygones be bygones did not move the ex-bureaucrat. He was also unhappy that Farooq had fielded his son from Ganderbal, when he had been promised the seat. He openly worked against Omar in the elections.

Pakistan's Role

Internal factors apart, Pakistan also played a key role in the defeat of the National Conference and in particular of Omar Abdullah from Ganderbal constituency. It pumped in huge amounts of money which was handed out not only to the militants but also to the various competing political groups. The money was spent extravagantly to ensure that Omar did not win. Islamabad was facing a great deal of flak internationally with Omar, a Muslim from Kashmir defending India's record on Kashmir all over the globe, with such a finesse that evoked envy even from seasoned diplomats and statesmen. Omar's speeches which reflected how Pakistan had been playing its devious role in fragmenting the Kashmiri society and using religion as a weapon to further its agenda of grabbing the territory of Kashmir and his strong denunciation of the terrorism unleashed by Pakistan in Jammu and Kashmir and the rest of India compelled the ISI to prepare special suicide squads to eliminate Omar. When those attempts failed, Pakistan attempted to kill him politically. The battleground of Ganderbal was chosen. This time Pakistan succeeded. Pakistan's men worked hard to generate hysteria against Omar. He was projected as a man who had no respect for his own religion. His having a Hindu wife was part of the campaign against him and his secular ways also came under fire.

Militant groups claimed that Pakistan bashing on the part of the Abdullahs was a sign of their loyalty to India which had stationed more than 700,000 troops on Kashmir's soil and who were now harassing the people of the Valley. In Kashmiris' eyes, the Indian face was now synonymous with that of a gun-toting soldier from whose lips would flow an incessant stream of obscenities. The soldier who frisked the men and young men in the middle of street was a public humiliation abhorrent to everyone. Now was the time to take revenge on India and the card was the ballot. And that is precisely what they did to Omar and the party he headed. If any evidence were needed about Pakistan's designs on the Abdullahs, it was clear from Pakistan TV and radio propaganda against the polls. It concentrated more on condemning the Abdullahs for their loyalty to India, showing them up as stooges of Delhi who were flourishing at the cost of the aspirations of the people. How the Abdullahs had joined hands with the Indian army and paramilitary forces and raised a force of 'murderers and looters' under Special Operation Groups (SOG) of the state police. In reality the SOGs had been set up in 1994 but no one bothered about that piece of information. It was attributed to the six-year rule of Farooq Abdullah.

Special Operation Groups

Farooq was himself to be blamed because he wittingly or unwittingly condoned even the worst acts of terror committed by the force. The SOG came to be known as the armed wing of the National Conference. The half- hearted effort with which, at times, Farooq tried to tame the force was unconvincing. He could not explain why the SOG had killed the innocent villagers and why it was detaining people without any reason and why it was resorting to extortions. In the situation in which the Abdullahs were trammelled, they needed the SOG as a counterweight to the army and the paramilitary forces and to provide security in situations where the threat of militancy was high. The SOG had built a reputation for itself of courageous fighters of the militancy and killers of the dreaded militants. But all these successes were over-shadowed by their excesses.

No longer did people remember the sacrifices that it had made to kill the militants who had made the life of the people so miserable; imprinted in their minds, instead, were stories of their excesses. That was what Pakistan exploited to its best advantage. Its electronic media churned out horror stories and its men in Kashmir spread them by word of mouth to all across the Valley. The price had to be paid by the National Conference. And it paid.

An Alienated Army

Ironically while the Abdullahs were at the receiving end for being fiercely Indian, the army turned against them because it felt that Farooq's fulminations against the army were anti-national. The National Conference was dubbed a party that was 'anti-army and anti-national people' which deserved to be defeated. The army could not bear the barbs that it did not have the guts to cross the LoC in the Kargil conflict and settle matters once and for all. Farooq had been ruthless in challenging the army's claim in the fight against insurgency. Farooq had made it known that the army had failed in its duties. There were stories galore that the army had remained stuck in its bunkers even while the militants were killing people. Rather than routing the militants, the army had compromised with them.

The army commanders could not bear the comparison that soldiers across the LoC were mutton eaters capable of dare-devil actions while those on this side of the divide were vegetarian and lacked the will and capacity to take on the mutton eaters even when the opportunities existed. He had pointed out at several forums that the Indian army had missed the opportunity of teaching Pakistan a lesson during the Kargil conflict. 'What is the point of constructing a huge road from Drass to Sankoo (a diversion) when the Indian army could have got rid of the two Pakistani posts that caused trouble on the existing roads?

We could not decide, because we did not have the guts. We were scared of America, and of what Bill Clinton would do. Did Pakistanis ask what they should have done when they crossed the LoC and occupied our territory?' Farooq's taunts were unbearable.

Farooq Abdullah had his own reasons. It was after the Kargil conflict that the era of the *fidayeen* (sacrificing) squads begun. The militants of Lashkar-e-Toiba had started *fidayeen* attacks on the security forces. The soldiers were unable to devise counter attacks apart from raising the walls of the cantonments and covering them with more barbed wire fences and by restricting the movement of civilians in and around their camps and cantonments. And whenever Farooq pointed out that the army was not taking up the militants' challenge the way it should have been, the soldiers seethed with anger against the Chief Minister and his party. They were the deciding factor in the countryside where they had their own men on roll. They would spread disaffection against the National Conference. Farooq could not publicly condemn the army for its acts of omission and commission but privately he was scornful of the ways of the army in Kashmir and its timidity in taking on the militants.

When elections came, the army also played its role. It told voters for whom to vote. The army barely concealed its threat to make trouble for the voters if they chose to vote for the National Conference, but if they behaved they could expect better behaviour from the soldiers. The militants were also working towards the same goal. The objectives of the otherwise warring sides converged on a single point: that of removing the National Conference. There were no fierce loyalists for the party on the ground and that facilitated their task. Even the Centre's benchmark was seeing NC out of power. Officials were removed from key positions, Army and paramilitary forces were made to work for non-NC forces. Yasin Malik's and Syed Ali Shah Geelani's arrests were attributed to ulterior motives of the National Conference even though Yasin had been arrested only after 100,000 US dollars were found on the persons carrying it for him and Geelani only after Sajjad Bazaz was arrested. In fact, the Government of India and some of the opposition groups in the state and the international media interpreted the arrests as a design on the part of the National Conference to jail the separatist leaders so as to remove opposition from the polls. These allegations were believed by many. The fact that the State government had chosen to arrest these leaders on the eve of the polls, was highly suspect since knowledge of their financial dealings and campaigning had been an open secret.

Mufti Instigates the Hurriyat Camp

Mufti knew what was going on in the Hurriyat camp. He condemned the arrest of Yasin Malik and Syed Ali Shah Geelani blaming Farooq Abdullah for setting up roadblocks ahead of the crucial Assembly elections. 'Farooq Abdullah was trying to sabotage the genuine political process in the state to perpetuate his rule.' He saw a design in the arrest of Yasin Malik, the man who had devised the plan of the abduction of his daughter Rubiya Sayeed in 1989.

British Foreign Secretary Jack Straw when asked about the extradition of Ayub Thakur, the king-pin of money laundering for Kashmir militants in the UK retorted: 'Why don't you take action against your own people first?' No one knows the answers to these questions.

The militants were already with the opposition. The NC candidates were targeted, but opposition members faced no challenges or threats. The Law Minister Mushtaq Lone had been killed, another minister Sakina Itoo was attacked eight times and the movement of the NC candidates was restricted. People were warned against participating in the NC rallies but the opposition faced little or no problems by comparison. This agenda was worked out long before the Prime Minister had pledged to the nation 'free and fair polls in Jammu and Kashmir' and 'talks with elected representatives' from the ramparts of the Red Fort in Delhi on August 15, 2000.

The participation of the People's Conference, one of the constituents of the All Parties Hurriyat Conference in the polls by proxy was an unexpected development. The contesting of Ghulam Mohi-ud-Din Sofi, a trusted aide of the assassinated People's Conference chief Abdul Gani Lone, from Handwara and four other men from four other constituencies of the Kupwara district in northwest Kashmir, proved to be a turning point in the electoral fortunes of the National Conference. It was a dire political miscalculation on the part of the National Conference that it lost the momentum in the campaign, living in the make- believe world that life would always be smooth for them and that there would never be a threat to their power. They were unaware that the opposition was getting emboldened and that each move was a calculated one, on the chess board of Kashmir politics.

Mufti Mohmmad Sayeed who was reluctant to contest when the polls were announced on August 2, 2002, found new opportunities when he saw that there were people willing to challenge the National Conference. He struck behind the scene deals and alliances that finally propelled him to the post of Chief Minister, the fulfilment of a long-term dream which spelt the fall of the Abdullah dynasty.

The PDP-Mufti's Offspring

It was one of those fine mornings of Kashmir summer in July

1999 when Mehbooba Mufti announced, at a hurriedly convened press conference, her resignation from the Congress Party and also her seat in the Legislative Assembly. It did not surprise any one. It was coming. The father-daughter duo had come to the parting of ways with Congress. They could not have continued in the party for long for the political posturing they had chosen was running counter to the ideology of the mainstream political party.

Mufti was calling for unconditional dialogue with the militants. He was seeking a soft approach towards them. He and his daughter were visiting the families of the militants who had been killed by security forces. The two were underwriting an agenda for themselves that they were peddling vigorously.

'No. Militants should not be killed. They need to be taken care of. No they should not even be asked to surrender, Mehbooba had told presspersons even when she was a Congress MLA. These statements and actions were at odds with the overall policy of Congress.

Pre-Empting the Role of the APHC

This was a deliberate move by Mufti and Mehbooba. They were projecting themselves as being different and were attempting to occupy a space in Kashmiri politics which would be something akin to that of the All Parties Hurriyat Conference which called for dialogue to resolve the Kashmir problem and in which Pakistan would have a central role as significant as that of India. There was a definite plan in the whole scheme of things. Mufti had seen the glimpses of success of his pro-secessionist strategy. It was not for nothing that he had chosen to emblazon the *kalam-dawat* (pen and inkpot) on his green party flag. It had its precursor in the Muslim United Front (MUF), the original version of the All Parties Hurriyat Conference that had contested elections in 1987. It is no secret that Mufti had helped the MUF in every way he could even while he was campaigning for Congress, the party which he then represented and under whose (Rajiv Gandhi) government he held the post of Tourism Minister. He was overwhelmed by his hatred for the National Conference and Congress' coalition with the party despite his strongest opposition. He could not stomach that insult. It was a matter of vendetta politics. This became more overt when he left his ministerial post to join hands with V. P. Singh, who made him Home Minister, the number two position in the government hierarchy in India.

He had now tasted the success of pandering to the secessionist sentiment and also the populist measures that had made him a household name. Using his position as a former Home Minister of the country, Mufti also maintained his links with the central leadership of the day. He knew that his ambitions could not be fulfilled without the help of Delhi. Who could have known it better than Mufti himself? He had been the protégé of Delhi in making and dislodging governments during Indira Gandhi's rule. He relishes recalling the days when he engineered the defections from the National Conference and brought Farooq Abdullah's Government to an end on July 2, 1984. Farooq's brother-in-law Ghulam Mohammad Shah would lie on the floor of the vehicles, to prevent detection, while on his journey to meet Mufti who had persuaded Indira to dislodge Farooq Abdullah from the government. He had played a role in removing the Shah Government in the belief that he would become Chief Minister. That did not happen. That failure continued to fester in his heart until he achieved what he had aspired for in 2002. Over the years, this wily politician came to realize that remaining in a national party would lead him nowhere. He was looking for a regional platform that could become an alternative to the National Conference, the party he hated because of its domination by the Abdullah family. After quitting, Janta Dal on being denied a ministerial berth after the 1996 parliamentary elections which brought the United Front Government to power with a rustic politician, from Karnataka, H. D. Deve Gowda as Prime Minister, Mufti also resigned from his Rajya Sabha seat. Since the Assembly elections were round the corner and it would not be possible for him to launch a regional political platform, he chose to bide his time and wait for the right moment to seek re-entry into Congress. Having tasted defeat in the previous Assembly elections in 1977 and 1983 in Kashmir, Mufti stayed out of the contest. But he could get tickets for his wife Gulshan and daughter Mehbooba. While his wife lost from Pahalgam, his daughter won from Bijebehra.

Mehbooba Mufti

Mehbooba, a young separated woman, has the sparks of an emotional politician. In her speeches she is long on stirring the emotions of her audiences and short on content.That is both her strength and her weakness. She struck an instant rapport with the voters of Bijbehra, a hilly constituency that her father had represented once. She spoke the language of the people, empathized with their woes and conjured the image of being a victim of the situation, like them.

The elections in 1996 were held against the backdrop of a violent past. The people were harassed by the bloodshed around them. Bijbhera, in particular, had seen and experienced one of the worst massacres in Kashmir history. Thirty-seven protesters were mowed down and 100 others wounded when the BSF men, unnerved by the full throated cries of the villagers coming out of Friday prayers calling for the lifting of the army siege around the revered Hazratbal shrine, opened fire on the procession. The mass graves of 36 of the victims are the stark reminders of the tragedy. The 37th victim was a Kashmiri Pandit youth who had taken part in the protest demonstration on October 22, 1993.

'I didn't know the ABC of politics. But when daddy wanted me to contest, I could not say no,' Mehbooba stated the reasons for her joining politics and becoming a candidate in those crucial elections which failed to turn the tide against secessionism, violence and the miseries of the people only because of the lack of seriousness on the part of politicians and the callousness with which they squabbled for their personal gains rather than working for the people.

The media riveted its attention on this young woman. Her speeches were covered extensively. Her campaign style was on the front pages. There were no satellite channels in those days to capture her political dexterity in campaigning. She was somewhat like her father but there were differences between the two as well. Her victory was a political marvel in itself. She had withstood the tide of the National Conference in the whole of south Kashmir. In fact, she was the only Congress candidate to have won from the Valley; the other, Moulvi Iftikhiar Hussain Ansari was for all practical purposes a National Conference candidate. (One cannot help noting, in passing, that there was not an iota of political or media attention paid to another woman contesting at that time: Sakina Itoo, daughter of the assassinated National Conference leader and former speaker Wali Mohammad Ittoo, who was contesting from Noorabad constituency in Anantnag district. Sakina also won but her victory was lost in the avalanche of victories of other National Conference candidates).

Mehbooba and Mufti went on to consolidate their victory in Bijbehra and started expanding with a zeal that caused ripples in the National Conference. But the ruling party would not wake from its slumber nor shake off its complacency. It had been lulled into the make-believe world of invincibility. Whenever there were worries causing big problems, it would poach on the MLAs of other parties.

Moulvi Ansari was already in the NC fold. He had been made a minister by Farooq Abdullah, a decision that aroused envy and anger from one and all. Congress men felt ashamed that despite having contested on the party ticket, Ansari, a businessman-cum-politician was sitting on the treasury benches. There was a dichotomy in the Congress-NC relationship. Congress was to play the role of the opposition. It was sharp because of the fact that Mufti had staged a coup of sorts against Ghulam Nabi Azad by getting Mehbooba elected as the Congress legislature party leader.

Barring Ansari, who in any case was a minister, the rest of the six Congress MLAs were first timers. Mufti utilized this fact for the benefit of his daughter. He convened a meeting of the Congress MLAs in which R. S. Sharma, who was elected from Nowhera, was kept out. There the deal was struck. Mehbooba was elected as the CLP leader, a fact that Azad would persistently dispute maintaining that there had never been anyone from the CLP acting as leader in the records of AICC.

Ansari

Ansari was Azad's man Friday and Azad was a close friend of Farooq Abdullah. That had prompted Farooq to induct Ansari into his cabinet as a minister. It was resented by his own partymen for whom Ansari was not only a rank outsider but also guilty of having hurled abuses at Madr-e-Meharban. Ansari had led a vicious campaign against the Abdullahs when he was close to Mufti in the 1980s. He was the CLP leader and one of the key players in toppling the Farooq Abdullah Government.

With anguish Sheikh Mustafa Kamal, Farooq's younger brother, who was known as mother's son, would recall the way Ansari had hurled abuses at his mother in the Assembly in the 1980s. The Begum herself was angry over the shifting stances of her eldest son. She gave vent to her anger and distress in one of her interviews with *The Indian Express*. She called Farooq 'irresponsible and 'non-serious' and threatened to resume active politics to campaign against her own son. She was pained by the fact that he had chosen the company of the very people who had decried her, her husband and Farooq himself. To her generation, this form of politics was not acceptable and unthinkable.

There were whispers against Ansari and often Sadiq Ali, another Shia leader, the Muslim sect to which Ansari also belonged, would publicize them in the Assembly. Questioning the seriousness of the National Conference leadership, Sadiq Ali eventually joined the PDP, which he maintained had deviated from its roots and principles.

Changing Status of the National Conference and the APHC

Two things were taking place in Kashmir politics. The National Conference had become arrogant and was distancing itself from the masses. The APHC had its own limitations. It was not in touch with day-to-day issues for it was working on a different and higher plane: seeking self-determination for the people of the Valley. The two extremes found their bases shrinking. Shrewd politicians that they were, the Muftis were stepping in and occupying that ground. Their stratagems were quiet and clever. They raised the day-to-day concerns and focused in particular on the atrocities committed by the security forces. They were media savvy, ensuring that all their actions received media coverage.

The anger against the custodial deaths and continuing violence and rising unemployment were ready-made issues. The APHC spoke of the excesses but could not talk of the roads, water and power. That agenda would have downgraded its role. Once we get freedom from the Indian occupation, everything would be smooth sailing. The APHC worked on that platform.

But the people were interested in their everyday necessities as well and they could not afford to look towards the APHC for deliverance as they had not even deigned to make any promises on such matters.

The Muftis highlighted the day-to-day needs of the people and the aspirations of the secessionists with a clear hint that the militants too would stand to benefit. This was both an anti-Delhi and pro-Kashmiri constituency. The Muftis' theme song found an echo in the hearts of the people. But the PDP itself was not willing to participate in a dialogue which the APHC had shunned. It was the classic example of adroitly identifying with the secessionist conglomerate and its ideology without making any noise about it. One such example occurred in May–June 2001, when, without announcing its boycott of talks with K. C. Pant, who was named as interlocutor by the Government of India to talk to Kashmiri groups, the Muftis did not talk to him. They put forward many excuses that the Pant mission was not mandated for something great. 'We need to discuss with our political affairs committee as to what to talk about,' Mehbooba, Vice-President would say in defence of her party's decision not to talk to Pant. Mehbooba is now President of the party.

Behind the refusal to talk to Pant, the PDP was implicitly telling the people that it was not talking to the Government of India. Pakistan's desire for involvement in the talks was also underlined. This was a clever ploy, that the PDP had constructed for itself after having seen and watched the course that the Hurriyat Conference had adopted. Are we any less than the Hurriyat was the message that was being subtly delivered. The recipients took it well. If, on the one hand, it was a strategy which pandered to the overwhelmingly separatist core of Kashmiri thinking, at the same time it was to blunt the Hurriyat. It was snatching a chance from the Hurriyat to criticize the PDP. The Hurriyat criticism of the Muftis participating in the polls was muted, while that against the National Conference and Congress was vocal and virulent. The PDP was gaining ground both geographically and psychologically. Its grip was tightening.

The tower of an alternative regional and political outfit was being constructed brick by brick. The masons—Mufti and his daughter—were assisted by trusted lieutenants whom the former Union Home Minister had drawn from Congress and Janta Dal, the parties where Mufti had his bitter-sweet stints. He had endeared himself to his loyalists and knew the art of politics well. He had his lobbyists in the bureaucracy and as he was always good with the media, he had his own men and women talking about him all the time. He would keep all his loyalists happy.

The Muftis' self-confidence was bolstered by the recognition they were getting in Delhi. They had access to the Prime Minister and the Deputy Prime Minister L. K. Advani. Farooq was amateurish in spilling the beans in his anger. He and some of his party men would openly charge the Centre with financing the Muftis to dislodge his government. His anger became his enemy. He was giving the Muftis the recognition that they were desperately seeking in the political arena of Kashmir. He was also annoying the Centre which, in any case had started looking for an alternative to Farooq Abdullah. The game had begun since the days of H. D. Deve Gowda. Although he had parted ways with Janta Dal, Mufti had maintained his links with Gowda, his successor I. K. Gujral and then onwards with Atal Bihari Vajpayee.

Farooq's fulminations were costing him dear. He was unaware that by his own acts and words he was creating a stronghold for his political rival. He lived in a world of his own where people had started deserting him for they thought that he and his men were taking them for granted. Nobody likes to be taken for granted. Farooq had failed to see the ground realities.

Mufti had given birth to the PDP but it was nurtured by Farooq Abdullah's mistakes. The stage had come when the PDP had outgrown its size because of the political shrewdness of the Muftis as well as the failures of Farooq Abdullah.

The birth of PDP became a turning point in the political history of Kashmir. The unexpected had occurred.

18

Multi-Party Coalition Government: New Political Experiment in Kashmir

Rise of PDF

The 2002 elections had thrown up a result that left the political groups with only one option: the formation of a coalition government. The National Conference, humbled at the polls, had only 28 seats, Congress was the next best performer with 20 seats and Mufti's PDP was the third with 16 seats. The surprise and shock in the NC camp was accentuated not just by the loss of power. Its President and the rising star of the new generation of politicians, Omar Abdullah had also lost.

The PDP had made its mark even though it had been placed in the third position in the final tally. It was only three years old and could not match the resources and the reach of the 70-year-old National Conference. Its 16 seats were a Major boost and a trend-setter in Kashmir politics. The story of the birth of the PDP is no secret nor are the issues which beset its leaders. There was always a secessionist tinge in Mufti's platform even though he had been groomed in the mainstream politics since the days of Jawaharlal Nehru and Indira Gandhi. His moorings were in that section of the populace which looked towards India for deliverance.

There was momentary uncertainty when it was announced that Mufti would be the parties'choice for the post of Chief Minister as absolute support from the political groups and the independent MLAs could not be guaranteed. Farooq Abdullah had refused to continue as caretaker Chief Minister beyond

October 18, 2002. He was advised that he could force things on the State so that it would become impossible for Mufti or Congress to form the government. Even the combined strength of the two did not add up to the magic number of 44, the minimum number required to form a majority in the House of 87. Congress with 20 and PDP with 16 were still short by eight members. Naturally the two were eyeing independents as well as members of other small parties. The Jammu and Kashmir National Panther's Party (JKNPP) under Bhim Singh[1] was aiming for the post of Chief Minister but also needed support. Bhim turned to the National Conference. The independents too were not far behind. Some had combined to form a group- Peoples' Democratic Forum. Its architect was CPI-M State Secretary Mohammad Yusuf Tarigami who saw his own chance of becoming a key figure in the government. But the party Politburo was against participation in the government, so Tarigami had to content himself with serving the government from behind the scenes.

Separatist Contests for the First Time

The PDF hoped to form the government. Ghulam Mohi-ud-Din Sofi, a close associate of Abdul Ghani Lone was keen on becoming Chief Minister. His plans to strike an alliance with the NC and other parties to cobble together the right numbers failed and as a result of this, the PDF had to join the Congress-PDP combination that is now ruling the State.

Sofi had broken with tradition in the 2002 Kashmir elections by jumping into the fray when the All Parties Hurriyat Conference and other separatist groups had announced a boycott of the polls. He contested from Handwara, a mountainous belt in Kupwara district bordering Pakistan-occupied Kashmir. The choice of Handwara was significant. It was the native town of Abdul Ghani Lone, the assassinated leader of the Hurriyat Conference and founder of the People's Conference. Sofi was known to be a close confidant of Lone. Lone was assassinated on May 21, 2002 at Idgah where the crowds were observing the 12th death anniversary of Mirwaiz Moulvi Farooq, who had been killed at his residence in Nageen in Srinagar that very day, in 1990. Sofi took advantage of the wave of sympathy generated among the masses, by the assassination of Lone. He declared himself Lone's real comrade. The people were exhilarated by this turnaround in the separatist camp. His entry into electoral politics would change the course for them.

The irony was that his supporters were shouting slogans for *azadi* (freedom from India) while hailing his decision to participate in the polls which meant direct acceptance of Indian sovereignty over Kashmir.

His victory was taken as a foregone conclusion. He won against the formidable National Conference minister Choudhary Mohammad Ramzan.[2] Thereafter, his ambitions soared. The National Conference sought to take advantage of his success and also played on the ambition of MLAs who were at a loose end, on the look-out for the most propitious platform to which they might align themselves.

PDP-Congress Coalition

The National Conference was desperate to stall Mufti from coming to power. Farooq had refused to continue as caretaker Chief Minister which made Governor's rule imminent-even though it was to be perhaps the shortest ever spell, lasting for 13 days. The NC watched with ill-concealed glee as Congress and PDP attempted to thrash out the arrangements that would lead to the formation of a government. The NC was also counting on the growing disillusionment of the Independents and there was no less frustration in the PDP camp. It saw no logic in Congress' claim that it should have the first shot at chief ministership. Mehbooba had spelt out the PDP's priorities and Congress' obligations in more direct terms. 'Congress is a national party. It has its own national agenda. It cannot be expected to implement the agenda that we are pledged to because that would be impossible for them to do without the risks at the national level.' She was right. Congress was about to face the toughest battle of elections in riot-hit Gujarat where BJP Chief Minister Narendra Modi was rolling over his *Hindutuva*[3] juggernaut.

Under the circumstances, for Congress to implement the disbanding of the special operation group of Jammu and Kashmir Police or to even talk of withdrawing the anti-terrorism law was a taboo. Congress, for its part, was striving to secure the requisite numbers to form the government on its own.

Mehbooba Mufti who had been taken to task by her father for her rigid stance which was proving to be an obstacle, decided to mend matters. She called Sonia Gandhi, Congress President in Delhi and expressed her party's willingness to discuss matters further. Talks between Congress and the PDP had been broken off when Mufti turned down Congress leader Manmohan Singh's[4] suggestion that he wait for a further three years before becoming Chief Minister. Talks were resumed in Delhi. The Panthers' Party chief Bhim Singh and CPI-M's Tarigami were also summoned; Congress duly appointed Mufti as Chief Minister. There were celebrations in Kashmir. This marked the end of the National Conference rule in the state.

Mufti's Triumph

Mufti was now Chief Minister. His lifelong dream was fulfilled on November 2, 2002. His unequivocal and repeated call for a solution through dialogue not bullets had impressed the woman who mattered most in propelling him to the topmost governmental position in Jammu and Kashmir. Sonia Gandhi , widow of Rajiv Gandhi, whom Mufti had left to join V.P. Singh's camp in the 1980s, rejected the advice of her own party colleagues and declared that Mufti would be Chief Minister for the first three years of the first-ever multi-party coalition government in Jammu and Kashmir, something to which Ghulam Nabi Azad could not reconcile himself. His reasons for not pressing his claim to Chief Ministership during the first phase appear plausible: it was their hope that Mufti would return to mainstream politics and be weaned from the secessionist viewpoint that was clear in the PDP leader's speeches. Mufti Mohammad Sayeed, who was Farooq Abdullah's *bête noire,* dismissed the NC's call for autonomy, in his response to the Governor's address in the State Legislative Assembly in November 2002. He pointed out that the Sheikh had not asked for any restoration of autonomy when he agreed to the 1975 Kashmir Accord. Sheikh Abdullah had obviously been more preoccupied with the consolidation of his power than with the issue of autonomy.

Having done that, he presented his agenda. He knew what was troubling the people most. Their lives had been darkened by violence and the electricity cuts at peak hours had only served to exacerbate matters. As the Lord would have it, he was being sworn in as Chief Minister on November 2, 2002 (days before the holy Muslim month of Ramzan). So he announced that there would be a drastic cut in the power shutdown. He halved it from 9 and a half hours to four and a half hours. The restoration of light was to make him a household name. People were delighted with the restoration of light in their homes. It was something to celebrate, when they had nothing else to feel good about. It was all part of the Chief Minister's long-term plan. He knew that he did not have numbers on his side so he undertook several populist measures such as maintaining the public medical units, at a heavy economic cost, and against the overall advice of the economists. He was building a vote bank for his party. Power reimbursements were reaching Rs. 2200 crores and the State Exchequer did not even have the money to pay salaries to its ever increasing army of government employees. Mufti was aware of this but he relentlessly pursued his agenda of expanding his independent base in the Valley, taking soft loans to maintain power supplies and to finance the health services. His daughter, Mehbooba Mufti pointed out that they had a duty towards the bereaved families of militants. These visits, which were highly profiled, thus prevented security forces from acting against the militants. Mufti went a step further by undertaking to procure their release.

The Jalil Abbas Gilani Affair

Pakistan's Deputy High Commissioner Jalil Abbas Gilani, in Delhi, had been found guilty of giving money to two Hurriyat leaders to finance terror campaigns in Jammu and Kashmir. India took what it deemed to be proper action and duly expelled Jalil Abbas Gilani. Islamabad had been quick to deny the charges and described them as part of the BJP Government's tactics to bolster its electoral chances. India said that the issue involved was one of 'national security.' The decision to expel Gilani was announced by Prime Minister Atal Bihari Vajpayee at a meeting of Chief Ministers on internal security. His attack was directed at Pakistan, charging it with having set up cells in Nepal and Bangladesh, two of the countries bordering India in South Asia, to inject terrorism into India. Events had unfolded in a dramatic manner. Anjum Zamruda Habib, a member of Khwatin-e-Markaz and Shabir Ahmad Dar, who was in charge of the Kashmir Awareness Bureau run by the APHC in Kashmir were key players. Habib, who—so her group claimed—was on her way to attend a human rights group meeting in Bangkok,

Thailand, was found with Rs. 3.75 lakhs. Habib admitted that she had been given the money by the Deputy High Commissioner. Her appointment had been fixed by APHC Chairman Bhat and Dar. That all this should happen at a time when the Mufti Sayeed Government was trying to rebuild bridges between the Kashmiris and the Centre so as to initiate dialogue and become a facilitator for subsequent Indo-Pak negotiations was a negative development and further jeopardized teetering Indo-Pak relations.

Mufti's Pro-Militant Profile

Mufti Mohammad Sayeed took matters into his own hands, preventing the Government of India from taking any action against the All Parties Hurriyat Conference Chairman, Abdul Ghani Bhat who was to receive the money given by Gilani. Mufti was worried about the political fallout that would follow upon the raid or arrest of the Hurriyat leader in this case. He told the Deputy Prime Minister L.K.Advani that any such measure would be disastrous. His line of argument was that this would enhance Bhat's image and the rest of the Hurriyat leadership and thus complicate matters at the international level. If the Hurriyat had to be sidelined, the best way, he argued was to do so by striking at their roots. Mufti had successfully occupied the ground that was shrinking under the feet of the Hurriyat Conference partly as a result of internal rifts and partly as a result of the strong measures which the Mufti Government had taken to isolate the secessionist conglomerate. It had already acquiesced to the impounding of the passport of the former Chairman of the APHC Mirwaiz Umar Farooq. His passport was impounded days before he was to fly to the United States with his wife. The charge against him was that he had received 2.50 lakh dollars to spread anti-India propaganda in foreign countries. This was a specious argument against him. Similarly, when Mufti opposed action against Abdul Ghani Bhat he succeeded in killing two birds with one stone: the latter was indebted to him and at the same time he was able to make political gain from the episode.

Mufti not only prevented Bhat's arrest, he also ordered the release of Syed Ali Shah Geelani, the Jamait-i-Islami leader who was undergoing treatment at Tata Memorial Hospital in Mumbai to which he had been transferred from Ranchi Prison as his health had deteriorated considerably. Mufti's action had been prompted solely by the interests of his party, even as the All Parties Hurriyat Conference was beginning to describe him as a surrogate of India and the Hizb-ul-Mujahadeen was challenging his role as the voice of Kashmir. He had taken this critical step in order to secure a political advantage in Pampore, a South Kashmir constituency, where the battle was tough. Abdul Aziz Mir, his party's MLA (Member of Legislative Assembly) had been assassinated in December 2002, barely six weeks after the formation of the Mufti Government. Mufti himself had been guarded. He had not contested in the elections for he felt that nomination to the Legislative Council was a safer route. He had slighted Congress by releasing Geelani. Congress had, in fact, requested that he keep the release of the separatist leaders on hold until the Himachal Pradesh elections. But Mufti had much more at stake at Pampore.

On the face of it, Gilani's release seemed to fit into the by now familiar pattern of Mufti's 'healing touch.' Mohammad Yasin Malik was the first to be set free, followed by Geelani. Then came the release of a series of other 'political prisoners.' The term 'political prisoners,' was a euphemism for the separatist leaders who were in jail on charges of receiving and distributing funds among the militant outfits which were furthering acts of militancy. Among these was Masarat Alam who was re-arrested upon pressure from Delhi. While the release of the separatist leaders bolstered the claim of the Mufti

Government that it was trying to bring about reconciliation and enlarging the scope of democratic political activity he was also achieving yet another objective that was close to his heart.

Nullifying the POTA (Prevention of Terrorism Act)

Having inveigled himself into power and having promised the militants a fair deal, Mufti now broached the possibility of unconditional dialogue. The POTA (Prevention of Terrorism Act)[5] came to a grinding halt. No prosecutors were assigned to the cases and, as a result, those accused of massacres were able to get away scot free. This was done with impunity in the case of those accused of involvement in the massacre of more than 30 slum dwellers on July 13, 2000 in Rajiv Nagar, on the outskirts of Jammu. The courts could do nothing because the state government had not pressed charges and legal proceedings could not be instituted. The security forces were told to go slow in operations against the militants. Any news of the killing of militant leaders was considered ominous. So, the Director General of Police and Additional Director General of Police (CID) was asked to discontinue the practice of giving him daily reports on the events of the previous night. This appeared highly irregular to the police force since it was a routine procedure to brief the Chief Minister, in every state, where the latter also acted as Home Minister. Mufti, had, however developed a special dislike for DGP A. K. Suri who had bluntly refused to comply with his, Mufti's, request to release a number of militants from jail. Suri had simply returned the list with the names of the militants to Mufti, requesting that he undertake their release himself. Suri was particularly appalled by Mufti's silence when informed of the killing of the chief commander of Hizb-ul-Mujahadeen, Saif-ul-Islam who had replaced Majid Dar. The death of every Hizb-ul-Mujahadeen leader added to the Chief Minister's displeasure towards his police officers. He knew how unhappy they were when he finally released Geelani. They were duly removed. Both Suri and Additional DGP (CID) Kuldip Khuda were given marching orders within a month of Geelani's release. Geelani, on his release, wanted Suri's removal. He accused Suri of defaming him.

On May 23, 2004, the Hizb-ul-Mujahadeen detonated an IED Improved Explosive Device at Lower Munda on the Jammu-Srinagar National Highway, about 90 kms. South of Srinagar, killing 29 BSF men, their wives and children. India's Prime Minister Manmohan Singh in his first cabinet meeting, on that very day, issued a statement condemning the incident as a cowardly act by terrorists. But Mufti, in whose state the incident had taken place, was singularly quiet about the matter. His silence on a terrorist act of this magnitude is all the more inexplicable and disquietening as he has been advocating the cause of dialogue with the Hizb-ul-Mujahadeen. These instances highlight Mufti's pro-militant profile.

Occupying the Middle Ground

It was Mufti's objective to occupy the middle ground in Kashmiri politics. He knew that he could not take extreme positions; he could not be on the side of the nationalist forces. He had seen the fate of the National Conference which had sided with the nationalist forces in India.

Neither could Mufti align himself with the separatists. He was able to exploit the secessionist sentiment, but assuming the role of a separatist was an altogether different matter. He would automatically lose the support of Delhi which had revived his fortunes. Mufti has not been able to reveal the source of his party's funding to date. Farooq Abdullah had accused Mufti of getting money from the Centre to destabilize his government. Mufti never denied these charges. Mufti proved to be a shrewder politician than Abdul Ghani Lone. Both Mufti and Lone were together in Congress. Both of them were ministers in the G.M.

Sadiq and Syed Mir Qasim governments. Lone became a separatist when he lost the Assembly elections in 1987. Mufti clung to his mainstream routes. However, he had helped the Muslim United Front candidates in his own way. While addressing the 1987 election rallies of the Congress and National Conference Alliance, in his capacity as senior Congress leader and also Tourism Minister in the federal government led by Rajiv Gandhi, he would touch his face and pen to indicate to that those sporting a beard and whose election symbol was the 'pen and inkpot' deserved their vote. Geelani, whom Mufti had known since the 1960s, was one of the MUF candidates who had emerged victorious. Lone lost his life because he could not subscribe to extremist secessionist ideology as propounded by Geelani. Geelani was always in favour of *Nizam-e-Mustafa* or the Islamic rule. Lone recoiled from it. And paid for it with his life.

Isolating the National Conference

Mufti was instrumental in persuading Congress that the Jamait-i-Islami should be made to contest the polls in 1972. It was the year when Sheikh Abdullah's Plebiscite Front had boycotted the polls. It was a move, typical of Delhi, of propping up alternatives to the Abdullahs in the Valley. It was repeated, subsequently, with Farooq Abdullah. When Vajpayee visited Kashmir in April, when spring was in full bloom in the Valley, there was effusive praise for the holding of free and fair elections in Kashmir, a land notorious for the'stuffing of ballots' when there were no voters around; where votes were cast for one person and some other would be declared winner. Vajpayee was at his poetic best in condemning all the previous elections. In the flurry of words beneath the swaying Chinar trees, he forgot that the 1977 Assembly elections had been held under direct Central rule in Jammu and Kashmir, polling for which had then been described as fair and free. Vajpyee was Foreign

Minister in the Janta Party Government in 1977 when elections were held in the State. But poets are apt to forget hard facts when they take off on flights of their imagination.

The desire for peace had asserted itself. Pakistan had to retrace its steps, if only temporarily. Mufti Mohammad Sayeed was going places talking of peace and applying the 'healing touch' to victims of militancy and violence. Tourists had started arriving. More than three lakhs visited the Valley and hopes soared. There was a revival of hospitality. Optimism filled the air. Kashmir was beginning to breathe more freely, moving away from the clutches of despair.

Prime Minister Vajpayee was again in Srinagar on August 27. Within an hour of the opening of the inter-state council meeting, a gathering of the top leadership of the different states of the country including chief ministers, the Lal Chowk area in Srinagar reverberated with gun fire and grenade explosions. The terrorists had struck and demolished the hopes of Kashmir. The BSF secured the victory by killing Ghazi Baba, the mastermind of the attack on Indian Parliament. Mufti, in the meantime, was working on another of his objectives.

Break-up of the APHC (All Parties Hurriyat Conference)

The inevitable had happened. The All Parties Hurriyat Conference (APHC) finally split up when 13 out of 25 of the constituents of the secessionist conglomerate walked out to form a parallel group calling itself the genuine Hurriyat Conference. The whole effort was initiated by Jamait-I-Islami leader Syed Ali Shah Geelani who was unable to reconcile himself to being one of the seven executive council members rather than the one who called all the shots. He had been disgruntled ever since he had to step down, very much against his will, as Chairman of the All Parties Hurriyat Conference in July 2000. He had become the Chairman in 1998 after having conspired to throw out

Mirwaiz Umar Farooq. The Mirwaiz, son of the assassinated religious scholar and Chairman of the Awami Action Committee had inherited the seat of chief priest of Kashmir and that of chief of the Awami Action Committee after his father's assassination, believed to have been committed by the fundamentalist militants opposed to the moderate stand of the Mirwaiz. The young man had probably been chosen out of a sense of gratitude to the memory of his father in the spring of 1993, when the Hurriyat was set up at the behest of Pakistan which was dismayed with the squabbling of the separatist leaders and the different groups.

The Hurriyat Conference represented an attempt to win back those living in the Valley who had begun to have doubts about the way and means with which the militants were operating and challenged the fact that gun-toting men be allowed to negotiate the future of the people. In the ensuing years, however, its relevance was enhanced by discussions between visiting diplomats and members of its leadership. Its ranks were expanded with the advent of Shabir Shah and Yasin Malik. But over the years, the Hurriyat Conference had shown itself to be a conglomerate of contradictions, and full of people with inflated egos. Its role was reduced to one of giving and calling off strikes. They had come to the parting of ways and Geelani floated a parallel outfit at his residence, on Sunday, September 7, 2003.[6]

The Hurriyat was enmeshed in contradictions. It was Kashmiri in origin but operated according to the dictates of Pakistan. The two could never be reconciled. People had placed their faith in the Hurriyat Conference; they had observed incessant strikes, suffered losses and sent their children across the border for training only to mourn their deaths upon their return. Disillusionment had begun to sink in especially when it was reported that the huge amounts of funds from abroad which filled the coffers of the Hurriyat had fallen into the grasping hands of its leaders. People were no longer willing to face the police batons and get hurt on behalf of leaders whose lifestyles and image had changed. They had become affluent. They had abandoned their old houses and shifted their bases from their villages to Srinagar where they now travelled about in luxury cars. 'They are the biggest thieves on the Kashmir scene' became a common refrain. People demanded to know what had befallen their sons and daughters. Fingers were pointed at Geelani. He had assured the future of his own sons and daughters who were ensconced in government service.His only son was in the forest department. Sajjad Lone, son of Abdul Ghani Lone wanted to know why Geelani's son had not been a militant. Nor had Sajjad himself gone for training. Ironically, it was his father who had first motivated and sent young men to Pakistan.

Internal Rifts

Abdul Ghani Lone explained that if he were to succumb to pressure and decided to contest in the elections or entered into negotiations with India, his very life would be threatened by those who had sacrificed their children to the cause. '...what of our sons, daughters and husbands buried in graves spread across the Valley? Why at the cost of their lives?' These were difficult questions to which he had no answer. As a leader, he wanted his people to recognize the reality of the changing times, but the fact remained that he was powerless to change their feelings-as he told me, in 2000, when vigorous efforts were on to persuade the Hurriyat to abandon its rigid stance and participate in the elections.

The Hurriyat leadership had always been afraid of itself. The leaders of the various parties also distrusted each other. They were never sure who was working for whom. What became obvious was that some of them were working for either the ISI or the IB and a few for both.

The IB would arrange meetings between the media and the jailed leaders. The money for air tickets were sponsored by IB. One such meeting was arranged in Jammu's central jail in 1993 for a separatist leader, who was to be set free a year later. The money from the sale of tickets was paid by the IB.

The ISI was becoming suspicious of Yasin Malik. So an attack was planned against him the day following his release. Yasin was flabbergasted. He showed the media letter written by Syed Salahuddin wishing him good health.

The rivalry between the IB and ISI had intensified and the Hurriyat Conference awoke to the fact that they were responsible for the deteriorating state of things.In November 2000, the Peoples' Conference had passed a resolution at its Srinagar conference calling for the handling of Kashmir problems to be taken out of the hands of intelligence agencies. Abdul Ghani Lone noted that they had become hostage to the machinations of the agencies,

The growing suspicion towards the Hurriyat Conference and its loss of credibility and relevance suited both Pakistan and India.

The split in the Hurriyat Conference also came as a boon to Mufti, paving the way for his brand of politicking to come centre stage. With Delhi's help, he had succeeded in undermining the National Conference, his main political rival and he now manoeuvred to split the Hurriyat Conference, discrediting it in the public eye. The extent of his success is partly manifest in the public outrage against the bickering among the leaders of the rivalling factions for the fulfilment of personal gain, ambition and interests.

People felt let down by the separatist leadership who had sold them dreams of 'freedom' for which they had sacrificed their sons to 'fight for the cause,' the legitimacy of which was being negated before its very eyes by their games of one upmanship.

Meanwhile, Pakistan was suffocating in its need for gun-powered air. Terrorists launched a suicide attack on an army camp in Jammu, killing 12 soldiers in June. Less than a month later, grenades exploded upon a group of pilgrims en route to the Hindu shrine of Shri Mata Vaishno Devi, killing seven pilgrims. There was another attack on the Tanda army camp in which a Brigadier and twelve soldiers were killed and on July 21, terrorists came close to wiping out the entire top brass of the northern command of the Indian army including Lt. Gen. Hari Parsad. Swift response was not available to India. It could not be. The year-long deployment of its troops on the borders had made it a laughing stock both at home and abroad. It had no option but to reconcile itself to the rising death census.

Islamabad was exultant over the helplessness of India and waited to deal another paralyzing blow. In the fortnight following the Hurriyat split, there was a terrorist strike and the symbol of Indian counter insurgency Kukka Parray was shot dead in his own home town of Hajjin. India was losing ground. It soon became evident that Kukka Parray's assassination on September 13, 2003 was part of a pattern of killings carried out in the Valley which coincided with the fragmentation of the separatist leadership and the upheaval in mainstream politics. The main separatist alliance All Parties Hurriyat Conference had been split in the middle. Jamait-i-Islami leader Syed Ali Shah Geelani had called for the split, urging the youth to rise and fight for an end to the military rule of India in Kashmir. Exactly 24 hours later, Kukka Parray was killed in his hometown Hajjin in the Sumbal area of north Kashmir district of Baramullah. Kukka Parray had remained a towering figure despite his defeat in the 2002 elections. He realized then that muscle and money would not suffice in the battle for heart and minds. And the people had made this clear by the vote they cast.

He sought to regain grace by immersing himself in social activities. On that fateful Saturday, he was on his way home from a cricket match when his Gypsy was waylaid by armed guerillas. He received a burst of bullets and died on the spot. With that, the chapter of counter insurgency in Kashmir was brought to a close. Parray had been used by everyone. He had died for a cause, the value of which he was not, himself, entirely convinced.

On the stage of mainstream politics, a senior minister in the Mufti Sayeed Government had been charged for alleged links with the militants who had attacked the Akshardham temple in Gujarat on September 24, 2002. Agriculture Minister Abdul Aziz Zargar proclaimed his innocence, saying that he had never met the militants nor was he aware that his native house in Manzgam in Damal Hanjipora area in the Shopian belt in south Kashmir was being used by them.

Laying the Foundation for the Mufti Dynasty

Kashmiris were becoming profoundly disillusioned with their leaders. They were beginning to see another betrayal in the offing. Mufti Mohammad Sayeed who had promised them the moon was falling into the mould of the Sheikh and his successors. Mufti proved to be a cleverer politician than many of his old associates had ever anticipated. Through his daughter, Mehbooba Mufti he dangled and beguiled Sonia Gandhi, the Congress President with the promise to strive for peace in the state vowing to provide the best government in Jammu and Kashmir. Having attained his lifetime dream of becoming Chief Minister, Mufti ruthlessly proceeded to finish off Congress, wiping it from the Kashmir Valley. Nor was this entirely unexpected. His twin objectives were to make the PDP the greatest political force among Kashmiri Muslims and to set the stage for his daughter to take the highest office in Kashmir.

Mufti kept his cards close to his chest. He ensured that there was division within his party to obviate the formation of a common opposition against him and the political dynasty that he was endeavouring to build. He opened up many fronts but stayed out of the battle. He lured others into the fight but he himself remained outside the fray. The results were invariably in his favour. Within his own party, he created two lobbies.

Muzzaffar Hussein Beig, a reputed jurist was appointed as Finance, Planning, Law and Parliamentary Affairs Minister.These were high profile portfolios which drew envy from all sides. Mufti availed himself of Beig's oratory, debating power, knowledge and his ability to turn every argument in his favour, to build an impregnable wall around himself, against the onslaughts of his political adversaries of whom there were many. On becoming Chief Minister, Mufti appointed Beig as President of PDP.

Everything was scripted according to Mufti's plan. Beig believed that his Chief Minister had rewarded him for the calibre and excellence of his work oblivious to the seeds of envy that the Chief Minister had successfully sown against him amongst his colleagues.

Ghulam Hassan Mir, a long time associate of Mufti, was given the comparatively insignificant portfolios of Housing and Tourism. Mir has a political head on his his shoulders and his moves are deadly. It was in April 2003-immediately after Prime Minister Atal Bihari Vajpayee had made a historic announcement at the Sher-e-Kashmir Cricket Stadium in Srinagar against the backdrop of the Chinar trees in Kashmir's spring air- that Mufti's designs were unfolded.On the eve of the PDP delegation's meeting with the Centre's interlocutor N.N. Vohra,[7] Mir struck. He said that there was no point in talking to Vohra. 'There is no purpose in our talking to Vohra unless the talks are held at the highest level with the Hurriyat Conference.' He did not join the party delegation in Srinagar but remained in Jammu.

Mir had marginalized Beig. He had defied the party president and at the same time made way for Mehbooba to take over as Chief of the party, which she eventually did. Beig was forced to quit his party post. Mufti had not sided with either of his colleagues but made it appear that matters were taking their natural course. No one realized that he had succeeded in his design of getting his daughter to the top party post without his having to lift a single finger in the exercise.

Mir's point that talks should be held with the Hurriyat Conference was pursued with vigour. Now, Mufti took the lead. He met the Prime Minister and Deputy Prime Minister and urged them to raise the level of the talks. And finally, in October 2003, Deputy Prime Minister, L. K. Advani was designated as the Centre's man to talk to the Hurriyat Conference led by Moulvi Abbas Ansari. Ansari lapped up the offer of talks and finally on January 22, 2004, the first round of talks was held between Advani and the Hurriyat Conference in Delhi.

Meanwhile, Delhi had also moved in the direction of improving its ties with Pakistan. The April 18 announcement of the Prime Minister for friendship with Pakistan was followed by the restoration of bus, air and rail links. This improvement in ties assumed historic significance when on January 6, on the sidelines of the SAARC (South Asian Association of Regional Cooperation)[8] summit in Islamabad, a joint Indo-Pak declaration was made in which the two countries agreed to discuss all issues including the most contentious one of all- Kashmir. Pakistan promised to stop all forms of terrorism on its territory and the areas under its control, a reference to Pakistan occupied Kashmir. A new chapter of bonhomie had begun. This found further expression in the cricket series arranged between India and Pakistan. Pak hosted the series and saw India win and Pakistanis saw themselves becoming part of the victory celebrations in Lahore where Indian fans danced with the Indian tricolour in their hands. The message of that spectacle for the Kashmiris was: Pakistan had changed. Prime Minister Vajpayee and President Musharraf were signing the declarations and Advani and the Hurriyat Conference were talking. That was happening because the leaders of the two countries were being pushed, by the EU and the US to work towards peace on the Indian subcontinent.

All this was not lost on Mufti who was bent on drawing political mileage from the situation. Since Prime Minister Vajpayee's offer of friendship to Pakistan had been made on Kashmiri soil on April 18, 2003 Mufti claimed that it had been mediated through him. No one challenged his claim. He had kept both Vajpayee and Sonia Gandhi happy striking a delicate balance between the two. With one breath, he praised Vajpayee and with the other he heaped praises on Sonia. Both Vajpayee and Sonia are bitter rivals in Indian politics.

Steady progress was being made in projecting the PDP as a Kashmir-based party that could guard the interests of the Kashmiri Muslims. The alliance partner Congress had had two major issues inserted in the Common Minimum Programme which became the policy document of the Mufti Government. One was the implementation of the Janki Nath Wazir Commission report that recommended the decentralization of power with the creation of three more districts in Jammu and one in the Kashmir Valley. Since, it was in the ratio of 3: 1 in terms of Jammu versus the Valley, the Chief Minister declared that the report was not valid and could not be implemented. Congress leaders sheepishly said that they would implement the report when the chair of Chief Minister rotated to them. One of the clauses of the unspoken agreement at the time of the formation of the government was that Congress would ensure Chief Ministership after the first three years of the six-year Assembly term. Mufti knew that he would never hand over power and that he would go to the polls before that, solely on the basis of the PDP's pro-Kashmir agenda. He did not implement the Wazir commission report. This brought him two advantages: Jammu did not receive anything and Congress was thus marginalized in what was its strongest bastion-giving it 15 out of the 20 seats it had won in the 2002 elections. It also made him a hero in Kashmir which is dead-set against Jammu's getting three districts.

Isolating Congress

The Chief Minister dealt another blow to Congress when he said no to the delimitation commission. The population of Jammu which almost equals that of the Valley with possibly a greater area actually qualifies for more seats in the Assembly. But Mufti had pre-empted Jammu from obtaining more seats. Congress had failed to implement any of the points on its CMP (Common Minimum Programme) an undertaking made by all the coalition partners in November 2002 and which forms the policy document of the Mufti government. Furthermore, Congress' most senior leader and Deputy Chief Minister Mangat Ram Sharma, wanted the seniormost IAS officer K. B. Pillai to be appointed Chairman of the Public Service Commission, a constitutional institution which selects men and women for the top posts in Jammu and Kashmir. Mir categorically refused and Sharma staged a walk out from the cabinet meeting, demanding that either Pillai be appointed or that the post remain vacant. The reverse occurred. The government quietly arranged for

Akhtar Murtaza to be appointed as the new Chairman of the PSC. Mangat Ram Sharma was left to lick his wounds. Congress had lost. Not only had the Congress leaders been humiliated - Mufti who had always enjoyed the best of relations with the media, ensured that every step of Congress' capitulation received wide press coverage.

Pandering to the Militants

The state is faced with the problem of unemployment but no scheme has been worked out and no project put forward to ensure work for the young, some of whom are highly educated and trained. The Chief Minister went on a Hajj, a Muslim pilgrimage to Mecca in Saudi Arabia in January 2004 and leaving Sharma in charge. The first cabinet meeting that Sharma chaired in his capacity as Acting Chief Minister approved and announced what it called the rehabilitation policy for the return of militants into the mainstream. Militants who agreed to surrender their weapons were entitled to Rs. 1.50 lakhs about $3500 in bank deposits and Rs. 2,000 monthly stipend in addition to job opportunities. This policy provoked outrage among the unemployed youth who felt that the gun-toting ruffians were being rewarded. Congress could not offer a legitimate reply for it was their man who had chaired the cabinet meeting which had approved the policy. Once again Congress had to take the blame. And yet again Mufti had killed two birds with one stone. He had not only marginalized Congress but also built his own constituency among the militants. His ally Bhim Singh said that this policy was meant for the PDP workers. PDP workers who had earlier worked in militancy would deposit their weapons, get money, a job, and bank loans and in return they were expected to strengthen and widen the base of the PDP. This was in line with Mufti's policy to set free the 'political prisoners' and according to which he had freed the Jammu Kashmir Liberation Front Chairman Mohammad Yasin Malik and Jamait-i-Islami leader Syed Ali Shah Geelani and a further 130 some of whom had been involved in murders and other heinous crimes. Mufti was doing all this with an eye to expanding his base.

Mufti spread the word among Kashmiri Muslims that it was he who was releasing their sons, fathers, from jail and was to be credited with reuniting the militants with their families. In return he expected their support. This kind of support had a double advantage. Mufti was seen as the one who championed the cause of Kashmiri Muslims among whom secessionist sentiments ran high. He was working on the expansion of the Islamic ways, but was fully empowered by the Indian Constitution in his official capacity as Chief Minister. Secondly, it got him the support of the men with guns or those who could control such men. And men with guns have always wielded control over political fortunes in the Valley. Bhim Singh made all these charges, some of which were substative. Mufti took account of Bhim Singh's charges. Bhim challenged Congress to quit the government over its humiliation, but Congress swallowed the insults and did nothing.

Permanent Resident Disqualification Bill-Out: Manoeuvring Congress

Matters came to a head when the Mufti Government very cleverly manoeuvred the passage of a controversial bill titled 'Jammu and Kashmir Permanent Resident (Disqualification) Bill 2004' in the Legislative Assembly.(9) According to the terms of the bill girls from Jammu and Kashmir who marry outsiders automatically lose their permanent resident status and all the rights accruing thereto.

In Jammu and Kashmir, it is mandatory to have a document called state subject or permanent resident certificate to get admission into schools, to jobs or to buy or sell immovable property, to vote or contest in polls. The bill completely nullifies the status of women who marry non-permanent residents. This anti-women bill was passed after the Jammu and Kashmir High Court had passed its ruling on October 7 2002, on an executive order issued in 1967 by the Government that girls were entitled to their state subject status until their marriage. Thereafter, they could acquire the state subject as per the status of their husbands. That meant that only girls marrying state subjects could retain their rights.

The High Court said that this was discriminatory and that girls marrying outside the state were also entitled to all the rights. The court dismissed the contention of the government lawyers that the notification issued by Maharaja Hari Singh, the last Dogra king of the state on April 20, 1927 had laid the foundation for the protection of the rights of the people of the state against the onslaught of outsiders.

The matter was allowed to rest for a while. The Mufti Government moved the petition in he Supreme Court challenging the High Court judgment and subsequently withdrew it with the stated purpose of bringing a law to nullify the High Court ruling. The petition was withdrawn in September 2003.

Mufti wanted the law to be enforced. But again he resorted to his usual tactics. He made the fact of the petition having been withdrawn known to the law makers during the budget session of the state legislature. Mohammad Yusuf Tarigami, a Communist MLA raised the issue in the Assembly seeking explanation as to what the government had done to reverse the High Court judgment. Again the two principal actors were to play their roles thinking that they were working on their own parts but inadvertently following Mufti's script. Beig in his capacity as Minister for Law disclosed that the petition filed in the Supreme Court had been withdrawn because, had the highest court in the country endorsed the High Court verdict then it would have been difficult to make a law on the subject. Mir dashed off a letter to the Chief Minister asking him why the cabinet had not been taken into confidence. The opposition National Conference members fell into the trap. They raised the issue in the House little knowing that Mufti was trying to reap political advantage at their expense. The bill was hastily drafted by the Law Minister who also discussed it with the opposition and alliance partners. The draft was approved by a panel at a meeting chaired by Deputy Chief Minister Mangat Ram Sharma on March 4, 2004.

The following day, the bill was passed in the Assembly, within a matter of five minutes, without debate. The media understood that an anti-women's bill had been passed and when satellite TV channels reported the matter, the issue generated a great deal of heat and light, sound and fury, all at once.

Sonia voiced her anguish and Vajpayee advised Mufti to find a way out. The bill had to go to the upper house of the state legislature—the Legislative Council—where it had to be passed with a two-third majority of the sanctioned strength of 36 of the House—before it could be sent to the Governor for his assent.

Protests erupted in the streets of Jammu against the bill, while in Srinagar the streets were filled with pro-bill women activists. Kashmir valley believed that the bill protected their indigenous rights and helped maintain their distinct ethnic identity, whereas Jammu's Hindus perceived this as a measure to prevent the entry of Indians into the state. They also feared that if the bill were ever to become law, it would force them to quit the state and they interpreted it as an instrument of political persecution which was forcing them to flee the state. In their eyes, then it was yet another means of transforming Jammu and Kashmir, into a purely Islamic state. Mufti knew that the bill could not be passed without the help of Congress. He also knew that the passage of the bill or its rejection in the Council, would seal the fate of his government. Any bending of the constitutional requirement to facilitate the passage of the bill would mean the withdrawal of Congress support, resulting in the fall of the government. If on the other hand it were rejected, taking the pure constitutional definition for the passage of such bills, he would have to face a tough time at the hands of the National Conference. For the first time, he was in a difficult spot. So he decided to let matters cool down till the Lok Sabha elections, were held. These elections had been partly responsible for snowballing the bill controversy, turning it into a major election issue, at the level of national campaigning between the BJP and Congress. This time the Chairman of the Council, Abdul Rashid, to the surprise of all, did not put the bill to vote after it was debated hotly in the House for more than six and a half hours. Instead, he adjourned the House *sine die*, keeping the bill alive. The bill lapsed after three months' constitutional life in June 2004.

The issue was whether the bill should be passed with a simple majority since it was Beig's contention that it was not a constitutional bill or whether it should be passed with a two-third majority. This gave rise to constitutional questions on which the Chairman said he needed to seek clarification. But there was something more to it. His judgment would have been final. He had stated in his media interviews that the sanctioned strength of the House was 36 and the bill had therefore to be passed by at least two-thirds of its members, i.e. by 24 members. The House's existing strength was 30 and those supporting the bill added up to 20 only. The National Conference had 15 members including the Chairman but that meant only 14 of them could vote because the presiding officer could vote only in the event of a tie, a system that the Indian parliament and legislatures follow on the pattern of British Parliamentary conventions.

Congress with eight and Jammu and Kashmir National Panthers Party with one in the opposition added up to nine. The PDP had four members, including Chief Minister. One communist and an independent also supported the bill.

Though the bill could not be passed, Mufti emerged victorious. He had dealt Congress a severe blow. Mufti had kept the bill alive and Congress could not have had it sent to the select committee. It became a subject of ridicule in the eyes of the electorate for the bill could not be stalled forever. In Kashmir, Mufti was able to get Congress painted as the villain of the piece—the party which had reversed its stand from one of supporting the bill on March 5 to one of opposing it on March 11 in council debate.

Congress was finished. He also rejected Congress' plea for a contest in Baramulla in north Kashmir and fielded his own candidate. Congress fielded its old war horse Ghulam Rasool Kar but the Kashmiris were not willing to look at Congressmen.

Mufti had decimated his supporting parties and raised his own and his party's profile. He was on his way to making Jammu and Kashmir an Islamic state.

Endnotes

1. Bhim Singh, Chairman of Jammu and Kashmir National Panthers' Party, a regional group that has its areas of influence in the Jammu region.

2. Choudhary Mohammad Ramzan, a senior National Conference leader who was a minister in the Farooq Abdullah government from 1987 to 1990 and 1996 to 2002.

3. Hindutuva, the movement that believes in spreading extremist Hinduism.

4. Manmohan Singh, a senior Congress leader who is now Prime Minister of India. He is the first Sikh Prime Minister of India.

5. POTA- This is the Prevention of Terrorism Act, a law enacted by the Indian Parliament as part of the global effort to curb terrorism. Congress party had opposed it at the national level when the Vajpayee government brought it up and PDP had raised its voice against the law in Jammu and Kashmir. Now with the Congress-led coalition government having taken over at the Centre (federal government), the POTA is likely to be withdrawn. Its implementation has already been stopped by the Mufti Government in Jammu and Kashmir.

6. The Hurriyat was divided when Syed Ali Shah Geelani demanded the People's Conference to explain why they had participated in the 2002 Assembly Elections by proxy. Close associates of Abdul Ghani Lone who was assassinated on May 21, 2002 had taken part in the elections. One of them, Ghulam Mohi-ud-Din Sofi was elected from Handwara in Kupwara district in north Kashmir, the native town of Abd ul Ghani Lone. He also became a minister in the Mufti Sayeed Government. He is still a confidant of Sajjad Lone, son of Abdul Ghani Lone and also Chairman of one faction of the People's Conference (not the Ansari faction of the Hurriyat Conference). His brother Bilal Lone heads another faction of the People's Conference (the Abbas Ansari faction of the APHC. With the assassination of their father, Sajjad became Chairman of the People's Conference and Bilal the representative of the Peoples' Conference in the executive council of the Hurriyat Conference. The head of a particular party automatically becomes the representative in the Hurriyat Conference. However, after the first round of talks on January 22, 2004 between the APHC (Ansari faction) and the then Indian Deputy Prime Minister, L. K. Advani, the two brothers felt that they could not accept the arrangement. They have parted ways and each accuses the other of betraying their father's legacy. The two are now bitter enemies.

7. N. N. Vohra, former Indian Home Secretary who was appointed in

February 2003 to hold talks with groups in Jammu and Kashmir.

8. Jammu and Kashmir has a bicameral legislature: The Lower House Legislative Assembly and upper House: The Legislative Council. The Permanent Resident (disqualification) Bill was passed in the Legislative Assembly on March 5, 2004 but when it came up in the upper house, i.e. the Legislative Council (March 11), it could not be passed because Congress by that time had turned hostile to the bill and without Congress Party's support the bill could not be passed in the LC. It is mandatory that both the houses of the legislature pass the bill before it goes to the Governor for his assent to become a law.

Conclusion

The search for a solution to the Kashmir crisis is desperate. India and Pakistan have made yet another bid to resolve the issue that has dogged their relationship. They have agreed to find a solution to the crisis by softening their heretofore inflexible and stand offish stance. India has agreed to discuss the Kashmir issue and Islamabad has responded by agreeing to stop all kinds of terrorist activities on its soil. Hopes of peace soared as this assertion found echo on the sidelines of the South Asian Association of Regional Cooperation (SAARC) summit in Islamabad in January 2004, preceded by a display of ceasefire by the Indian and Pakistani armies along the contentious Line of Control and the international border in Jammu and Kashmir. It would appear that the leaders of the two countries have acknowledged the will of the people for peace and are moving steadily towards the meeting table, though in taking this step forward it remained important to the people of both countries to know whether their leaders were acting of their own volition or under pressure from the west.

Jarring notes continue to be heard now and again. And neither tangible efforts nor wide agreement has yet been reached on Kashmir. Though it may be too soon to expect any results, the real anxiety is it takes only a single big bang on the part of the *jihadis* along the pattern of 3/11 in Spain or the attempted assassination of Pakistan President Pervez Musharraf, who has already survived a couple of serious attempts on his life, for the whole effort to go to waste.

The Western public is not immune to such misgivings for fears that Kashmir could trigger off a nuclear clash have not died down.

Such a complex issue which has been variously described

as a vicious mix of insurgency, terrorism and proxy war, cannot be resolved by a single summit meeting nor even a series of summits. The politics of prestige and the turf war between India and Pakistan, on the one hand, and the limelight of international attention on the other have added to the complications that exist within the Himalayan territory which is also undergoing a metamorphosis from within. Even as the Valley has become exclusively Muslim, and intolerance towards Muslims is increasingly conspicuous in Jammu, tensions are also mounting between Buddhists and Muslims in Ladakh.

Communal and regional tensions are on the rise. The Valley is increasingly becoming the launch-pad of the Islamic movement where the aspirations of Jammu Hindus are perceived as threats. The Valley views Jammu and its Hindu population as partisans seeking to extend the Indian-infidel agenda- in Kashmir. This represents a direct clash between Kashmiri Muslims who are influenced by pan-Islamic sentiments and the *jihadi* cult and the Indian Hindus. All this means a sharpening of the confrontation between Jammu Hindus and Kashmiri Muslims which has complicated the process of finding a solution. While the best brains across Asia and the western world are engaged in that exercise, nothing seems to be succeeding.Cautionary words of wisdom have failed time and again. The desperate need for a solution and the frustration of not finding one might draw both countries willy-nilly down the path of nuclear war and such wars are not bilateral issues.

The tentative steps forward can all too easily be retracted by a return to the unyielding, empty rhetoric of the past.

Both India and Pakistan are unaware of the passions gnawing at the vitals of their populace. India does not know how to analyze the problem in Kashmir. It is not a problem of maintaining law and order; it is not terrorism alone and it is also not purely an issue of insurgency as such.

There are aspirations within a section the people which impel them towards a struggle. But these aspirations have been hijacked by fundamentalist elements and outsiders who have sought to expand their agenda at the expense of the original wishes of the people in the state.

Jihadi elements have come in. Post-9/11 has turned it into an issue of terrorism versus insurgency. The world is in a dilemma as to which side to take.

Pakistan is unaware of the realities in Kashmir. The Kashmiri movement is not a religious movement alone; nor is it a question of the assertion of political will. Pakistan cannot think of hijacking the agenda of Kashmir all on its own. It too has to look at the problem as it exists where the popular sentiment is to dismantle all forms of occupation and where the people are wary of sliding into another occupation.

India and Pakistan have tried to outwit each other in the past, without exactly looking at a possible solution. Pervez Musharraf's obsession with the right to self-determination has been considered an advantage in his championship of the cause of Kashmiris. It was also true for all Pakistanis who believed that such a situation would inevitably deliver Kashmir into Pakistan's hands. But he stunned this school of thought when he said that the UN resolution which offers such an exercise could be set aside and other solutions explored. That was to put pressure on India to talk.

India, when confronted with this suggestion asked Pakistan to indulge in self introspection. India's recommendation to Pakistan to 'practice before preaching' democracy had become the hallmark of the speeches of Prime

Minister Vajpayee. 'If you will talk of Kashmir, we will talk of Pakistan-occupied Kashmir (PoK).'

The friendships are conditional. Pakistan wants to grab the hand of peace but refuses to show friendly gestures towards Kashmir. For Pakistan, Kashmir remains the core issue. India refuses to accept that. The international community under the spell of the might of the United States is equally oblivious to the grimness of the situation. Merely saying that the place is dangerous is not enough for Kashmir. It can ignore Kashmir and the threat it poses only at its own peril.

The intellectuals are working over time, churning out solutions which may bedazzle the onlookers. But on the ground, these are impracticable. Some of the solutions are worse than the crisis; they can barely be contemplated, let alone be put into action.

The status quo is the cause of the trouble that the Valley is now witnessing, so naturally it is unacceptable as a solution to the crisis that has left both sides embittered and the people of the State –more angry.

If people like Syed Ali Shah Geelani and Syed Salahauddin have their say, Kashmir should become Pakistan going by the logic of numbers. The majority of Muslims, it is presumed would vote for Pakistan. But the urge for independence is far greater among the Muslims. It should not be forgotten here, that these are people bent on independence and if forced to join Pakistan, would rebel. These voices are already audible in the Pakistan controlled part of Kashmir. That cure would be worse than the disease. As it would be, equally so, if Kashmir happens to join India. The clamour of pro-independence and pro-Pakistan voices would be raised in alarm. So, what then is the objection to an independent Kashmir? Hindus in Jammu will not accept it.

Buddhists in Ladakh would reject it. Both India and Pakistan are not willing to give up their territory. Neither of them wants an eyesore on the borders with the US emerging as the biggest beneficiary. There are other potential dangers if the two parts of Kashmir with a Muslim majority were to unite leaving out the predominantly Buddhist and Hindu parts of the State for this would mean the birth of yet another Islamic nation on the map of the world. This is obviously not to the liking of India and Delhi would oppose any such move. The US, votary of an independent Kashmir, for it is understood to be behind the campaign of the JKLF in building a pro-independence mood, in Kashmir would also lead to the birth of another Islamic nation in south Asia. Such a state, the terrain of which is ideal for terrorists, is the last thing that the US would bless as a Kashmir solution. In the modern-day world, nothing stirs without US consent. In this case too, Pakistan would not be willing to cede its territory. If Pakistan could not keep Afghanistan as its colony, how then might it have Kashmir?

The Chenab formula, joining all Muslim majority parts of Jammu and Kashmir to Pakistan is as reprehensible as making the whole of Jammu and Kashmir a part of Pakistan. India would not give even an inch for a formula which makes the river Chenab the natural boundary between Hindu-dominated parts and the extended boundaries of Pakistan.

So where do we go from here? Live within the current boundaries with India and Pakistan guaranteeing self-respect to the people and opening the frontiers. Is that perhaps the way out?

Kashmir cannot be left alone. The global terrorist threat is as worrisome as ever. Kashmir is that rare combination of a place in which India and Pakistan can flex their nuclear muscles.

Islamic terrorists too are also eyeing it as a potential base.

Its geography of high mountains, endless meadows covered by impenetrable forests make it an ideal location for terrorists to operate in. The wires of Lashkar-e-Toiba, Al-Qaeda and Jammiyah Islamiah are connected; some have already occupied parts of the place and others are on their way to doing so elsewhere in the country. These terrorist outfits have the capacity to take on the US and Europe.

They can prove the worst fears of the world right by acquiring nuclear weapons or heightening the tensions between India and Pakistan embroiling them in a conflict in which atomic bombs are put to the devastating use for which they have been designed. The world must wake up.

Further Reading

Books

Aiyar, Mani Shankar, *Pakistan Papers*, Delhi: UBS Publishers and Distributors Ltd.

Akbar, M. J., *The Shade of Swords*, Delhi: Roli Books

Ali, Tariq, *The Clash of Fundamentalisms: Crusades, Jihads and Modernity*, London: Verso, 2002.

Anand, A. S. Justice, *The Constitution of Jammu and Kashmir-Its Development and Comments*, Delhi: University Law Publishing Co. Pvt. Ltd.

Atal, Hira Lal, Maj.-Gen., *Kashmir Diary: Psychology of Militancy*, Delhi: Manas Publications.

Baweja, Harinder, *A Soldier's Diary: Kargil-Inside Story*, Delhi: Books Today, 1999.

Baweja, Harinder, *Most Wanted Profiles of Terror-Compilation of Profiles of Osma bin Laden, Hafiz Saeed, V. Prabhakaran, Maulana Masood Azhar, Prakash Barua, Sayeed Salahauddin*, Delhi: Roli Books, 2002.

Behra, Ajay Darshan, Matthew Joseph C. 'Pakistan in a Changing Strategic Context,' *Knowledge World*, New Delhi in association with Centre for Strategic and Regional Studies, Jammu: University of Jammu, 2003.

Collins, Larry and Dominique Lapierre, *Mountbatten and the Partition of India*, Delhi: Vikas Publishing House.

Dass, Durga, *India from Curzon to Nehru and After*, Delhi: Rupa and Co.

Ganguly, Sumit, *The Origins of War in South Asia, Indo-Pakistan Conflicts Since 1947*, London: West View Press.

Gill, K. P. S. and Ajai Sahni, 'Faultlines,' *Writings on Conflict and Resolution*, Vol. 6. Delhi: The Institute of Conflict Resolution, August, 2000.

Gupte, Pranay, *Vengeance-India After the Assassination of Indira Gandhi*, New York: W. W. Norton and Co.

Hewitt, Vernon, *Reclaiming the Past:The Search for Political and Cultural Unity in Contemporary Jammu and Kashmir*, Portland Place, London: Portland Books.

Hussain, Altaf, *The Wounded Paradise*, Srinagar.

Jagmohan, *My Frozen Turbulence in Kashmir*, Delhi: Allied Publishers Ltd., 1991.

Jain, Pramod Kumar, 'J&K Votes' *A Statistical Report on the General Election to the Jammu and Kashmir Assembly, 2002*, Election Department, Government of Jammu and Kashmir, 2003.

Jha, Prem Shankar, *Kashmir 1947 Rival Versions of History*, Delhi: Oxford University Press.

Kapur, M. L., *Studies in History and Culture of Kashmir*, Jammu: Trikuta Publishers, 1976.

Lapierre, Dominique and Larry Collins, *Freedom at Midnight*, Delhi: Vikas Publishing House.

Margolis, Eric S., *War at the Top of the World*, Delhi: Roli Books, 2001.

Maley, William, *Afghanistan and the Taliban: The Rebirth of Fundamentalism?* Delhi: Penguin Books, 2002.

Misra, Neelesh, *173 Hours in Captivity, The Hijacking of IC 814,* Delhi: HarperCollins, Publishers 2000.

Muju, G. K., *Pakistan's Proxy War Explodes Myths about Kashmir,* Jammu: Sahyogi Publications.

Neve, Arthur, *Thirty Years in Kashmir,* Lucknow: Asian Publications 1982.

Ray, Arjun, *Kashmir Diary: Psychology of Militancy,* Delhi: Manas Publications 1997.

Rashid, Ahmed, *Jihad,* Orient Longman Pvt. Ltd.

Sands, *The Villain of Peace,* Jammu: Sands Publications.

Schelling, Thomas C. and Morton H. Halperin, *Strategy and Arms Control,* Pergamon-Brassey.

Schofield, Victoria, *Kashmir in Conflict-India, Pakistan and the Unending War,* Delhi: Viva Books.

Singh, Jaswant, *Jammu and Kashmir, Political and Constitutional Development,* New Delhi: Har-Anand Publications.

Singh, Karan, *Heir Apparent, an Autobiography,* Delhi: Oxford University Press 1982.

Sinha, S. P., *Jackals of the Himalayas-Kashmir Hostage Mystery,* Delhi: Applied Media.

Yusaf, Mohammad and Mark Adkin, *The Bear Trap-Afghanistan's Untold Story,* Jang Publishers, 1992.

Zahir-ud-Din, *Did They Vanish into Thin Air?* Srinagar: Sabha Publications.

Zakaria, Rafiq, *The Man Who Divided India-An Insight into Jinnah's*

Leadership and its Aftermath. Mumbai: Popular Prakashan.

Government Publications

Jammu and Kashmir Assembly Secretariat, July 2000, Assembly Debates on Autonomy Report.

Jammu and Kashmir Human Rights Commission, *Annual Report, 2000-1.*

Jammu and Kashmir Information Dept. Publications, 'Accession-Much Ado About It,' *Newsline,* February, 1994.

Jammu and Kashmir Information Dept. Publications, 'Hazratbat-A Turning Point,' *Newsline, December, 1993.*

Jammu and Kashmir Information Dept. Publications, 'Plot to Make Kashmir Unhappy Valley,'*Youth Information,* January 1993.

Jammu and Kashmir Information Dept. Publications, *'Selected Speeches of Gen. K. V. Krishna Rao, Governor of Jammu and Kashmir'.*